LETTERS FROM CAMBRIDGE
1939-1944

LETTERS
from
CAMBRIDGE
1939–1944
by
A. S. F. GOW

JONATHAN CAPE
THIRTY BEDFORD SQUARE
LONDON

FIRST PUBLISHED 1945

JONATHAN CAPE LTD.   30 BEDFORD SQUARE, LONDON
AND 91 WELLINGTON STREET WEST, TORONTO

PRINTED IN GREAT BRITAIN IN THE CITY OF OXFORD
AT THE ALDEN PRESS
BOUND BY A. W. BAIN & CO. LTD., LONDON

PREFACE

THE letters in this volume were originally written, and are now printed, in circumstances already sufficiently explained on pages 48 and 253. The name which they early acquired, 'The Parish Magazine', is some indication of their scope; they aimed at recording the vicissitudes of the University during the war, and their other themes are often drawn from Cambridge, where the majority of their recipients had recently been in residence. If such matter now proves of interest outside the circle of friends for whom it was intended I shall be pleased.

I have corrected a good many slips of pen and typewriter, and for one reason or another I have slightly modified perhaps a dozen phrases; otherwise the letters are unaltered. I have, however, equipped them with an occasional footnote, and I have compiled a desultory index, wherein, among other things, may be discovered the significance of those strings of initials from which few war-time documents are immune.

Some of my correspondents have not lived to see the publication of this book. I should naturally wish to associate it with their names, which are printed overleaf.

A. S. F. G.

Trinity College, Cambridge
September 1945

M. S.

M. H. ANDERSON	R.A.F.V.R.
D. S. H. BURY	R.A.F.V.R.
P. B. N. DAVIS	R.A.F.V.R.
R. G. A. GOW	R.A.
D. H. JACOBSON	Rifle Brigade
J. S. W. JARVIE	R.N.V.R.
H. LIVERSIDGE	R.A.F.V.R.
W. M. MACKEAN	N. Irish Horse
L. NICHOLSON	Oxf. & Bucks. L.I.
A. P. PEASE	R.A.F.V.R.
J. A. PRYCE	Queen's R. Regt.
P. SEAGER-BERRY	Home Guard
L. P. SHAND	R.E.
A. J. STUART	R.A.F.V.R.

ὥσπερ εἴ τις τὸ ἔαρ ἐκ τοῦ ἐνιαυτοῦ ἐξέλοι

FIRST LETTER

Trinity College,
Cambridge.
8.9.39

I HOPE you will forgive a letter which resembles a circular. It seemed to me that in these uncheerful times those in foreign parts might perhaps like rather more gossip than they usually get out of my correspondence, and that as the gossip would have to be more or less the same for all, it would be a good thing to duplicate it rather than write it all out separately for different people. Then I thought that I might send it also to some people not in foreign parts with whom I don't usually correspond, though these, if in England, will be apt to find in it a good deal they know already. My present idea is try and keep up the service until a bomb or some other obstacle puts a stop to it, but if you don't like the idea you have but to say so and it can easily be stopped.

I meant, on ceasing to be Tutor, to have a thoroughly idle Long Vac., but that plan, like a good many others, came to nought. I was kept here until August 14 in order to have a practice air-raid, and then I went down to Wales. I meant to go on to Scotland on the 23rd, but by that time Scotland had begun to seem rather far from my base as I should have had to drive myself back, so I stayed two more days in Wales and then came home, thinking at the moment that Hitler was going to announce in his Tannenberg speech that he was about to invade, or had invaded, Poland. The speech was cancelled as you know, and things hung fire for a bit, but it was as well I came back, for, though there wasn't very much to do, there were oddments of A.R.P. and discussions of one thing and another, and there was some point in my being here. It would also not have been much fun trying to take a holiday. By the time the fat was fully in the fire quite a lot of people were back, and our precautions, such as they are, were pretty well complete.

We have sent away some of the more important pictures and books; the Porters' Lodge at the Great Gate is strutted and sandbagged as our chief Wardens' Post, cellars in Whewell's and Nevile's Courts have been made into quite good shelters, and something is being done to the cellar under Hall which isn't so good for the purpose but will serve at a pinch;

as it contains a good deal of beer, some may even prefer it. We started with a false alarm of a raid some days before war began. This was due to a Warden in Chesterton switching on the siren instead of switching off the electric light, but he stopped soon enough not to cause me (at any rate) to get out of bed. On Sunday, the first day, there was a real alarm, due apparently to a mistake about some unidentified machines, which blasted me out of bed at 2.45; and there have been others since. They have been tiresome, but not useless, for they have given us an opportunity of seeing defects in our arrangements which may presently be useful. The College Wardens take it in turn to be primarily responsible and my hours are 11 to 2 at night. I go to bed, but have disposed at hand clothes suitable to the purpose and can get to my post in about three minutes with my gas-mask, a tin-hat (much too small and very uncomfortable, but there is a shortage of larger sizes), and in my pocket a copy of the *Inferno*, which seemed a suitable book for reading while waiting for something to happen. As a matter of fact the chief, and almost the only, duty of the Warden so far has been to answer telephone enquiries as to where Kitson Clark is. He is a Warden belonging to a town post, not to the College, and sleeps soundly through the uproar made by the sirens so that an expedition has to be made to collect him.

The most surprising thing about this affair is its utter unlikeness both to 1914 and also to last September — both here and, I am told, in London. In 1914 those who didn't think we ought to be keeping out altogether were excited and in many places hilarious; in September last year everybody had the jitters. This time I have seen nobody either excited or alarmed, and though I suppose we are mostly fairly depressed at the prospect, very few people are showing it. Probably most think (as I do) that one can't go on as one has for the past two years, that Hitler's behaviour in regard to Poland shows that he meant to go to war with us sooner or later, and that one may as well swallow one's pill now rather than sit looking at it. People are going about their business in the town much as usual except that most of them carry their gas-masks and that the children, according to instructions, are attached to luggage-labels. The Fitzwilliam is closed, most of the chief treasures having been moved out of Cambridge, and some buildings (such as Addenbrooke's and the police station) are heavily sandbagged. The University is wondering how many men will be up, and how it will accommodate them in addition to various bodies evacuated from London, and different committees meet from time to time to discuss these problems. The medical students are coming up on September 14 to begin their studies together with the students of two London hospitals. Others will come, if they do come, at the ordinary time. I hope myself that quite a lot of freshmen will arrive and make a start before they are called up for conscription, for we are told that the youngest classes will not be summoned first. There is a University Recruiting Board sitting and sorting out those suitable for commissions from those unsuitable; also, I hope, those whose technical knowledge of one sort or another — medical, mechanical, or scientific — would make them more useful in non-military capacities. In the last war all and sundry were bundled into the army and the waste of brain-power was appalling. I hope we shall avoid that blunder this time.

My general impression so far is that things have worked with surprising smoothness. Of course the evacuated mothers and children have led to some misfits. The Director of the Fitzwilliam, a bachelor who lives in a large house on the Grange Road, was consigned a cargo of females suffering from scarlet fever and dug his toes in; my Bedmaker tells me that the table-manners of the little boy in her house leave much to be desired but that as his mother is there she can't say so — and one hears things of this sort from other parts of England. However with a little sorting out and goodwill they will be got over.

23.9.39

To continue. The war, as no doubt you have observed, is still hanging fire at this end, but we have been getting things straighter here. It now seems plain that in October we shall have about two-thirds of the University up, and that the first and second year may well be here for quite a long time as those under twenty will not be called up just yet. Of course this may change, but that is what we are budgeting for, and the principal difficulty at present is to find rooms to house them and lecture-rooms to teach them in when there are so many other people in the place. However we shall manage somehow or other though the amenities won't be what you were accustomed to. I have become a Tutor again, partly because Evennett, my successor, is liable to be called away on Government service, partly because this is no time for swapping horses however jaded and spavined the old one may be. In any case much of the recent business has been writing reports on men coming up to see the Recruiting Board, and as I knew them and Evennett did not, this fell to me even before I resumed the strings. Thanks to Hitler the said strings had got a bit tangled in my two months out of office, but I have now got the hang of them again and am not at the moment terribly busy, though what with A.R.P., University business, and other things I am so by fits and starts. When term really begins in October I suppose I shall be up to the eyes, for the absence of various lecturers will mean a good deal more teaching for us all, and there will no doubt be a lot of last minute adjustment due to the arrival of people not expected and the absence of some who are; so I had better get this first budget off before then even if it contains very little of interest to those of you who are still waiting for their orders. Since I wrote the last instalment I nipped up to London for a few hours to attend to family affairs and thought the balloon barrage a considerable ornament. I was also pleased to read somewhere of an old lady who said that if the Germans thought they could frighten her by sitting up in them there balloons all day they were much mistaken. In a similar vein I heard of a notice issued to billeted troops saying that all ranks were to arrange to take baths with their landladies, and that in case any difficulty was experienced the Sergt. Major would interview the landlady. It only shows how difficult it is to say what you mean.

I hope you will find time to let me know how you are and any news that won't bring the censor down on you (I hoped in 1918 that I should never again receive a censored letter, but I have already had more than one). In such times as these it is more than usually pleasant to hear from one's friends even if it is no more than a line, and if you want any more of this sort of thing a good many of you will have to tell me how to address the envelope.

SECOND LETTER

2.10.39

I HAVE been reading the British Diplomatic White Book. Much of it is speeches by Chamberlain, Halifax, and Hitler which one has read before, but the dispatches from Berlin, Danzig, and Warsaw are interesting, and Henderson's from Berlin would in places be amusing if it were not so far past a joke that the destinies of Europe (to say nothing of yours and mine) should be at the mercies of a parcel of neurotics, bullies, and megalomaniacs. Hitler I take to be a dreamer who really persuades himself that what he is saying at the time is true, and is equally persuaded next week

of something quite different. But whether he is that or a cynical oppor-
tunist, like Ribbentrop and Stalin, you can't do business with such a man,
or even live comfortably in the same street. The *Times* record called *A
Grammar of Aggression*, which I dare say you saw, is a really appalling
document. The Poles seem to me to have behaved well. No doubt there
were frontier incidents and even atrocities (under great provocation), but
the government showed extraordinary forbearance throughout. The
Russian affair, which isn't touched on in the White Book, remains
mysterious, though by the time you get this it may be less so. I don't
myself believe in a lasting Russian-German agreement except by way of a
Bolshevik revolution in Germany (which might happen); how incon-
venient a temporary agreement may be remains to be seen, for but those
of you who are in the Far East I hope it has some advantages.

I read in some paper the other day that the remarkable exploits of Mr
John Cobb with his Railton car had been 'somewhat overshadowed by
the war'. This caught my eye both for its happy phrasing and because
J.C. was for a time a pupil of mine at Eton; and as Capt. Eyston, never
having taken a degree and being therefore still nominally *in statu pupillari*,
is also nominally a pupil of mine here, my tutorial record in speed-kings
is *hors concours*. I mention it, however, because I am aware that my last
letter was mostly about the war and you might (since the war is still
hanging fire in these parts) like to know that the front of Christ's and also
Nevile's Court were cleaned in the Long Vac. and are now as bright as
new pins. I don't hold with the modern passion for washing buildings
myself (unless the dirt is doing serious harm) and prefer the honest grime
of centuries to the spurious cleanliness so much admired in Cambridge,
which is, incidentally, very expensive to produce. Hence if we are
presently told to camouflage Nevile's Court with zebra-like streaks I shall
secretly be a good deal amused; and it has come out so astonishingly
white that the order really wouldn't be altogether surprising.

9.10.39

I go on as occasion presents itself. I am at the moment addressing myself
to the task of interviewing freshmen and hoping that I shall remember
who they are the next time I see them. This is an annual test which I was
looking forward to having to do no more, for it is really difficult; if one
does it right one gets no credit, and if one does it wrong the victim feels

insulted — as I dare say some of you remember. Most of the Fellows are still here. Two, I think, have gone away on more or less hush-hush jobs, and a number of others are awaiting summonses. Lapsley, who always goes back to America in the Long Vac., having no duties here, is very sensibly staying there, and his gyp (Penny) is loud in admiration of the foresight which inspired him to pack his winter clothes in July. We know (more or less) what undergraduates will be here, and the Lecture List, though belated, is about to appear. The threat that we should have to start lecturing at 8.30 and might have to lecture in the afternoons has not been realised. It was made because, owing to the number of alien institutions here and the shortage of lecture-rooms, there seemed likely to be a great difficulty in finding places for all. However the aliens, who seem to like lecturing in the afternoon, have, I believe, been given our leavings in lecture-rooms, so all is well. I have spent the last week in sessions of the General Board considering emergency University legislation — for instance, for people who hope to be up two but not three years and want to change their courses of study. In the intervals I have been taking some A.R.P. work off the shoulders of the Junior Bursar who has more than enough to do in assigning rooms and lodgings to people and arranging about furniture, the Board of Works having commandeered the New Court and Hostel. I have drawn up some masterly notices telling those in College down which hole they are to go, and how they are to deport themselves when they get down, asking for volunteers for this service and that, and adumbrating what the duties will be; I have also interviewed firemen and first-aid experts and found out what they want in the way of helpers and materials. It all seems very remote, but I suppose it is necessary, especially as I am told that a recent German broadcast in English mentioned Cambridge as a good place to bomb. My trembling spirits are somewhat fortified by the fact that, having flown over it a good deal, I know it to be not at all an easy place to detect from the air. I don't like holes myself and am glad that my duties require me to display courage and presence of mind on the surface. (*A.R.P. Handbook No.* 8: 'The keynotes of the Warden's conduct should be courage and presence of mind'.)

To revert to three subjects mentioned in my last, viz., refugees, balloon-barrages, and the difficulty of saying what you mean. I hear that Brighton is full of expectant mothers who walk up and down the front and are locally known as the Brighton balloon-barrage. As to saying what you mean, I read of an A.R.P. circular (not local) which said 'If Wardens patrol after the warning has been given without their clothes, the tendency of the public is to come out of doors'. On reflexion, however, I am not sure that I know what this writer did mean unless it was that the Wardens were to wear what I haven't got myself, namely jacket and trousers, anti-gas, light. (I remember, during the last war, at Eton helping to draw up a bogus military notice, of which I can now only recall one item. It was — '*Words, order of*: the right order of words will be wrong.' It was not, alas, one of my contributions.)

22.10.39

Term being now ten days old, and it being near a month since I concluded my last letter, I will make an effort to wind this one up. As to term, the numbers here are about what I expected, or it might be rather more. In normal years I have from 150 to 160 pupils, and now 120. I haven't enquired of other Tutors, whose numbers are probably about the same, nor have I seen any tables for the University as a whole, but I suppose this is a fair fraction for all except those Colleges which discouraged men from returning — perhaps I should say rather 'that College', and leave you to guess which. The absentees are nearly all in the third year, not many of these having returned except people in reserved occupations such as medicine. My lecture class, which would not be attended by third year men, contained its average numbers of fifty to sixty, and I have been lecturing in a normal manner except that my course began by informing the audience where to take refuge in the event of my being interrupted by a siren — the University having decided that for the present lectures are to be broken off for air-raid warnings. No doubt if we have many warnings and no raids we may reconsider this decision. The Junior Bursar has penned his flock with less difficulty than was anticipated, and could still take in some more if necessary. He has, it is true, got a good many people sharing single sets of rooms in College, but this is not altogether a disadvantage because the commandeering of the New Court and Hostel (whose prospective occupants have so far only made inventories of furniture and draped the place with telephone wires) means that the number of cheap sets in College is much reduced, and a good many men are glad to share for reasons of economy.

At present, so far as I can judge, things seem to be proceeding fairly normally except that it is pitch dark at night and we shut up at 11 instead of 12, and that cars have been forbidden by the University. Also we have two Halls only, the last at 7.45. The Proctors were in some doubt how they could function in the dark, but I gather that moonlight is more useful than they expected. Whether those who are here will find it easy to lead normal lives remains to be seen. I hope very much that they will, and preached a little sermon on this theme in what is known (to Tutors at any rate) as the Speech from the Throne on the first day of term — saying that the War Office had announced that men were expected to go on with their studies until they were 20, that their services were now at the disposal of the competent authority and there was nothing more that they could or should do about it, and that they would best serve everybody's interest by making the best use of whatever time they might have here. I don't usually preach on these occasions, as I dare say you will do me the justice to remember, but I feel very strongly about the effect of war on the intellectual life of a nation, and remember with horror the boredom and intellectual inertia which settled on those who took part in the last. Goodness knows there was excuse enough, but if it were possible to compute the man-hours between 1914 and 1918 spent playing Jazz on the gramophone and reading the *Sketch* in Messes, the total would probably give pause even to those more partial to these entertainments than I. However I read a letter in the *Times* from an undergraduate of this College (unknown to me) who says he 'is engaged on a monograph on the evolution of the term *O.K.*' — so in one young hand at least the sacred torch of research is still uplifted.

I have had a lot of very welcome letters as the result of my first bulletin, and as none have come back through the Dead Letter Office, I suppose those from whom I haven't heard nevertheless received their dose; but you might remember to keep me posted as to your addresses if you want more. I have numbered this letter mainly for my own convenience, but the number might also serve to show whether you have missed one. I am also putting my name and address on the outside of the envelope because I have read that I must for all foreign correspondence. I gathered from those of you who wrote that you would like me to go on, and I shall try and do so, but I don't expect I shall be able to run to the length of these first two, not because I am unwilling to spend the time but because, day in and day out, life here doesn't provide very much to write about, and I don't suppose I shall be able to think of things to say. However we shall see.

Postscript

On seeing the stencil from which this is to be duplicated I am appalled to find that it overflows on a fifth page — and I thinking the while that I was halfway down the fourth. I promise that this shan't occur again.

THIRD LETTER

1.11.39

THE *Cambridge Review* has now published its annual statistics, from which it appears that (apart from M.A.'s, whom you do not, and I will not, count) there are in residence 4353 men and 465 women, as against 5491 and 513 last year; so my 120 pupils against 150-160 proves to be a fair section. In addition to these, however, there are 1649 evacuated students from other colleges and seminaries, so that the total is altogether rather above than below the normal. I see nothing of the visitors myself, for our Classical lectures are too advanced for them, but some faculties, such as economics and architecture, are being more matey, and the lectures are pooled and attended by both groups. I suppose some of our total have already drifted away, but only one pupil of mine has gone, and he not because he was called up but because the Recruiting Board told him that he would be well advised to learn some accounting with a view to a commission in the R.A.S.C.

One or two of you, having read in the paper that I had been elected a member of the Council of the Senate, have congratulated me on this elevation. It was a kindly thought, but in the first place as the other candidates were an aggressive communist and an aggressive pacifist, consumed as I may be with conceit, I cannot count the poll as a wholly impartial tribute to my merits; and, in the second and more important place, it is rather a matter for condolence than congratulation. The Council meets for two hours (or more) every Monday morning, serves out a wad of literature to be read in advance, and has a number of committees which one cannot well escape; the General Board, of which I was already a member, meets for two hours (or more) every Wednesday afternoon, serves out a much larger wad of literature, and has nearly as many committees. As I must attend other two-hour meetings two Thursdays out of three, and a number of committees which meet less regularly, I have a good deal more of this sort of thing than I should choose or is my fair share, and I should not have consented to stand for the Council if I had not been rather urgently pressed to do so, and if I did not count it as a sort of war-work, or at any rate the nearest I can get to it at the moment — and, as a matter of fact, a good deal of the work just now is concerned with emergency rules and regulations. What do the Council and the General Board do? It would be hard to say. When some years ago Jeans produced a best-seller entitled *The Mysterious Universe*, the Registrary threatened to write another to be called *The Mysterious University*, to which, if it existed, I might refer you. As it does not, let it suffice (for the first lesson) that all University business comes before one or other body and much of it comes before both. They are exhausting to sit upon because it is no good being on them unless you are prepared to try and understand the business, and much of the business concerns departments of the University with which one is quite unfamiliar. Hence by lunchtime on Monday and by tea-time on Wednesday, I am apt to be wilting a bit. What with tutorial business, lecturing, and more College teaching than usual (owing to people being away), I really am rather hard-driven, and you will infer that the immortal work on which I have been engaged for ten years or more makes but slow progress. In fact it makes none, and this term I have not so far even got out the books to pursue it. However I do not at the moment find connected thought very easy, and am not discontented to be driven from pillar to post.

8.11.39

I am told that the amiable broadcaster from Hamburg has looked forward with pleasurable anticipation to the bombing of King's Chapel. This takes me back to 1912 when I was working in Berlin museums, and a stranger, seeing me reading an English paper in a café, forced his conversation on me in order to tell me of the damage Zeppelins would one day do in England. On the whole I have liked Germany and Germans, but there is no denying a taint of odious brutality which we used to consider Prussian (though it was much less evident in Berlin after the war — at least to a casual visitor) and may now, I suppose, consider Nazi. Evidence in plenty, if you want it, in the White Paper on atrocities. This consists mainly of reports from British consuls in Germany and Austria on conditions in internment camps; it made me feel physically sick, so unless you like horrors I don't recommend it. I do recommend Sir N. Henderson's *Final Report* which will cost you 3d. King-Hall's News Sheet has fallen foul, perhaps rightly, of its opening paragraphs, but it is very interesting on Hitler and his immediate entourage, and it comes not far short of being well-written. He attaches major importance to the mésalliance of Field-Marshal von Blomberg and the consequent disgrace of the more moderate military advisers — so here is another face which has launched a thousand ships and I dare say none of us can remember the new Helen's name. Another three-penny-worth you might read to supplement Henderson is *Who Hitler is* by R. C. K. Ensor.

Question by one of our foreign Fellows (whom I will not particularise): 'What is to wutter?' For the honour of the College I am glad to report that on hearing that this verb was spelt wuther, Simpson and I, to whom the question was addressed, instantly and simultaneously guessed that he was considering whether to go to a film of *Wuthering Heights*. A pardonable mistake, but our foreigners are not always very industrious in learning the tongue spoken by their colleagues. I remember another, no longer with us, who regularly referred to the knuckles of the atom (meaning the nucleus), and once intervened in a conversation on heraldry to say that his crest was 'a crow with a bag in his hand and a clock in his mouth'. These surprising attributes proved, though the speaker was Russian, to be somewhat hasty renderings of the French *bague* and *cloche*.

14.11.39

The University has issued its first notice about allowances of terms and examinations to people absent on national service, and as this concerns a good many of you I had better summarise it here, boring as it may be to those whose academic wings are fully fledged. However skipping is said to be a healthy exercise. Roughly speaking, then, the University is prepared to allow to those who produce evidence that they have been absent for three terms on military, or on other approved national, service, three terms residence; and if they have passed the appropriate examinations during their period of residence, they will be allowed also the suitable ration of examinations for the terms allowed. This means in effect that those of you who were called away at the end of your second year having passed the proper exams. up to then, will, if you are away for a year, be able to take your B.A. degrees without further residence or examination. (I hope some of you will come back notwithstanding this generosity.) This is only a summary of an extremely complicated report — as I have good cause to know, having helped to draft it — but I think it tells you all you need to know at present. As a matter of fact the University curriculum is now so complicated and flexible that omnibus reports are appallingly difficult to draft, and it is much easier to think of cases whom any given report does not cover than to devise a form of words which will cover them. So far only the simple cases of men who disappeared at the end of an academic year have been considered; those who will disappear in the middle of one remain for future consideration and will present some pretty problems.

20.11.39

It is time that I wound up this number, for the last is a month old and, more important, I shall be engulfed this week in papers for the University Scholarships exam. in January. As I have no great confidence in my own judgment in such matters, and take no pleasure in deciding that A is a better scholar than B, I hate examining, and am landed in this particular job out of kindness of heart, having, before I resumed the tutorship, undertaken to replace a colleague who was ill. It is a tiresome job too, for the papers have to be difficult and when one looks at the pieces set by one's colleagues (or they at yours) one is apt to think that what one can construe at sight isn't difficult enough, or if one cannot make head or tail of a passage (as not infrequently happens), that it is too difficult — and neither conclusion is necessarily right.

There is, I am painfully aware, precious little news in this number. However I warned you that that was likely to be the case, and those of you who spent three years at Cambridge without ever hearing of the Council, the General Board, or the University Scholarships will, if you read so far, enjoy the melancholy satisfaction of uprooting some of your wild oats. Nothing in particular has happened since the first instalment except that a few people have been called up (three, I think, of my pupils) and that one (not my pupil) has been interned. I have no particular reason to think that he was a spy, but he raises the pretty question whether being interned is to count as approved national service for University purposes.

FOURTH LETTER

28.11.39

THE other day a Fellow of this College who was going to France asked for suggestions as to books to take with him, the requirements being that they should be i. good, ii. long, and iii. cheap; and with thought I produced some ideas suited to what I believed to be his tastes. About the same time one of you said that as I had expressed the hope that your war-reading would not be confined to the *Sketch*, I ought to make some positive suggestions. This threw me into a slight twitter, partly because I am always rather chary of advising anybody to read a book unless I know that it is likely to appeal to his particular taste, and partly because these letters already bear sufficient resemblance to the Parish Magazine and I didn't wish to increase the resemblance by anything in the nature of a sermon. However the two incidents together caused me to get from my bookseller a list of Everyman's Library (as qualifying under conditions ii and iii above) and to look and see what books in it had served me in foreign parts — for when I go abroad I usually take some fairly substantial reading for the evenings. I will put down the result of this enquiry here, but you must regard them not as a sermon but as an autobiographical fragment which might chance to be useful to somebody else.

In biography, then, I have used with content Boswell's *Life of Johnson*, and his *Tour to the Hebrides*, Benvenuto Cellini's *Autobiography*, and Lockhart's *Life of Scott* (in Everyman this is an abridged edition): for travel and science, Darwin's *Origin of Species*, and *Voyage of the Beagle*, Bates's *Naturalist on the Amazon*, and Ford's *Gatherings from Spain*. I usually take also some poetry — Shakespeare (Tragedies much more frequently than Histories or Comedies), Milton, Homer (*Odyssey* more often than *Iliad*, not because it is better but because it is more varied), Dante — but I don't recommend the Everyman crib to Homer, and for Dante one must have the Italian as well however little of that tongue one knows, so I use the Temple edition. I don't usually take English novels, relying in France or Italy, where I mostly travel, on the local products. However Everyman is well equipped with all standard novelists from Jane Austen to Dostoevsky and you can take your choice. I noticed, however, two less standard that I have used — Conrad's *Lord Jim*, and Herman Melville's *Moby Dick* — a very queer book. If anybody thinks of trying Herodotus, let him not be deterred by the fact that it was written in Greek. It loses something of course in a translation, but for varied information and entertainment it can have few rivals in the world in whatever tongue you read it, and I have recommended it successfully to the Greekless before now. I am not a strong reader of modern English novels (which are of course not in Everyman), but I read *Gone with the Wind* two years ago with pleasure. It is true that I was in a nursing home at the time, and it might be argued that it was necessary to retire to one before embarking on a work of such length; more recently, I forget on what provocation, I read another almost as long by Somerset Maugham called *Of Human Bondage*, and thought it good. But the fact is that I don't read novels very much, not because I disapprove of them in the least but because here I never have time to read for amusement except in bed, and for the nightly half-hour or so which I there devote to the matter I chance to prefer travel or biography. Hence, as I said at the beginning, I am reluctant to advise people who may have other tastes lest I should be thought to disapprove of theirs or they should disapprove of mine. Whatever they might do, I shouldn't disapprove of theirs, taking the view that as long as the book can be called literature and not mere reading matter it doesn't matter much what one reads. Nor am I really shocked by those who read little but detective novels, for though I am not addicted to them myself I have known many of the wise and good who were.

I noticed the other day, in a review of a book about Germany, that Hitler had issued an order that in future his portrait was not to appear on toilet-paper. This is one of the perils of excessive popularity which, I confess, had not occurred to me.

9.12.39

Term ended two days ago and we are now in the throes of the Scholarship Examination, in which, thank heavens, I am not examining. When, in bed last night, I collected my thoughts and considered in retrospect what the term had been like, it seemed to me that from the undergraduate point of view, it had, apart from externals such as black-out, earlier hall, and so on, not differed very much from the normal. The O.T.C. has been busier than usual and members, who are doing 1 hr. lecture and 2 hrs. parade a week, are much seen about the streets in overalls and forage caps with a blue band. People have been going away much less than usual, and have been dining much more regularly in Hall. This is no doubt due partly to the Pitt being shut, but it is a welcome change, for though I sympathise with those who dislike dining at 6.30, I hold that nobody can really afford to pay for two dinners nightly. On the whole it is my impression as a Tutor, and it is also that of lecturers and supervisors in most subjects, that men have done more rather than less work. A few have said they could not concentrate, and there are always some freshmen who do not get started in their first term, but in general they seem to me to have belied the alarm I expressed in my second letter, and quite a number even of those who are in their third year and liable to be called up at any moment have been showing a real determination to make the most of the time available. Of course this is partly due to the reduction in the number of distractions, and I dare say also that the situation would change if the war became more active, but even one term snatched from the burning is all to the good.

As to myself, I reflected that whereas term usually goes like a flash this term had not. That, however, is not surprising since it ought to have started in October and for all practical purposes started for me at the end of August. Secondly, I never remember to have been so exhausted by bedtime as I have regularly been for the last two months. This is partly due to old age and infirmities creeping on, but more to the fact that, as I said in my last letter, I have been extremely busy, and busy with odd jobs, which are always more tiring than settled occupation. Thirdly, there has been no term in which I have done so little of my own work. In the last fortnight I pulled myself together and used what odd hours there were in putting together a paper for a learned journal, but the material was mostly collected some time ago and it involved no great effort beyond that (always considerable) of thinking of the right words and putting them in the right order. Previously odd hours had been devoted to a little spade-work on a subject on which I had undertaken to lecture in 1941. This lent a certain unreality to the proceedings, but the subject was off my usual beat and it was as well to see soon how much research it would need. Further thoughts that occurred to me were that I had done practically no entertaining during the term. This was partly a matter of economy, and partly due to the fact that it hasn't been easy to foresee a day on which I shouldn't have to do a good deal of work after dinner. On the rare occasions on which I did order a meal I was received by the kitchen-manager with open arms, the private-supply business of the kitchens being practically dead. Also I reflected that the closing of the Fitzwilliam had been unexpectedly depressing to me. It was unexpected because, apart from meetings of the Fitzw. Syndicate and from business connected with them, I didn't go there very often — perhaps twice a fortnight for half an hour — and came away not noticeably uplifted, and not having seen any object which was not familiar before. However the tonic proves to have been more than I realised, and I am glad that I resisted my first impulse to hide away the few objects of art of any value which I have in my rooms. I decided that if a bomb dropped on my rooms and I not in them, the satisfaction of knowing that I had a few drawings still to live with would not be considerable, and that in the meantime I might as well enjoy them in case the bomb fell on me and not on them.

The Mysterious University: lesson 2. Q. What is the Fitzwilliam Syndicate? *A.* The Committee which manages the Museum. Some University committees are called Syndicates, some Boards, and some simply Committees. Q. What is the difference between these? *A.* There is no appreciable difference. Q. Why, then, do they have different names? *A.* Nobody knows.

15.12.39

I shall close this instalment earlier than usual because, for the first time for very many years, I am not staying here for Christmas, and shall therefore have to send it out before I go away. This will have the advantage that it will reach more of you in time to wish you a happy Christmas. Some of you, I know, it will not reach until far into the New Year. But, at whatever time or place, and however long behind the time, it does wish you a very happy Christmas, and a much happier New Year than the last has been.

FIFTH LETTER

20.12.39

I HOPE you have raised your glasses to *Exeter*, *Achilles* and *Ajax*. The chivvying by those three cruisers of a ship that ought to have sunk the lot of them seems to me one of those feats of arms that tighten the heartstrings and come near to deluding one for a moment into the belief that war has after all some merits — the most inspiriting event for many weary months.[1]

1 The pocket battleship *Graf Spee*, engaged by these three cruisers in the south Atlantic on Dec. 13, took refuge at Montevideo, and was there scuttled four days later.

As I said in my last letter, I am breaking a very long-standing habit of spending Christmas in Cambridge — a pleasant place for the purpose if you have no overpowering itch for crackers and paper caps (and, as perhaps you may have guessed, I have none). It is very quiet, but on Christmas Day there is a Feast, smaller and more domestic, and therefore more agreeable, than term-time Feasts. We usually sit down about 40, and therefore dine in the Combination Room, which again is less formal than Hall. Formerly Colleges feasted continuously from Christmas to Twelfth-night, and as a relic of those heroic times Trinity provides its Fellows for twelve days with free lunches off a sideboard groaning with boar's head and other olde worlde viands; but this I find rather liverish myself, and I usually go away on the 26th or 27th. This year, however, my hostess, whom I did not want to miss, had to go to London immediately after Christmas so I forced myself into an appallingly crowded train and came down on the 23rd to N. Devon where I am writing this instalment — on a hill near Instow which looks over the Torridge and the Westward Ho peninsula to Bideford Bay. It is a lovely situation, there have been some fine sunny days, and though it has sometimes been cold, the western air is kindlier than the dank chill of Cambs. at this time of year. I have taken a good deal of air and mild exercise, done a little (very little) work, and read in a desultory manner—among other things *Why we are at War*, by Harold Nicolson (Penguin), a sensible and readable sixpenn'orth which one of you mentioned to me; *Down Stream*, by L. Mosley, a lively account by a journalist of recent European crises which he reported on the spot; a Life of Horace Walpole by Stephen Gwynn, cursory but readable (provided you are interested in H.W.); *In Good King Charles's Golden Days*, a dullish play by Shaw; *Theatre*, a novel by Somerset Maugham, as usual extremely competent, amusing, and rather disagreeable; and *Jack and Jill*, by E. Weekley, not as you might guess a novel, but a somewhat indigestible book about Christian names. Altogether a very agreeable respite after four depressing months, and though I do not find the war long absent from my thoughts even in the country, one is much less insistently reminded of it here than in Cambs. As a matter of fact, even after a term of normal length and content, I always find it a relief to stay in a private house. Life in College is all very well, and no doubt one is spared by it a deal of trouble; but it is a comfort to escape for a while from restaurant food, to have a bell to ring in case of need, and, more important than these, to have one's meals under the same roof as one's bed. Moreover my room, having the Cloister under the floor, is at all times hard to keep warm, and I reduced the size of the hearth in Sept. in order to economise coal. Consequently the parts by the window where I work have been arctic, and in cold weather you may picture me swathed in shawls, complete with mittens and foot-muff, struggling with nerveless fingers to hold the pen straight.

John Christie, with whom I am staying, has handed over his house and Opera-premises at Glyndebourne to evacuated infants, and the Opera Company is about to produce the *Beggar's Opera* in the provinces and afterwards in London. This ought to be fun. I haven't seen it for ages, but I used to enjoy Playfair's production at the Lyric in 1920 and the following years, for the music is charming, and the dialogue, as I have lately reminded myself by re-reading it, both unexpectedly witty, and, for 1728, unexpectedly modern. I have not in the past been a habitué of the Glyndebourne Opera, for, being highly unmusical, I have not, at the exhausting end of the summer term, felt sufficiently enthusiastic to dolly myself up in a tail-coat at tea-time and set off from Victoria to Lewes. Last July, however, when I was undergoing treatment in London, I took some nights off, found beds in Sussex, went to *Figaro*, *Così*, and *Macbeth*, and enjoyed myself very much. In the future (if there is such a thing) I shall be more enterprising.

7.1.40

I have also, for the first time since the war began, spent some odd nights in London — two before Christmas and four on my way back here. The inhabitants find it depressing, and I can see why, though even now in the matter of traffic, shop-windows, and so on, it would give points to any other European capital. Still, there are too many closed premises, barricaded or brown-papered windows, A.R.P. notices, and bedraggled sandbags; and unless one is prepared to walk further or take more taxis than suits arthritic and impoverished Dons, getting about is difficult owing to the reduction in omnibus and train services. Moreover soldiers in full battle-array, of whom there were a good many about, make nubbly neighbours in a crowded vehicle. At night it varies; when it is cloudy and moonless one can get along the main streets by the light of passing cars, and one soon learns the technique, but the quieter streets are like the Pit — much darker than Cambs. owing to the greater height of the houses — and walking is unpleasant and even alarming; and if one takes a bus it is difficult to make out where one has got to and when one has reached the destination. By moonlight of course it is easy enough, and surprisingly beautiful even in unlovely parts, for the moonlight, unbroken by harsher lighting, gives the blacks a velvety softness and delicacy. Some of the views of Cambs. by it have been astonishing, and I have never seen either the Great Court or Nevile's look better than with one side lit by a low moon, the other dark. I had a good deal of business of one sort and another to do in London and little time for diversions, but I contrived to attend an Alsatian lunch given by the Wine and Food Society (rather solid for my frugal taste), and to see a few pictures (the stationary kind). The dealers, however, like the Museums, have hidden their more important works in the country, and a diet of secondary works by secondary British painters is not very sustaining; and when, as at the United Artists' Exhibition at Burlington House, there are some two thousand of them, it is also highly indigestible. I paid an amusing visit to the headquarters of the Railway Executive Committee which from the bowels of the earth controls all the train-services. They are housed in a disused tube-station in quarters like the cabins of a ship behind numerous gas-proof doors of scarlet steel — altogether very impressive.

20.1.40

I have been busy with various odd jobs and with looking over University Scholarship papers. There are fourteen candidates, against twenty-two last year, a proportion which reflects the absence of all but one third-year man. The shortage saves the examiners a little trouble, but not so much as you suppose because in this exam., after each examiner has marked the papers he set himself, a select list is made and each examiner marks all the papers of those left in, who will presumably be as many as usual. It makes examining troublesome because little bundles of papers keep turning up just as you have settled down to something else. For the Chancellor's Medals there are no candidates (three last year); this, however, was to be expected for they are usually fourth-year men, and it was a sign rather of low cunning than of high intelligence on my part to select among my papers the only one which is done by the Medal-candidates alone. It might be thought to save the Chancellor a pretty penny, for his two medals (he gives also two more for other things during the year) used to contain in gold-standard days £10 worth of gold apiece, and, though I think they have lately been made of lower-carat gold, they must cost a good deal more than £10. However the Chancellor, having elicited from the Treasury the opinion that gold should not be used for such purposes in war-time, was proposing to strike them in bronze. I should not myself turn many stones to save the Chancellor's pocket because I do not think he pays dearly in money or trouble for his high honour, but gold medals are a silly form of prize. You couldn't wear them even if you wished, you hesitate to melt them down, and wilting self-esteem is little buttressed by the thought (if it occurs to you) that cached in a safe or a bank you possess such objects. The Treasury will, however, have saved the University a little money because it too gives some (smaller) medals annually and will now feel obliged to strike these in bronze.

I got back from London on Jan. 6 and Full Term began on the 15th. It has been bitterly cold and the pipes in my bathroom have been frozen. My reflections on this recurrent event you can supply for yourselves, and any that the new term may suggest had better be postponed to the next number. And if you think, as you well may, that there is little news in this, be pleased to recollect that it is a vacation number.

SIXTH LETTER

28.1.40

As to the new term (postponed from my last instalment), four of my pupils were called up last term and seven more in the vac.; and two medicals went off at the end of their seventh term to embark on clinical work elsewhere under a war-time regulation. Against these losses two men absent last term came back this, and I have admitted eight freshmen, most of whom would have come up normally next October. The wastage therefore is slow, and I see from statistics published in the *Review* that in the whole University there are 111 fewer male undergraduates than last term but 153 more refugee students from other seminaries. The authorities concerned are at present showing a willingness to allow people to postpone calling-up until after their exams., and if they continue our problems will be eased. At present, however, it looks as if there might be a shortage of freshmen in October. Even allowing for those admitted in advance my lists are a good deal shorter than usual at this time of year, and there was a falling off in the number of candidates for entrance scholarships which would appear to indicate that some didn't feel that they could send their sons up even if they got scholarships. What with increased taxation and the uncertainties of the times this is hardly surprising, but it is possible that a good many may come up at the last minute. The party for whom the Office of Works snaffled half the College still tarrying, the O. of W. has lodged another party of forty in the New Court, but I suppose I mustn't say who they are. They dine in Hall (to the advantage of the kitchens) but do not otherwise impinge upon us.

With the gradual removal of scaffolding and rubbish-heaps it begins to be possible to form some idea of the new John's building. This is a three-sided, four-storied, building opening on Bridge Street, the two short sides not rectangular but splayed outwards. East of this, running parallel with the Chapel up to the cross-road, is a very odd two-storied flat-topped building (to contain offices and garages) which will take a lot of getting used to. It is early to judge the court for there are hoardings in front of it still, but I suspect that I shan't like it very much for the windows are rather meanly designed. However with some grass and a tree or two it may not look so bad. We were told, if I remember, that the general aspect of Bridge Street was hardly to be encroached upon. In fact every house on that side from the corner to the bridge has been pulled down, and already a new shop is building next the bridge — apparently a garage. This complete reorganisation of the street is the most extensive alteration in Cambridge since the Caius building and the Guildhall transmogrified the Market Place. There are some other changes too that you will notice when you are here next. A large building is going up next the University Arms — a telephone exchange, I am told; and the town, hitherto idle about air-raid shelters, has lately been busy. Consequently the river bank in Chesterton is riddled with dug-outs and there are others on other open spaces; also one in Green Street on a site belonging to us which we lent for the purpose. Contrariwise, whatever we had intended to do on the site behind Matthew's (and in spite of undergraduate rumour our plans hadn't got very far) is now postponed and Matthew's are staying put for the duration — just as well, for one would like to know what the University will look like after the war before embarking on housing-schemes.

Term began with a tragedy. A pupil of mine, who was not indeed fit but not in any sense ill, was seized with a pain in the chest while dressing and died within the hour, the cause, apparently, collapse of a lung. Nobody could have foreseen it, and though the nurse was on the spot in five minutes and a doctor with oxygen in ten, they could do nothing. I remember some years ago a case of an undergraduate who went for a gentle run rather too soon after a modest lunch, collapsed, and died almost on the spot — this time from a failure in the spleen — though he had done nothing that I should hesitate for a moment to do myself. These calamities leave me, and must leave any Tutor, with a sense of insecurity; they do not happen often, but happen they do, and since they are unaccountable one wonders why they do not happen oftener, and to whom one will happen next.

11.2.40

As it is no longer a state secret that it has been cold, I may say that the weather reduced the plumbing and sanitary arrangements of the College to a pretty pass. My bathroom pipes, reported in my last as frozen, shortly afterwards burst — an occurrence ambiguously reported to the Junior Bursar in the words 'Mr Gow's burst and flooded the rooms below' (o shades of Arius); and those above shortly after retaliated by bursting and flooding my waiting-room. After the snow came it was filthy, for though there wasn't much, it froze into three inches of dirty ice over everything, and as the cold was unnaturally combined with an outbreak of influenza I spent a good deal of time slithering gingerly from sick-bed to sick-bed. Before that it wasn't so bad for there were some lovely sunny and windless days, and not so long since I should have enjoyed it; but I daren't any longer trust my damaged hip on skates, and as I now weigh something less than ten stone (as against thirteen) I am ill protected against cold, which I dislike very much. Moreover, as second childhood draws nearer, I have reverted to chilblains, an affliction I haven't thought of these thirty years. So if you have pictured me, in the somewhat unpoetical phrase of the poet, biting the blue finger, correct the impression; some of them are red or green, and too sore to bite. There has also been a difficulty in getting supplies of the particular kind of fuel required to warm University buildings (technically and ridiculously known as washed peas), and one has tottered to meetings laden with coats and rugs in case the heating had broken down — though, as a matter of fact, it hasn't as yet. For the first time, I think, I have noticed a seagull or two on the Backs and even in Nevile's Court, and one day, when there was ice on the river and a powdering of snow, I found the track of an otter running from water below John's to water above King's. No doubt it knew its own business, but I was very much surprised; and in case any

of you think I don't know an otter's track when I see one, let me add that
I got someone to confirm this diagnosis.[1]

As to my avocations (a perennial theme, I fear, in this correspondence)
I am in theory less busy than last term for I am lecturing less. In practice
it hasn't proved so, and the immortal work remains in store. I have
been engaged with University Scholarship papers, which are unusually
troublesome this year because one has got to keep up the standard though
there are fewer candidates; and, though this is easy in, say, a Tripos, where
there are standards of marks, it is much harder in a competitive examination where the standard must vary a good deal with the strength of the
competitors. We shall make our awards next week, I should guess not
awarding all the scholarships. I have also had to spend a good deal of
time on examination entries, which are always tiresome, and at present
much more so than usual owing to emergency regulations and the uncertainty of prospective candidates as to their future; and on correcting
proofs — a book by someone else, and an article by me. The latter
would have been no great matter but that it has involved me in a brawl
with the Clarendon Press which has lately taken over the publication of
the Classical journals and has a maddening habit of imposing its own
whims of spelling and punctuation on its contributors. I happen to dislike
such spellings as judgement and realization, and my gorge rises at being
made to write Jones' nose when I mean and say Jones's; hence I have been
composing courteously nasty notes on the rights of self-respecting authors.
In addition to these pursuits I have been a good deal occupied on the
Exemptions Committee, which, in normal circs., costs no great labour.
The Mysterious University: lesson 3. Q. What is the E.C.? A. The E.C.
is a committee of the Council which deals with such matters as allowances
of terms and examinations, remission of fees, etc. It has been busy with
applications from people who were away, or came back late, last term for
reasons connected with the war though not obviously national service.
They held this or that erroneous opinion as to what would happen; could
not get passports, or passages, or their ship was delayed; one was asked to
censor letters in Arabic, another to broadcast in Afrikaans; this one is
working with the National Allotments Committee, that one is in Finland
with an ambulance — and so on and so forth. It can't be called very
entertaining, but some of the cases take a good deal of discussion, and the
committee, which in normal times meets seldom, has been kept fairly busy.

[1] See p. 30.

17.2.40

A native of Ceylon, taking his degree from this College the other day, disclosed in doing so that his first name was Nanayakkaragodakandéarach-chige. A facetious friend has written to ask whether I addressed him as Nan, or God, or Earache, but so far as I know I never addressed him at all. If any of you, as a relief from the usual weary contents of the papers, have been reading the case in which a young woman sued her husband's parents for enticement, you may like to know that, however little else you may have had in common with the husband in the case, you at least had a common tutor.

SEVENTH LETTER

28.2.40

I HAVE been contemplating the *Altmark* affair[1] with diversified emotions — admiration for a ticklish undertaking carried out very efficiently; satisfaction at the fury it has evidently caused in Germany; some sympathy with the Norwegians, who are in a very awkward situation; amusement at the diversified pleas of the Norwegians, who say the ship was naval and could not be examined, and of the Germans, who say that it was an innocent and outraged merchant-vessel; some regret that we should have been forced into an action which, if legal, is somewhat high-handed; and at the same time some approval of our showing that we cannot indefinitely stand on the letter of laws to which the other side pays no attention at all. Our international lawyers are not agreed on the legal position, which turns, apparently, on whether legitimate passage through territorial waters can be held to cover a long voyage down the Norwegian coast in a kind of safety rat-run. Since the Norwegians seems to have been unduly complaisant about the torpedoing of ships (including their own) inside their three-mile limit, my sympathy with them is tempered, especially as no Norwegian came to any harm.

The otter who was stated in my last letter to have surprised me should perhaps have done so less than he did; I mentioned the matter to the Master of John's who told me that when he had rooms overlooking the river he used often to see otters playing at night between the two bridges.

---

[1] On Feb. 14 the *Altmark* was located in Josing Fjord. H.M.S. *Cossack* entered the fjord and released 299 prisoners from ships sunk by the *Graf Spee*.

This was no doubt some time ago, but it must have been within this century for he is not more than five or six years senior to me. So I suppose that I might have seen them too if I had looked; but I never did, nor do I remember ever to have heard of otters on the Backs in my undergraduate days.

9.3.40

I went a week or so since to a meeting of the Arts Society and was amused to notice that all the questions put to the reader of the paper were in guttural German accents. It wasn't quite a fair test for the reader was a German-Jew refugee, and refugees are good at rallying round when one of them is performing; and indeed it was that motive which took me there, for he was one Ruhemann, formerly picture-restorer to the Berlin Gallery, whom I have known and liked for some years now. But it is true that there are an awful lot of German refugees in Cambridge and I am constantly overhearing scraps of Hunnish in the streets. There were already a good many before the war, some of them rather bores, poor dears, partly because it is their nature, and partly because they are on their beam-ends and bound to be often asking if nothing can be done for them; and I suppose the increase of German in the streets, which I seem to have noticed of late, is partly due to more having arrived with the London institutions to which they had attached themselves. Another consequence of the arrival of London in our midst is the growth of undergraduate soviets of one sort and another, fostered, I fancy, largely by the London School of Economics, whose left-wing predilections incline them favourably to soviets. And, apart from that, in a non-residential University such as London undergraduates naturally organise more for themselves than they need do here. Perhaps too the seed fell on ground partially prepared, for the questionnaires and memorials which circulated here before the war about the teaching in the different faculties looked somewhat symptomatic. I cannot say that the movement alarms me, or that I hear a menacing roll of approaching tumbrils, for I believe in the fundamental good sense of most undergraduates; and I even think that some good may result, if not as much as the reformers anticipate. The trouble is that the ardent and youthful are inclined to go off the deep end before looking to see whether there is any water in the bath, and that their communications often display more vigour than urbanity. Thus the General Board not long since received from one undergraduate body a

31

letter roundly denouncing our supine acquiescence in a number of abuses which in fact had never existed, and the Librarian of the University Library, which has been carrying on with great difficulty owing to the absence of a third of its staff, was not particularly gratified to receive a curt notice that another undergraduate body 'has decided that the Library shall remain open for longer hours'. Undergraduate Hampdens, too, are rather apt to fire the beacon of freedom and reform, and then go off and forget all about it. The Classical Board last year received a memorial containing the results of a questionnaire about reforms in teaching and examinations, and though quite a small number had answered the questionnaire it took a good deal of pains over it, made one reform asked for, and appointed a heavy delegation of Professors and others to meet the complainants — of whom only one took the trouble to turn up at the meeting. There is, in short, an element of absurdity about all this, and it doesn't shock me at all; but such things take up the responsible body's time, and just now responsible bodies have a good deal to do. Moreover, like enough, it will all die down. I note that the recently formed College Union, which had a hundred at its first meeting, has dwindled at its second and third to fifty and twenty, and you may rest assured that the College is no redder than before in consequence of its deliberations. Indeed, so far as I know, all it did was to appoint the members of certain committees previously appointed rather (but not much) less democratically by the Junior Combination Room Committee.

17.3.40

Term came to an end two days ago, unlamented by me, for, what with the weather and this and that, it has been pretty beastly. When I last wrote of the weather we were having a thaw which I fondly assumed to be the end of the frost. In fact it lasted only for four days, and though it melted the snow, and converted the courts and paddocks into lakes (as the water could not penetrate the frozen ground), the snow was shortly afterwards replaced by some slightly cleaner which lasted a long while though this time it did not cake up the streets with ice. We never had here the frozen rain which did so much harm to trees, but the long cold has had a disastrous effect on grass, paths, and in some places on stone-work. The Ketton stone of which Cambs. is mostly built, if you look at it under a lens (as no doubt you were constantly doing), looks like caviare, with little grains so closely cemented together that you cannot easily get one out. The cold and damp have undone these bonds so that the surface of the stone has powdered away and at the bottom of some walls you see little mounds of sand. However fortunately the only part of Trinity which has suffered badly is the Hall steps which are in a sad mess but do not much matter. When the thaw arrived in earnest the epidemics, which had unseasonably begun in the frost, really took hold, and I never remember so many victims as were simultaneously laid up with influenza, German measles, or bad throats — so many that the doctors, who are much reduced in numbers, have been hard put to it, and there has been no getting the measly into homes or the Isolation Hospital despite the lamentable outcries of some of their landladies who pester me on the telephone. I am apt to escape influenza myself, and have in fact not caught measles, but I have had a foul throat and have in consequence been less conscientious than usual in visiting the sick, not wishing to exchange complaints with them — though I could in any case hardly have got round the lot.

The University Scholarships were awarded about the middle of last month, or rather one was awarded and three were not. This was not unexpected for the standard had to be kept up; and as it is unusual for more than one second-year man to get a scholarship, and there was no serious third-year candidate, the result might be said to be plausible however stingy it looked. In other capacities I have also failed to award five prizes for Greek and Latin composition. This is more surprising, but there were very few candidates and their works more deserving of penalties than prizes. By all this the University benefits a bit, for under its emergency statutes it is taking power to annex unexpended balances of trust funds (such as finance prizes and scholarships) and pay them into a general emergency fund, to which will also go the stipends of professorships and other posts vacated by death or retirement and left vacant for the duration — as almost all will be. This is our device for financing the University, which will, if the war goes on long, be no easy task since we are faced with a reduction in income from fees of the order of £50,000 this year, and the deficit may well increase. Also until the other day we were uncertain whether we should get the usual Government grant though for the present this is now assured.

Rations have set in here as elsewhere and give the steward a lot of trouble (meat began too late to affect the term), but I do not hear complaints from undergraduates, and make none myself at present since I do not eat meat, hardly eat butter, and never have sugar in my drinks.

Consequently the High Table is so far the better for my ration-card on which I have as yet drawn nothing myself. Gates are put back again to 12 (instead of 11) as the result of a petition from undergraduates; and corduroy trousers are all the wear though I haven't taken to them myself. They serve to distinguish the males of this University from the females of others now resident here, who favour blue serge or grey flannel.

With these items of social intelligence I shall close — rather earlier than usual, for though I have no plans for the vac. I shall have to go away for a few days to try and shake off my sore throat, and it will be convenient to get this number off before Easter.

EIGHTH LETTER

28.3.40

THE passage in my 4th letter about war-time reading reminded me that in the last war I kept Gibbon as a stand-by and read him through in bed; and it caused me to think I might select some similar work for bed-side literature in this — somewhat on the principle of Mr. Soapy Sponge (a character whom I do not otherwise much resemble) who always carried in his pocket Mogg's *Ten Thousand Cabfares* in case he should need intellectual refreshment. I couldn't read Gibbon through again, for though it is amusing and interesting from page to page, the cumulative effect of the style is stupefying. I therefore began with Lockhart's *Life of Scott*, which I had recommended to you, but after about two volumes changed to Byron's letters. Both are favourites (a short selection of Byron in Everyman by the way), and either would have done very well but for the fact that their print is smaller than I can now conveniently read in bed. Hence, being as yet without the ideal Mogg, I have read various oddments of other sorts — most of Yeats's collected poems, bits of the French Diplomatic Yellow Book (more detailed than the English White Book, but, the milk being spilt, my interest in a slow-motion picture of the overturning jug does not reach to 400 pages of bad French print), *Amurath to Amurath* (travel and archaeology in Asiatic Turkey by Gertrude Bell), her *Letters* (which can be obtained in two Pelican vols. and are interesting), Chesterton's *Autobiography* (amusing in parts), Rothenstein's *Memoirs* vol. 3 (not exciting), *The Wandering Years* (an entertaining autobiography of adventure by Weston Martyr with matter about the last war which might be useful in this), *A Naturalist on Rona* (by F. F.

Darling; essays, mostly about seals and birds — interesting if you like that sort of thing), *The Land of the Blessed Virgin*, and *Don Fernando* (both by Somerset Maugham, the first about Andalusia, the second about Spain in the XVIth and XVIIth cents.) The last two remind me to say that when in letter 5 I called a novel by S.M. competent, one of you supposed me to be criticising him. This was a mistake for I am far too conscious of the difficulty of constructing even the simplest paragraph to use the word disparagingly. Some time ago I read a book of S.M.'s, called *The Summing Up*, about the relations of a novelist and a playwright with his public; it happened to interest me (though it might not you) but in particular it impressed me by the unobtrusive efficiency of the style. I had read next to nothing of his before and have since read most of his non-dramatic works and think him a very good writer — if you want fiction you might well do worse than the omnibus volume of his short stories called *Altogether* (better on the whole than his novels). I do not think him a great or important author because he doesn't seem to me to have anything very important to say, but that is another matter. You might, by the way, do worse than read a sixpenny booklet by him called *France at War*.

You will infer from this that I read the two books about Spain (which are quite interesting) rather because they were by S.M. than because I am a Hispanophil — and in fact I am not, and have only been there twice. The first time, in Madrid and Castile, I disliked it more than any foreign country I have been to — I disliked the people, their ways of life, and the hideous chocolate landscape of Castile hemmed in by jagged mountains with no nobility of outline. The second time I went again to Madrid, but also to Andalusia and liked it better, for the country was greener and the mountains had more shape. Moreover, though I hold no brief for Moorish architecture, the mosque at Cordoba is undeniably a remarkable building, and the Alhambra seen from outside — a rose-red fortress crowning a hill set with poplars and cypresses against a background of snow-mountains — fairly takes the breath. Of course the pictures in the Prado reconcile one to a fortnight in Madrid which must otherwise be the least interesting and agreeable of European capitals, and has, besides, a vile climate with scorching sun in one street and a blast off a glacier in the next — and it may be that my dislike is partly due to the devastating colds I caught there.

I got back to Cambs. three days ago after a brief holiday which began at Eton, where I usually go at this time of year having still old friends there besides several ex-pupils. I did not notice many new signs of war, for the dug-outs were mostly complete a year ago and the principal sign of change is that the boys go into school bare-headed so that they may repair to the said dug-outs without a preliminary fight over their top-hats. Some Government Department has erected at the Slough end of Agar's Plough a vast series of Ladies' and Gents.' latrines; nobody seems to know exactly for whose use they are intended, and though the playing fields of Eton have a good reputation for winning battles, I do not myself see that these additions to them will assist greatly in winning the war. However, though no great ornament to the landscape, neither are they any great dis-figurement. About eight of the junior masters have gone off and have been replaced by substitutes (of whom two chance to be former pupils of mine), and more are going before next Half. I recall with amusement the motley procession of Ersatz-beaks who featured there during the last war and don't envy the Headmaster the task of finding competent substitutes.

From Eton I went to Lewes for four days. Why Lewes? Well, I had reason, which proved to be well founded, to believe there was a comfort-able hotel there, thought that a draught of air off the sea might be good for me (as perhaps it was), and knew that the Downs on either side of the town were good to walk on; and this I knew because I used to stay at Glyndebourne (long before there was an opera there) and had often walked on them before. It was pleasant enough but not an unqualified success, for I was too lame to walk very much, the said draught off the sea was too cold and violent to sit about in, and I rather badly wanted a car to potter round the country. There was hardly a sign of spring in Sussex, whereas here not only the willows, which are always very early, but also most other trees are already showing green.

There being at Lewes a good deal of time between the hour at which I could walk no more and that at which I could with decency go to bed, I did a certain amount of desultory reading — a book by G. Rivière about Degas (who as a man amuses me, and as an artist interests me much more than any other painter of the last hundred years); a work by a writer with the resounding name (or pen-name) of Antoine de Saint Exupéry called *Terre des Hommes* and about the experiences of a commercial air-pilot

(R.A.F. readers please note; but they might prefer an earlier work by the same called *Vol de Nuit*); *Adventures Before Thirty*, by Algernon Black-wood, hitherto known to me only as a writer of ghost-stories (struggles for a living in America; I thought it very interesting. You can buy it in the Travellers' Library for 3/6), and three Penguins: *The Southseaman* by Weston Martyr (see above; about building and sailing a boat; readable but too technical for me), and two novels about country-life — *The Lonely Plough*, by Constance Holme (Westmorland, mainly cheerful), and *Fontamara* by Ignazio Silone (Abruzzi, mainly gloomy), both goodish. Perhaps you thought that you would get off any more literary chitchat in this number? You were wrong — partly because this is vacation, partly because I can now include two novels, and one of you complained of Our Literary Corner on the grounds that it contained no fiction and he was immutably determined to read nothing else. I also read half the *Iliad* and will not conceal from you that it is better value than any of the above-mentioned works.

In addition to these excursions I have spent odd days in London and shall have to spend two more before term begins, attending to bits of business and seeing people. In the intervals of these pursuits I have been to various exhibitions of pictures, of which the best is one of British Painting since Whistler which occupies nine rooms of the National Gallery. It might perhaps be better balanced but it is quite a good show, the pictures look very well in the ample space which the N.G. affords them, and it is nice to have the N.G. open again. I also visited a military hospital at Roehampton to see a pupil invalided home from France with pleurisy, and formed the impression that if any more of you should be unlucky enough to suffer a similar fate you would be comfortable and well looked-after. And, for the first time for I do not know how many years, I went to a London theatre — to see, as I advised you to do, the Glyndebourne *Beggar's Opera* which has now reached the Haymarket. It is a much more finished production than Playfair's and I enjoyed it very much though vexed to see it staged in the 1820's instead of the 1720's. Playfair's setting was not all that realistic and it should not have been difficult to stick to Gay and Hogarth without seeming to copy him; and, whatever Gielgud may say, his evocations of Dickens and Cruikshank seem to me incongruous. However I am, as you know, a pedant both by instinct and profession, and you need not fear that considerations of this kind will prevent you from having a very agreeable evening.

19.4.40

Since the above was written term has begun and much else of more moment has occurred and is impending.[1] All this I leave for the present, but as the war seems to have taken a turn for better or worse (better I hope), I should perhaps say now that though I intend to continue this series as long as I can, it is not difficult to imagine circumstances which might delay or stop me. Hence if your monthly dose doesn't arrive don't immediately assume the reason to be catastrophic. And if in fact it proves that a bomb has dropped on my head (or the like), whatever other reflections such an incident may suggest, be pleased to remember that it will at any rate have saved me a deal of trouble.

NINTH LETTER

28.4.40

Full Term began on the 19th (the date of my last instalment) but has so far produced no startling news. I have lost three pupils (one from calling up, one from illness, and one from a too fond mamma), and regained one, invalided out after a week in the Navy; one or two freshmen have been admitted, and in numbers we are much where we were. The most exciting local event is the arrival at the Fitzwilliam of some pictures which reached us from the bequest of one Hindley Smith who had a large and quite good collection of modern French and English pictures. He had no connexion with Cambridge but left his collection to be distributed by the dealer from whom he had bought most of it; and the dealer, seeing Oxford and Cambs. to be deplorably lacking in modern works of any significance, divided the bulk of it between us, giving Cambs. about thirty pictures and some drawings and sculpture. The plums among ours are by Degas and Renoir, but there are other decent pictures by important artists and good ones by less important, and the gift is a deliverance indeed. Most of us had been praying for something of the sort for thirty years, but the late Director of the Museum, who had a talent for begging, couldn't be got to take any interest in modern painting, and the prospects were growing dimmer and dimmer; we shall now have quite a respectable show, and, what is perhaps more important, a nest-egg. The nest-egg principle is vital in museums like the Fitzw. If you have something of a

[1] German troops occupied Denmark and entered Norway on Apr. 9. British and French forces landed in Norway on Apr. 11.

sort, the private collector says 'Here is a good museum very weak in so and so; I shall bequeath my collection to it; it will there cut a dash which it wouldn't in a London Museum.' If you have nothing, he says 'These fools don't know what is worth having', and disposes of his things elsewhere. We had known for some time that these pictures were to be ours, but the fly in the ointment had been that they were to be stowed away in a place of safety and it had seemed necessary to survive the war in order to see them. However the Museum opened in the middle of last term with a loan collection of modern English pictures (not exactly my cup of tea but refreshing in a drought); and, as we were open, we thought we might risk these for a month before consigning them to a cache. We shall shortly have also an exhibition of printing to commemorate, as well as one can at present, the 500th anniversary of the invention of that dangerous craft. We are now paying a price for having opened the Museum because a Government Department, having seen its inside, is threatening to bag it. However we are resisting.

My time has been somewhat occupied, and was occupied in the vac., with various committees. One was a committee of the Council on the allowances for war service to be made to people who have not yet matriculated — not, you might think, an urgent matter, but in the last war a trickle of casualties began to come in fairly early and it is as well to be prepared. Another was a committee on the College Kitchens which are in a proper mess financially. I am well aware that most of you believe (erroneously, I may add) that you could run the kitchens better yourselves, and will merely say that the College has never aimed at running them at a profit, and that our fundamental difficulty is that men are only up for six months in the year while most of the overhead charges go on for twelve. However with reduced numbers, rising costs of provisions, almost complete disappearance of the private-supply business, abolition of feasts, calling up of porters, etc., etc., the situation had become desperate. We have therefore reduced the undergraduate dinner by a course, limited private supply to dishes on the lunch and dinner menu, and given notice to our more highly paid chefs, who under present conditions have little to do. Since you probably believe also that the High Table dinner is paid for by undergraduates, I add (a) that this is not the case, and (b) that it also has been reduced by a course. Among our troubles has been the amount of clerical work entailed by rationing. I don't hear any complaints of this or of the shortened dinner from undergraduates, and I myself am positively the better off. As I eat no meat, when it was served I used to go without; now on the nights when rationed meat appears I get a vegetarian substitute.

If you want to know what those who sometimes dine in Hall and sometimes not do about rations, I can hardly do better than quote the local Food-Executive Officer: 'Non-resident Fellows who wish to retain their meat coupons for use in their private houses will not be required to give up their meat coupons to the College, notwithstanding that they may dine regularly in Hall, subject however that, in such cases their right to take meat dishes in Hall must be postponed to Undergraduates and resident Fellows who have given up coupons, being limited to the supplies of meat being available in College' — or perhaps, if I really tried, I could do better. This reminds me to say that my observations on military English in letter 2 have brought me from one of you the proper description of a wheel which you may happen to have detached from a wheelbarrow; it is 'Barrows, wheel, large, steel — less barrow 1'.

9.5.40

Some of you will shortly receive a notice about taking your degrees in virtue of war allowances. In case you are feeling doubtful whether or not to do so, I will say (regardless of the boredom I shall cause to those not confronted by this choice) that though I do not feel very strongly about it, I should myself be inclined to take the degree. The arguments against are, I suppose, that the glory of a B.A. is not at the moment very useful to you, and that if you come back after the war to complete your courses, as I hope many of you will, you will have paid Capitation Tax for three terms which you will subsequently keep over again. The last argument, however, is fallacious, for if you come back as B.A.'s you will save much more in the reduction of fees than you will now be charged for Capit. Tax, and you will have the advantage of not having to keep terms, and also the other privileges of B.A.'s. Another argument, though it is not one that I should wish to weigh heavily, is that the conditions offered are generous, and that, as the University finances are in Queer Street owing to the war, you would do it some service by taking the degree now. However don't think that I am pressing you if you don't want. The notice will be received not only by those who have already three terms war service to their credit but also by those who have two or one. Further generosity: but the Council, confronted by the dilemma of allowing a year's examinations on less than a year's absence, or else allowing the examinations to those absent for a year but refusing them to those who had spent part of the year working for them (or so it is hoped), preferred to impale themselves on the first horn. The Council spends a good deal of time confronting dilemmas just now, but the horns of this one are not very sharp for it seems unlikely that those now favoured will not presently have a year's war service to show.

Spring has been very lovely here. The crocuses indeed got so nipped and buffeted that they were below form and the editors, so far as I observed, prudently left their stock picture of our Avenue in its drawer, but the other spring flowers — daffodils, fritillaries, cowslips and so on — and the blossom (including the wistaria in the Great Court) have been better than usual, and one has perhaps appreciated them the more for the current vileness of man. They came on with a rush owing to one or two warm days at the end of last month, and the only thing I have missed is the convoys of ducklings on the Backs. The ducks seem to have decided that the Upper River makes a better nursery, for there are plenty there, but they were a pleasant addition to the amenities nearer home, like the ducks themselves, who are comparatively newcomers to the river. I have always supposed that it was the drying up of some of their fenland haunts in two recent summers that brought them into Cambridge. And this reminds me to say that when in London I was surprised at the vast numbers of tufted ducks on the river by Westminster Bridge. Whether they are always there, or came owing to the hard winter, I do not know, for in the days when I had a home in those parts and walked the Embankment more I was even less observant of such matters than I am now. As I write the swifts are swishing round this Court for the first time. I count them always as the beginning of summer, and they are patterns of punctuality for year after year they appear on May 9 or 10.

17.5.40

I sent out my last letter when Norway was just developing, wrote the last section of this in a political crisis, and dispatch it while Holland and Belgium are in the toils and we are facing a new version of August 1914.[1] Neither strategy, nor politics, nor prophecy, are within my competence; and, if they were, the function of these letters is rather to provide relief

---

[1] German troops entered Holland and Belgium on May 10. A national War Cabinet was formed on May 11.

from the war than to discuss it. Therefore I say only of the first that I think anxiety and disppointment[1] have led some to forget the substantial goods delivered (as usual) by the Navy; of the second, that some of the criticism (not all) seems to me either stupid or dishonest (for where initiative consists in outrage, you must either advocate outrage or refrain from blaming those who lack initiative); and of the third — well, 'All thoughts to rive the heart are here, and all are vain: Horror and scorn and hate and fear and indignation'. But if I do not write of these things do not suppose I do not think of them. I find it an effort to think, and therefore to write, of anything else; so if this letter is even duller than usual, make allowances.

P.S. On Mussolini see a proverb recorded by Bacon in his *Promus of Formularies and Elegancies*, a work with which, it may be, you are not very familiar — 'He doth like the ape that the higher he clymbes the more he showes his ars'.

TENTH LETTER

24.6.40

I HAVE found it impossible during the month since I last wrote to you to sit down and chronicle the small beer usually handed round at this party, but if I write the less I have been thinking of you the more, and especially of those who have been in the thick of it. It is the privilege of my profession to have many friends and acquaintances much younger than ourselves, and to take in their welfare a warmer interest, perhaps, than we are always credited with. In times like these it is not a privilege which makes for peace of mind, and if this letter is shorter and more serious than its predecessors that must be my excuse. It would be a kindness if those of you who had addresses in France, or are in the R.A.F. or R.N., would write me a line at least of news.

I will begin by answering a question one of you asked me a month ago — whether I was pessimistic about the war.

Events since the question was asked have not conduced to optimism,[2] but I had not then seen any reason to think that we should be defeated,

---

[1] The evacuation of Norway had been announced on May 2.

[2] The evacuation of Dunkirk was completed on June 4; Italy entered the war on June 10; Germans entered Paris on June 14; Marshal Pétain asked for terms on June 17, and signed an armistice five days later.

and, provided that we lose neither heart nor head, I still decline to contemplate that possibility. But even if I did so, I should still say, taking a long view, that I was no pessimist. I will not attempt to define the cause for which we are fighting, and probably we should not agree in detail about it, but at least it includes reasonable liberty to the individual to think and act for himself, and, in international relations, such standards of decent behaviour as in civilised society a man expects of his neighbour. The dictators are necessarily hostile to the first of these ideals and have proved themselves hostile to the second, but I have no doubt nevertheless that the ideals will survive, in other continents if not in this, and that the outrages of the last five years, which have now put the meaning of Nazi and Fascist beyond question, have roused men to the realisation of what is at stake, and will ultimately ensure not only the survival but the victory.

On the short view, whatever the outcome of the war, I am not cheerful about the prospects in Europe for many years to come, at any rate for those who by reason of age or health can no longer adapt themselves easily to new ways of life. But most of these, I hope, are aware that nothing that can happen to us can have any real significance, and if it is unpleasant we must reflect that some part of our lives has been spent in easier and happier times than are likely to return for long to come. We may be 'strangers and afraid', but not 'in a world we never made', for, however little any one of us has contributed, we share collectively the responsibility for what has happened — and by 'we' I mean my own and older generations not only in England but in all the greater nations of Europe and America. For my own part provided we win this war I do not care what happens to me; and if we should chance to lose, the thought of surviving is intolerable — and this equilibrium of the spirit, though not exactly optimistic, should not be called pessimism.

I read some time ago, and should have mentioned in my last letter if I had had room, Henderson's *Failure of a Mission*. It is somewhat too much a personal apologia, and though it has been called well-written, I do not think it so — even in this cliché-fed and mealy-mouthed age it shocks me to read that if he had known his dispatch about Goering's tapestries was to be published he would have substituted 'nude figures' for 'naked ladies'. Still, if not distinguished in style, it is easy to read, sets out the whole horrible story quite lucidly, and draws a clearer picture of the people chiefly concerned (especially of Goering and Goebbels) than I have seen elsewhere.

The impression it left on my mind was that nothing we could have done in recent years would have prevented war, and this has been amply confirmed in the last month by the accumulating evidence of long premeditation and preparation — preparation so thorough and efficient that one cannot but feel some admiration for it. The future historian will no doubt be in a more favourable position for admiring it than you and I, but I think he must add that up to the present we have not been lucky. We have been unlucky in the weather, unlucky in the extraordinary miscalculations of the French, and unlucky in Belgium — first that Albert should needlessly break his neck, and secondly that Leopold should have been neither sufficiently pro-German not to ask us in nor sufficiently pro-ally to make advance arrangements or, when once committed, to see it through. I suppose that the Old Harrovians, who are already somewhat above themselves at the number of O.H.'s running this country, will derive further uplift from the behaviour of that unhappy young man[1] whom I remember well as a shy nice-mannered boy at Eton. I am glad, however, that we have been more reticent than his own countrymen and the French, for I dare say that when the smoke of battle lifts we shall see more cause for pity than for anger. On Italy I will perhaps write something in another letter.

Arrears of Cambridge news must keep. The next three numbers are vacation numbers and if they get written at all will be hard indeed to fill. Present indications suggest a variety of causes which might prevent them getting written, and in case one of these should intervene between us I take this opportunity of sending you every good wish.

ELEVENTH LETTER

7.7.40

My last month's letter contained no Cambridge news and I shall go back to recount the effect of events in the outer world upon this microcosm. The racket began on May 12 when my Sunday lunch was disturbed with the tidings that the police had arrested three of my pupils. They had in fact arrested and interned all male enemy aliens under 60. It was the sensible thing to do, but it was uncommon hard on some of them — on one of my three, for instance, who had often and vainly tried

[1] King Leopold asked for terms on May 28.

for a commission and was about to get a first in the Tripos. It was also hard on others besides the aliens, for the wives of some of the senior men were left without support and had to be provided for locally. A certain number of University Lecturers were also removed and there was a shortage of examiners in Law. About the same time the Chairman of Examiners in the Natural Sciences Tripos was in danger of being jugged . owing to the indiscretions of the Peace Pledge Union with which he was connected, and though this danger was averted, 'Examiners in Prison' made a novel agendum for the General Board.

The next item was the formation of the L.D.V.'s and the Home Defence Battalions, which at once put us in a difficulty. Up to this point men had been encouraged by the Govt. to go on with their education until 20, and as the Govt. could, if they wished, call up the 18's and 19's at any moment, it was plain (at least to me) that it was not the business of an educational establishment to urge anyone to abandon his education. What advice to give those so minded was less clear, but in the end we ascertained that the authorities wanted medicals, engineers, and other technicians to go on with their work, and that though they didn't want all Arts students to volunteer, they did want a sprinkling of keen ones who would make good officers. What we shall be doing in October is for other reasons wrapped in mystery (though of course we shall be carrying on unless we are forcibly prevented; please contradict rumours to the contrary), but even if nothing else intervenes the formation of these two bodies will make a considerable difference to our numbers. In the middle of last term, when things were still quiet, it seemed probable that we should have nearly as many men up next year as last, and my tenure of the tutorship was in consequence prolonged for another year. At the time this was an obvious step to take, for though during the last year smaller numbers have meant less routine work for Tutors, the complexity and difficulty of the work which remained had increased enormously owing both to the number of emergency regulations and also to the extreme difficulty of advising one's pupils in a situation where some of the factors are incalculable. Consequently there was still ample work for four Tutors and it would have been a mistake to reduce the number. At the moment the matter rests there, but by the autumn things may well look different. The University Grants Committee has lately enquired how many men will be in residence in October and has been told to ask us an easier one.

The next incident was that the Heads of Houses (whom you perhaps call Masters of Colleges) met and decided that men should go down as soon as they had finished their exams. This was not in fact a panic-stricken decision and in itself there was a good deal to be said for it, but it was reached too late, and it was so worded and announced that in some quarters (not in Trinity) it produced something like a panic. As the Heads of Houses are an entirely unconstitutional body with no powers to commit their own Colleges, let alone the University, and as this ukase caused a great deal of inconvenience to everyone concerned, their action came in for some very acid criticism and I should be surprised if they met again.

The collapse of France marked the beginning of air activity, about which I suppose I mustn't write much. Suffice it, then, that at the date of writing the University is intact, that we have had a great many warnings of one colour or another, and that I am no longer a stranger either to the explosion or to the whistle of a bomb. I have been busy with A.R.P., for these experiences suggested some changes, and the problem, with a constantly fluctuating population, requires a good deal of looking after. It cannot indeed be very effectively solved, but one must do one's best to protect the buildings and their occupants, and I shall be engaged this week in arranging for the Long Vac. term, during which there will be a fair number of men — mostly medicals — in residence.

The Mysterious University: lesson 4 (a long time since we had one). Q. What is the University Grants Committee? *A.* It is a committee of the Treasury which deals with Govt. grants to Universities. Normally it impinges on a tutor's life only in the Long, when it demands a tiresome return of one's pupils classified in various ways. The inexperienced tutor spends a long time trying to get the totals on the different pages to agree. The more experienced (or one of them), knowing that precise accuracy cannot matter, has thought of some unprincipled devices for facilitating this task.

17.7.40

I said in no. 10 that I might presently write something about Italy. That was partly because I foresaw that I should be short of matter, partly because I have known and liked it better than other European countries. I don't mean that I really know the people intimately or speak Italian at all fluently, but I have been there a great deal in the last 35 years, mainly for the purpose of studying pictures; and if you do this seriously in Italy you must visit not only most towns but also many villages, so that from

Rome to the Alps I do know the towns (other than the purely industrial and the watering places) and much also of the countryside.

I never banked much on Italian neutrality myself, partly because Mussolini hates England, and at intervals, when it has not seemed more opportune to talk of something else, has talked of destroying the British Empire, partly because the Allies had nothing to offer, and Hitler, if he won, would have a lot. On the other hand unless M.'s mass meetings and the bombastic slogans with which he disfigures every wall have had more effect than I think, the war will not be at all popular. Fascism arose in northern Italy as a reaction against Socialist and Communist disorders which, in the post-war period, affected both the industrial towns and the countryfolk (a good picture of the agrarian unrest in a novel by Panzini called *Il Padrone Sono Me*, which was published, and read by me, about 1923). Hence N. Italy remains the stronghold of Fascism; but N. Italians hate the Germans. S. Italians, a very different and unattractive people, do not distinguish them from other foreigners, but they dislike war and are not at all strongly Fascist. No doubt propaganda has done something, but the Italians, though enslaved, are not, like the Germans, slaves by choice, and as they are quite good at spontaneous demonstrations and many of them quite good liars, I doubt if bogus demonstrations impress them very much or if they attach much weight to press propaganda. I don't anticipate either mutiny or revolution, at any rate until things begin to go badly, but I certainly do not think their hearts will be in the business. I was last in Italy in 1938 during the Czech crisis — taking mud-baths at Abano near Padua. The place was full of Germans and the papers most offensively anti-British; the people as friendly as ever and not concealing their dislike of the Germans. I am sorry for the Italians for I like N. Italians very much; and if I thought Hitler was going to win I should be still sorrier, for not only would their domestic fetters be tighter riveted but they would be the serfs of the Germans, who regard them with insolent contempt and would presently eat them up. I do not of course mean that Mussolini did not do his country some good. In the early days at any rate he did quite a lot; so did Hitler, and Napoleon, and so can any dictator, though I dare say that the improvements in public order, railway services, and so on gave mere visitors an exaggerated idea of M.'s achievement. The trouble of these disjointed times is that when our dictators have done their bit we no longer send them back to their ploughs or their paper-hanging but allow them to become tyrants.

TWELFTH LETTER

As I am short of material, and as the Parish Magazine comes with this number to the end of its first year, I propose to inflict upon you something of its history. Know, therefore, that when I began it last September I was moved by recollections of the last war. I remembered how one lost touch with one's friends, uprooted as they commonly were from their usual avocations; and I remembered also the devastating boredom to which many, the soldiers in particular, fell a prey. I thought that if I lost touch with the recipient of such a periodical letter the fault at any rate would not be mine; and, though I did not flatter myself that I could dispel any great amount of boredom, that seemed no excuse for not dispelling the little I could. I undertook these two enterprises, however, with a good deal of hesitation, for those of you who have excused brief and infrequent letters with the defence that letter-writing came easier to me than to them are far astray. I have never been a willing or copious letter-writer, and, if I had been, years of tutorial correspondence would long ago have cured me of the taste. Moreover even a facile writer must have something to write about, and though I myself like to know in detail how my friends spend their time (correspondents please note), I did not see how the daily life of a Don could provide monthly pabulum even for the most inquisitive. Still, though I have never finished one letter without wondering what on earth there could be to put in the next, that problem has so far solved itself somehow or other, and however tedious the solutions may have proved they have at any rate not been brief — indeed I am astonished when I look at the bulk of the back numbers.

The first letter was sent out to about 80 people, but subsequent issues have gone to about 100 — usually to rather more. The circulation went up partly because people (including, somewhat to my embarrassment, one complete stranger) who had seen copies asked if they might receive them; more because men were called up from here or went away, and if I had known them well they were put on the list. Not all the recipients were members of this College, but the great majority were, and of these the great majority again were my tutorial pupils. The total has varied very little from issue to issue, but the 100 odd have not been quite the same throughout the year, for those who let three or four months go by without a word, unless there is an obvious explanation, get dropped. This is partly because I have found it curiously and unexpectedly depressing to sit down and dispatch letters to those who will not send an occasional line in reply — unexpectedly, for I had foreseen from the outset that there would be such, and if there were less else to depress me I should no doubt mind it less. At the same time such letters are obviously failing to keep me in touch, and if, after due notice, their recipients still don't write, it is reasonable to conclude that they don't much want any more; hence, as there is a limit to the numbers I can cope with, it has seemed more sensible to make room for others than to pursue my failures beyond a certain point. Casualties, I am relieved to say, have reduced the roll less than I feared they might, and indeed I do not know for certain that any recipient has been killed, though of four I very much fear that it is likely. Apart from these I know only of two wounded and one invalided home from France, but a territorial gunner, after a year in the army and an expedition to Dunkirk, has been released to resume his medical studies, and, being now in residence again, no longer needs bulletins of local news.

The circulation has touched many parts of the world — Gibraltar, Cyprus, Palestine, Egypt, the Sudan, Nigeria, Natal, Rhodesia, Nyasaland, Tanganyika, Kenya, Iraq, various parts of India, Malaya, Sarawak, Hongkong, Tokyo, Australia, and the U.S.A. South America still sits in darkness for I have had few pupils thence (being, between ourselves, not very partial to Latin Americans as pupils), and, for reasons beyond my control, most also of Europe — and indeed I do not know whether the Mediterranean recipients still get their copies.

Looking back on the year I do not regret having adventured. I have not found the writing of the letters as burdensome as I expected and it could be done at odd moments. The issuing of them, certainly, has been a heavy job especially at busy times. I have aimed at posting the whole batch simultaneously, and as soon as might be after the date at the head of the last section — lest the rapid movement of events should make the number out of date before it was born. Usually I have got the copies off within a couple of days, and this explains why I have often not been able to add more than a word or two of a personal nature to each. I have had a lot of interesting letters in reply, and even where my correspondents have been brief and uninformative their letters have kept me, as I wished, in touch; and I hope I am right in inferring from some at least that the writers have been glad to receive mine. Some months ago I dipped into a volume which contained letters sent out in rather similar circumstances by a schoolmaster during the last war and since imprudently published. It caused me to wonder whether I was exposing myself as blatantly as he appeared to do. I reflected, however, that, if I was, the damage was already done, and so, though chastened in spirit, I decided to go on and chance it.

17.8.40

The Long Vac. term is just drawing to a close and has not produced much incident. We have had about 70 men up — some two thirds of the usual number — almost exclusively medicals and scientists, for whom alone courses were provided. Arts students, of whom there are some in normal Long Vacs., have mostly taken up swords, saws, or sickles. I have not really been very busy, though in addition to the tasks which regularly befall a tutor in July and August (more than you are aware of) a good many committees have been meeting, and the Exemptions Committee has been hard worked for it has had to vet applications for allowances of terms and examinations on the score of war-service. The first large batch of war-degrees (which included a dozen of yourselves) was conferred on August 3rd.

Since the Junior Bursar is likely to join the Navy[1] before next term I have formally taken over from him the A.R.P. business of the College, though, as he has been very busy throughout the year, I had been informally doing a good deal of it before. The Tutors made it a condition that those who came up in the Long Vac. should undertake A.R.P. duties, and consequently I had a good deal to do in sorting them out into First Aid and Fire Parties, etc., and getting practices going. Almost all the people were really keen, and the two or three who were not, on making the macabre discovery that I was apt to attend practices myself and to ask absentees for explanations, became at least regular. The First Aid Party has been organised into four stretcher parties and a dressing station, and it has been no unusual thing to find the courts strewn with casualties labelled as suffering from the most appalling injuries and being splinted and bandaged by the stretcher parties or borne away to the Chapel for the attentions of the dressers. The Fire Party has also been busy (sometimes in conjunction with the F.A.P.) trailing hoses over roofs, lowering the injured in slings, and the like. Its constitution amuses me. Its leader, a German refugee Fellow, was interned in May; now the chief stalwarts

[1] See p. 61.

are an Irishman, an Estonian, a Hungarian, a Siamese, and a Chink — and this is no accident, for these folk, being unable to return to their native countries, are very glad, in return for free rooms and dinners, to stay up over vacations and so solve our most serious problem. The absence of the F.A. Party in September doesn't matter for there are only a few decayed Dons like myself to become casualties, but the Library (for instance) is as liable to become a casualty then as in term-time, and the really empty times of year are an anxiety for that reason.

Both these parties have been largely left to organise themselves, and both have done it very efficiently — so efficiently in fact that my task has been rather to check them from being too ambitious (and wishing, for instance, to equip the dressing-station with oxygen cylinders and anaesthetics and to add a demolition squad to the Fire Party) than to ginger them up; so that though I have spent a good deal of time on them I haven't disliked the job, and as many of the men will be up in October we shan't have to start all over again from scratch.

We have had a lot of A.R. warnings, yellow, purple (a local innovation, I think)[1] and red, but not many of the last. Experience in June, when warnings were more prodigally distributed than they have been lately, led to a modification of the system by which the Wardens had each so many hours per night, for this resulted in all Wardens being disturbed on most nights and in their being unable to leave Cambs. We now have a week on full duty, a week in reserve, and then an interval with no duties. When on full duty one gets all warnings; when in reserve one reinforces the Wardens' post if there is a red warning; and as my rooms are a good way from the post at the Great Gate I sleep, for the fortnight, in shirt and trousers instead of pyjamas. I won't pretend I like it, but it is a mild inconvenience to endure in such times as these. When off duty one may please oneself, and I, if I did so, should stay quietly in bed. As a matter of fact, being to some extent responsible, I have so far got up and gone round the F.A. and Fire parties and inspected the shelters, showing, I hope, becoming courage and presence of mind (see Letter 2).

A bomber brought down near here some time since was said to have contained a German ex-undergraduate — a pretty example of German thoroughness though I doubt if an undergraduate career at Cambs. would help you much to find your way about East Anglia at night from 20,000 ft.

[1] See p. 52.

THIRTEENTH LETTER

5.9.40

I AM writing this in Radnorshire, from a lonely house on the empty hills between Llandrindod and Builth where I usually come about this time of year. I hesitated a good deal about going away this Long, for holidays depend on mood as well as leisure and I haven't felt like casting care aside, but I was pretty jaded for, except for an odd night in London on business, I hadn't been away since March. I hadn't much excuse for being jaded, for in this extraordinary summer August was less oppressive than usual in Cambs., but those who live in their rooms and do their work elsewhere, or, alternatively, work in their rooms and go home to their families at night, have the advantage of a daily change of scene denied to those who, like me, live in their offices. When I had a car I used it here chiefly to leave by the roadside while I went for a walk in the country but my car was laid by at Christmas, and since then I have hardly been beyond the streets; so, what with one thing and another, I thought I had better freshen myself with a change of air and scene and society before term began. And when the time came I was glad to go, for the last week of August was rather restless. At night purple and white A.R. messages succeeded each other like the crocuses on the King's avenue, and during my last day on duty we had six sirens during the daytime. I spent some time on the top of the Great Gate, like Ajax defying the lightning, but I saw nothing of interest; and though during the week a number of bombs were dropped on and near Cambs., they only broke a few windows in the town and, so far as I know, did no damage outside it. I discovered that if I hired a car I could get enough petrol to take me to Wales and back, so on Sept. 2 I set off in an Austin 10 (which gave me cramp) spending on the way a night near Pershore, where I was treated to a fine display of searchlights trying to find raiders going up the Severn valley Here too one hears Huns snooping round after dark, but one is out of sound of sirens and can only see one very distant searchlight, beyond the hills toward Hereford — and this is a real rest, for at Cambs., whether on duty or off, I have got into the habit of sleeping with an ear half-open for telephone, siren, or bombs and the subconscious is foolishly apt to mistake other sounds for one of these. It doesn't worry me, but it is pleasant to know that one cannot be roused by the first two and is unlikely to be roused by the third. Several of you have corrected my belief that purple messages were a local innovation; the local innovation was to issue them on occasions for which they were not intended. However the Cambs. authorities have now mastered the rules, issued a number of obscure notices, and toed the line.

As I have a car I have also been able to get over for a week-end to a still more familiar house in Montgomeryshire, on the still emptier northern spurs of Plynlimon. Here you may climb close on a thousand feet straight out of the garden and walk all day on grassy or heathery uplands, not seeing a soul or hearing a sound except a buzzard or raven overhead, with astonishing prospects of tangled ridge and valley, especially northward towards Cader Idris and the mountains of Merioneth. 'Solitudes of shepherds High in the folded hills' are not everyone's choice of scenery, but they are decidedly mine; and these, partly because I have known them longer and better than others, are my favourite in that kind. Autumn is early this year, and these hills, lovely at all times, are never lovelier than when the turning bracken and bilberry splash their sides with russet and scarlet. War has touched them little: a few aeroplanes by day and night, a little more ground in the valleys under plough, and here and there on the higher points an L.D.V. look-out post. Some plantations are being cut, but I have no love for conifers where they are not really at home and I shall not miss them. The hardwoods which grow round the streams on the lower slopes would be another matter, but they are so far untouched.

Cambridge news since last I wrote is scarce. The Master, as no doubt you have seen, is dead, but he was 83 and had long been failing, and no friend in such times could have wished his life prolonged. Our Mastership is a Crown appointment and we are therefore spared the debates and consultations which rage in other Colleges on these occasions; they must often be very unpleasant, particularly when among the electors there are those who hope to be elected. Naturally Trinity awaits the head imposed upon it with interest, but one may hope that the Prime Minister will make no appointment until after the war. Our Master, unlike those of most Colleges, discharges little but ceremonial duties, and many months ago the late Master ceased to discharge even the simplest of these, so we are used to doing without; the choice of a successor might well be limited by the war; and in time of grave financial difficulty we should be glad enough to economise his stipend.

The College kitchens have effected further economies of staff and service, and during the Long Vac. Term experimented with an inclusive charge to undergraduates for breakfast, lunch, and dinner which seems to have been a success. The Fellows, for whom there was available a small club lunch in the Combination Room, are now provided only with the undergraduate lunch; and since this, though good enough, often consists of dishes which I do not eat, I have been driven to lunching frugally in my rooms.

Partly for that reason, partly because when roused from my beauty sleep by an A.R. message on a telephone within six inches of my pillow I do not drop off again very readily, I have done more desultory reading than usual in the past few months, but though you haven't been stood in the Literary Corner of the P.M. for some time I shall not set out, and indeed cannot remember, more than a small part of it. Here, however, are a few books which I do remember: Winstanley's *Early Victorian Cambridge* (amusing in places but rather minutely parochial for non-residents); *A Buried Life*, by P. Withers (about A. E. Housman; not a bad picture but not very informative for those who knew him); *Reaching for the Stars*, by N. Waln (a dispassionate account of Nazi Germany by an American woman educated in China who has also written an amusing book about China called *The House of Exile* which you may buy as a Penguin); *A Prisoner in the Forbidden Land*, by G. Krist (surprising adventures of an Austrian prisoner of the last war in Central Asia); *Spanish Prison*, by G. Elstob (by a man who went to Spain to fly on the Govt. side and spent his time in a Govt. prison instead); *The Eager Years*, by L. Ker (narrative of an adventurous life; rather good); *Country Contentments*, by M. Westerling (about the Cotswolds; agreeable in a quiet way); *The Young Melbourne*, by David Cecil (amusing, though in my opinion over-praised; however I have always thought Lady Caroline Lamb a poor joke). I have also read *Down and Out* by G. Orwell (a pseudonym), and *Caribbean Treasure* by I. Sanderson, not because washing up dishes in Parisian restaurants or collecting animals in the W. Indies (their respective themes) appeal to me much but because both authors were my pupils though not in these subjects. My Welsh holiday I occupied with an immense novel about a Welsh mining village by Richard Llewellyn called *How Green was my Valley*, of which I thought very well. At odd times I have also read three much older books: Lord Stanhope's *Conversations with the Duke of Wellington* (interesting and sometimes entertaining), Charles

Grant's *Tales of Naples* (a lively picture of Naples in the heyday of the Camorra), and Stendhal's *Chartreuse de Parme*. The last, if I had been properly educated, I should no doubt have read long ago, and indeed I had made the attempt. Having now achieved it, I think the book overrated and much inferior to *Le Rouge et le Noir* on which I should advise intending Stendhalians to begin; two thirds of it are first rate.

18.9.40

I came back to Cambs. three days ago, a day or two before I had intended (for while bombs are showering on London[1] the heart agrees reluctantly with the head that for all one can do to prevent them one may as well pursue one's original plans) but much refreshed in body and mind by contact with favourite scenes and old friends. As I drove homewards I reflected that a number of the P.M. was about due and that much was still to write. Here, however, I was wrong, for having indited the above not all on Sept. 5 but at odd moments while I was away, I found, on typing it out, that I had been more garrulous than I thought. Nothing much has happened here during my absence, so before commenting adversely on the contents of this number be pleased to recall that it takes garrulity to squeeze twelve pages out of a Long Vacation, and that if garrulity is a vice, so also is taciturnity. I could name some who are addicted to it.

FOURTEENTH LETTER

29.9.40

I MEANT before term began to go up to town for a couple of nights to see various people and to have a Turkish bath, but one was bidden to keep away unless one's business was urgent. Mine was not, and though many eminent persons from Agamemnon to Marat (whom the author of the *Times* crossword cannot, I regret to see, distinguish from Murat) have perished in the bath, I would sooner be bombed, if I must, in some less ignoble posture. Consequently I have stayed here, and have been uncommonly busy too, for the onset of indiscriminate bombing has involved a thorough reconsideration of our A.R.P. arrangements. My time for the past ten days has been entirely occupied with such things as the protection of the Hall windows and various skylights, devices for getting people out of Hall in an emergency, provision of sleeping quarters for

[1] The Battle of Britain began on Aug. 11

the Fire Party (who don't fancy sleeping every night in a cellar), painting
the lead on the Library roof (said to be too conspicuous from the air: the
Fire Party, whom I turned on, made a capital job of it), rewriting the
College A.R.P. notices (now a substantial literature), etc., etc. These are
tasks for which I have neither aptitude nor liking but somebody must do
them and I dare say that I am no more incompetent than another. The
fact is, here as elsewhere, that since the contingencies which may arise
are so various no provision to meet them can satisfy, and our troubles are
increased by the seemingly capricious way in which warnings are issued.
On one night we have a 3 hr. warning when no Hun is within the county
boundary; on another, while the sirens hold their peace, an obvious alien
buzzes about overhead for half an hour and presently shakes my windows
as he relieves himself over the countryside. No doubt the explanation is
that the authorities have decided not to rouse the population for a lone
raider — and quite right too; but those who have to make rules for
crowded Halls and lecture-rooms must needs reflect that if one of these
is picked off it will make little difference whether it is by a single spy or
by a whole battalion. I know that we have spent a lot of thought and
trouble on our problems, I think we have done the best we can, and I
hope if we are tested we shan't be found wanting; but it takes more than
hope to generate peace of mind. The way in which London and other
towns have met their emergencies fills me with admiration both for the
A.R.P. services and for the people in general.

The Long Vac. usually produces some changes in the outward appearance of this place, but has naturally produced less than usual this year.
The most startling is the effect on Bridge St caused by the removal of
most of the hoarding from the new John's building, which confirms the
suspicion voiced in Letter 6 that I shouldn't like it very much. I don't;
and its oddity is increased by the fact that though the buildings have been
set back a lot the kerb has not, so that there is an asphalt pavement considerably wider than the roadway in front of it. The interior court,
though not beautiful, is fitted to the W. end of the Chapel with some
ingenuity, and it is embellished with a nice coat of arms by Eric Gill —
not so nice however as that in Jesus (I wonder how many of you have
ever looked at it). In Trinity the approach to the Great Gate is obstructed
with cement-mixers and piles of gravel because we are constructing a new
A.R. shelter under the cycle-shed, meaning, when circs. permit, to remove

that unsightly shanty and shelter the cycles underground. Otherwise you would notice only that the sandbag defences of the Porters' Lodge and of the Hall cellar, which were becoming sadly dishevelled, have now been neatly encased in concrete; and whereas it was previously believed that they would withstand high explosives, it now seems improbable that they can be removed without them. King's, who have been gradually taking the stained glass out of their Chapel at a cost of £75 per window, have desisted, leaving only four out of twenty-six windows, the rest being partly plain glass but mostly boarding. I suppose they were wise though I sometimes wonder what they will do with the windows if the Chapel is demolished. In other Colleges I have noticed only that Peterhouse is putting up an odd building on round brick pillars in their third court, but most Colleges, having hush-hush contents of one sort or another, are closed to the public, so what may have gone on in their interiors is more than I can say. In the town the new Cavendish Lab. is more or less finished but does not show itself unless one penetrates the mysterious purlieus behind Free School Lane, and the telephone exchange next the University Arms has cast aside its veils and looks like a Noah's Ark with an ill-fitting lid, but I haven't observed other changes. A prying eye might detect (for instance at Fenner's) some inconsiderable pits, scars, and pock-marks, but it would have to pry. I leave you to guess what caused them.

The Fitzwilliam has staged an amusing exhibition of some 70 modern drawings of University worthies. It is quite an interesting show and will provide our local Philistines with a fine opportunity of letting off steam, for though they have never used their eyes intelligently on a drawing or, for that matter, on a human head, they are always ready to pronounce at a glance upon that most delicate question whether a portrait is a likeness or not. Why is it delicate? Because A, B, and C, do not see X with the same eyes, and the artist may not see him with A's or B's or C's. Nevertheless if the artist has put down accurately what he sees, his drawing is a likeness; and if A, B, and C are competent to judge, and they study, or better live with, the result, they will realise that it is so. And this I learnt painfully because once upon a time the College drawings used to lie about in my rooms, and usually those which shocked me at first unpacking and were most loudly denounced by the l.P.'s grew upon me until it was plain that though not one's own idea of the sitter they were nevertheless good and truthful portraits. And I have no doubt that if the artists were not Rothenstein, Dodd, and the like, but Holbein and Rembrandt, the l.P.'s would clamour the louder in proportion as they are the less capable of seeing with the eyes of the greater men.

18.10.40

Full Term began on Oct. 8, and I had meant to complete this letter with a survey of the situation here, but this will have to stand over until my next when I hope to have had a little time to collect my facts and thoughts. I knew that the beginning of this Michaelmas Term would be more of a rush than usual because in addition to the regular business of identifying freshmen, and so on, I should have also to see everybody living in College on A.R.P. business, and, since we are doing a good deal of supervision for absentee Dons, a number of Classics from other Colleges besides. Furthermore the first week of term happened to coincide with my week on Warden's duty and I was likely to be up a good deal at night (as I was). Things turned out even worse than I expected for two reasons. One was that my mother's house in Hampstead got a bit damaged, and as the neighbourhood was being peppered a kind friend whisked her off to Oxford on the spur of the moment. She is an invalid and well over 80 so that this was something of an upset; it went off most fortunately as it happened, but I had to go over to Oxford and was thus two days behindhand at a critical moment. My arrival in that seat of learning was greeted with a salvo of high explosive in the neighbourhood (not very near) which caused me some malicious amusement, for the Oxonians have so far been less molested than ourselves and are darkly suspected of having lured away some of our freshmen by promises of greater safety. However what you gain on the bombs you may lose on the babies, and I have heard grim tales of Oxford Quads. a-flutter with diapers. I hadn't time to investigate them, but certain it is that the place is crowded with evacuees.

The other circumstance was that I had forgotten that I was examining in the Seatonian Prize and that the exercises came in in the first week of term. *The Mysterious University: lesson 5.* Q. What is the S.P.? *A.* The S.P. was founded in 1738 for a poem, the subject of which 'shall for the first year be one or other of the Perfections or Attributes of the Supreme Being, and so the succeeding years till that subject be exhausted; and afterwards the subject shall be either Death, Judgment, Heaven, Hell, Purity of Heart, etc. or whatever else may be judged by the

Vice-Chancellor, Master of Clare Hall, and Greek Professor to be most conducive to the honour of the Supreme Being and recommendation of virtue'. After seven years those three authorities could apparently think of no more attributes of the Deity, and by 1774 they had sunk to 'Duelling' for the subject. Modern examiners, no longer *ex officio*, confine themselves to themes more obviously, if sometimes only mildly, edifying — this year it was 'Glastonbury'. You may well ask what my qualifications may be, but though I have examined several times I know only that it is a piece of preferment I would willingly forgo, for the poems are of unconscionable length and commonly of dreadful badness. Since there is no upper limit of standing for competitors it is reasonable to conjecture that incumbents of country parishes occupy their declining years upon their composition, and indeed, when no award is made, there sometimes comes from a remote rectory a letter of pained surprise that the examiners should be so lacking in appreciation. But, award or no, the conscientious examiner must read the stuff, it is too soporific, I find, to be read with profit at the Wardens' Post, and it forms a very unwelcome addition to a Tutor's duties at this time of year.

FIFTEENTH LETTER

15.11.40

I PUT all this no. under one date not because I wrote it all to-day, but because the statistics which it contains are less easily come by than the egotistics which are your usual portion, and though I have jotted things down at intervals during a very busy month I have only now had time to put them together.

I provided you at this time last year with figures of residents, and now do the same for this year. Not counting M.A.'s, there are, it seems, 2908 men + 497 women in residence, as against 4353 + 465 in 1939, and 5491 + 513 in 1938. Apart from B.A.'s and other seniors, this year's total includes 412 3rd year men, 1174 2nd year, and 1124 freshmen; last year's figures for the three years were 911, 1326, and 1624 respectively, but here the comparison is a little misleading for a number of men were admitted in January and a few in April. These are now swelling the 2nd year total but are mostly men who would in normal times have come up this term. The figures for the University are not available but this College last

October admitted 206 freshmen as against 136 this year; since however about 40 came up in by-terms the difference is less than it seems.

Our own numbers (334 as against 710 in 1938) have shrunk more than those of the University as a whole, partly because our total in normal times includes a larger proportion of B.A.'s and research students than that of other Colleges, and partly, I think, because it also includes more of those whom some would call the idle rich; and these last have mostly not come up, or, having come, have volunteered for service before their time. On the whole, however, I should say that the intake both in the College and the University is not keeping up too badly, and it presents a great contrast to 1915 when, under the volunteer system, there were less than 1000 men up in the whole University. No doubt we should have diminished more markedly if the War Office had not announced that men who obtained Certificate B through the O.T.C., now called the S(enior) T.C., would be eligible for posting straight to an O.C.T.U. The S.T.C. course involves 150 hrs. parades, and in consequence one complete morning a week; and as this scheme was sprung on us long after the Lecture List was complete beyond hope of alteration it is at present causing some difficulty. It should be eased next term, but we are so short of Lecture Rooms owing to the presence of evacuees that the L.L. is no joke to arrange anyhow. The Air Squadron has just come to life again and will function on the same sort of basis as the S.T.C.

In addition to our own folk there are just over 1500 students from evacuated London institutions — about 100 less than last year. At the end of August and beginning of September all the bodies (I think) who were here last year announced their intention of going back to London. It seemed even then an idiotic decision, and of course they reversed it a fortnight later, but it would have served them right if they had found their places filled. As a fact they did not, and all but one are back. The Office of Works, also, has found some occupants for our New Court which they annexed (probably they said 'hypothecated') a year ago but have since left empty except for birds of passage; and they are there erecting some rather unsightly surface A.R. shelters of pallid bricks. The Leys School, on the other hand, has retired to Pitlochry, not from pusillanimity but because their premises have been commandeered.

Turning from undergraduates to Dons, there are now over a hundred University teaching officers away on war work of one kind and another. From Trinity, Butler, Evennett, Knight and Vyvyan disappeared during last year, and they were joined in the Long by Dean, Hamson, Logan, and Hinks — the last not, as no. 12 said, in navy blue but in khaki. With nearly a quarter of the staff away and quite a number of vacant lecture-ships and professorships suspended, the Lecture List begins to look a bit thin in places, and supervision is not always easy to arrange. Rattenbury, Sandbach and I, for instance, have on our hands, in addition to our own Classics, those of Clare, Corpus, Pembroke, and Sidney, those Colleges being without any Classical lecturers. The burden is not overwhelming, for of course the falling off in undergraduate numbers is much more marked in the humane than in the scientific subjects, but we have all three got more supervision to do than we want. Contrariwise the Home Office, after 5 months' shameful bungling, has begun to release respectable aliens. Our Italian economist is back; our German mathematician is released but has joined the Pioneer Corps; and a German engineer whom we elected to a Fellowship while in a concentration camp in Canada is to be let out — as you have perhaps read in the papers, which consider him good copy. Meanwhile a number of undergraduates languish in camps in the Dominions, and one University teacher, an Italian, was drowned in the *Arandora Star*. As I said in no. 11, the rounding up of aliens in May seemed right; but the incompetence and stupidity with which the matter has since been handled are beyond words.

Apart from numbers things go on much as they did last year and the only change which seems to deserve record in this meticulous chronicle is that our undergraduates have all their meals in Hall at an inclusive rate of 30/- a week (or 25/- if they breakfast in their lodgings). Trinity would not be Trinity if its members, Dons and undergraduates alike, did not complain of their meals, but the complaints are not loud or substantial and on the whole the system seems to be giving satisfaction. It has caused me some anxious moments because meals go on during A.R. warnings and I have had to organise a service of observers who stand outside Hall at such times and ring an alarm if they think those inside should go to ground. Of course this does not abolish the risk of a bomb falling on them, but it is difficult to see what more one can do, and at any rate the observer can see and hear if anything is going on, whereas inside there is such a din that sirens are totally inaudible and it would take a bomb in the Great Ct or Nevile's Ct to drown the clatter of knives and forks. Under-graduates observe for breakfast, lunch and First Hall; a Warden for Second Hall. It hasn't happened much so far, and I have usually been out myself, sometimes on a watch of my own, at others because if there is warning during First Hall I have so far reinforced the undergraduate observer — more for my own information than because I mistrust him. Indeed I think that undergraduates, if you pick the right ones (as I hope I have), are more competent in such a matter than Dons, whose habits of mind do not dispose them towards quick decisions — as you would readily learn if you sat on University committees.

Last, but not least, we have a new Master. In no. 13 I said I thought the appointment might well be postponed until after the war and I shall not unsay it now, but it was then commonly believed that Trevelyan would decline. This was no idle speculation for he had frequently said so himself; and his change of mind makes a difference, for he was the obvious choice and, failing him, it was less plain whom the Prime Minister should, and much less plain whom he would, appoint. There is much to be said for having a Humanist for a change, G.M.T. is a distinguished one, and I have no doubt that he is generally welcome. He is to be admitted tomorrow by a ritual which, if it was not, no doubt would have been invented during the Gothic Revival. The College gates are locked: the new Master beats on them: he is interrogated through a crack by a porter and hands in his Patent which is conveyed on a silver salver to the assembled Fellows in the Combination Room. They, having satisfied themselves as to its contents, process to the gate, receive him, and escort him to the Chapel, where he takes the oath behind closed doors. The public are then admitted to hear the Fellows (or it might be the choir) sing a Te Deum; after which the Fellows deposit the Master in the Lodge. These picturesque proceedings offer hostages both to the weather and to the Luftwaffe, but we have escaped one contretemps and may escape others. The Crown Lawyers, failing to remember that we were given new statutes in 1926, made out, and got the King to sign, a patent appointing G.M.T. for life; and if he had presented this I suppose we should have had to keep the doors closed and turn him away. Luckily, however, the blunder was detected in time. One sacrifice to the Luftwaffe we make in any case, for the proceedings end with a lunch not a dinner to suit their convenience — a heavy sacrifice for those who dislike ceremonial lunches as much as I.

I hope none of you were unduly perturbed by a report from Berlin published in the *New York Times*. This said that Cambs. had been heavily bombed, that much damage was visible, fires were raging, and clouds of smoke trailing far beyond the city; also that reconnaissance on the following day showed that the flames had become wholesale conflagrations. Probably I may say without indiscretion what Mark Twain said of the account of his own death — that the report was much exaggerated.

SIXTEENTH LETTER

1.12.40

THE installation of the new Master went off quite happily on Nov. 16, uninterrupted by precipitations either of moisture or of H.E. His solitary wait outside the Great Gate is, I think, somewhat undignified and should on another occasion be curtailed; it must have lasted for five minutes, and would have lasted longer if the Head Porter, charged with the Patent, had not legged it across the court more nimbly than befitted so ceremonial an occasion. The dignity of this proceeding was not enhanced by the ludicrous mace which he carried — a wooden handle surmounted by a pinchbeck crown, the whole not more than eight inches long. This preposterous object I guess to have been made for the installation of Whewell in 1841 or perhaps of Wordsworth in 1820,[1] but, whenever made, we shall do well to lose it before it is next wanted. I do not know how Trevelyan supported the embarrassing interval, but when the gates were thrown open he made quite an impressive entry, and, at the lunch, a speech which was both audible and appropriate — and those accustomed to speeches in our Hall will welcome this innovation. The procession of Fellows to meet him was, I presume, ridiculous, for august and venerable as are our individual deportments, when called upon for concerted movements we go to pieces. I hope, however, that we were not more ridiculous than usual on such occasions, and the actual admission ceremony in Chapel was more dignified than admissions of Fellows and Scholars had led me to expect. There was quite a good show of spectators (for it was a fine day), and in both Halls that night the undergraduates had a glass of fizz to drink the Master's health, so, though not there to see, I imagine they were content. It is a minor misfortune of the times that there is so short an interval between the two occupations of the Lodge, for from garret to cellar it is in sad need of renovation, and the large rooms present formidable problems, particularly of lighting, over which it

[1] See p. 120.

would have been fun to ponder and experiment. The big drawing room, though not a friendly room, could be made a stately one, for it is spacious and has character, which it mostly owes to an elegant and not over-elaborate Elizabethan plaster ceiling. The dining room, suitable for parties of forty and highly unsuitable for anything else, would be a real terror to make habitable, and some day, I fancy, it will have to be divided into two. However, even if we had time to think, we couldn't now get labour or materials for elaborate redecoration, let alone rebuilding, so these riddles must put up for the moment with makeshift answers, though even to answer them so will take until well after Christmas. We shall seize the opportunity of getting out of the Lodge a few pictures to improve the showing in Hall and elsewhere, but even so we are under disadvantages for some of the better portraits both from the Lodge and the College were sent away on the outbreak of war, and to plan a wall from one's memory of what the pictures look like is a chancy and unsatisfactory business.

14.12.40

In a general retrospect the term, which ended on Dec. 7, offers me little material. The weather has not been too cold, and there have been some lovely days, but I have known better Cambridge autumns, for the gales in September and October, which perhaps checked an invasion, brought down the leaves, and the trees in the Backs were not at their best. What they were like about the countryside I do not know, for being car-less I could not go to see, but perhaps for that reason I noticed more than before some aliens in the Botanic Garden — maples and sumachs — which put on astounding pinks and reds.

Business has been much as before. University committees may have been a trifle, but only a trifle, less active than last year, but their proceedings, fortunately perhaps for readers of the P.M. but unfortunately for its writer, are not of much general interest. There is, indeed, one considering whether, to spare candidates unnecessary travelling, the Little Go and one or two other exams. could be taken away from Cambs., but emergency legislation was mostly got through last year and we are now less occupied with general principles than with their application to particular cases. So and so has left his Belgian equivalent for a school certificate in Brussels; shall we accept his evidence as to its contents? An American, north or south, wants a Cambs. degree but is not allowed by his Govt. to return to that seat of learning; may he count a year's work at some trans-Atlantic seminary towards it? May a conscientious (but refractory) objector now in jug have leave to degrade until he emerges? Is an un-exploded bomb in the back garden an adequate substitute for Latin in the Little Go? — and so forth. These and their like are nice rather than interesting questions, and it is wonderful what a time may, quite properly, be spent in resolving them. Another committee of a very different kind, though it does not take up much time, has been unusually active, for the march of events has set the College Wine Committee some problems. The Wine Committee, however, unlike others, meets over the dinner table, and might be said to combine business with pleasure, though when there are many samples to taste the pleasure is mixed in more senses than one. We usually carry a large stock of port and champagne but of nothing else. Port doesn't matter, and our successors will, if the cellars are still intact, be better off than we were in 1918, for owing to foolishness over 1908 and cowardice over 1912 we were then left badly off, and consequently have now no old port but lots of young which will keep. Champagne is more difficult, for as there are now no feasts we have far more than we want. However as it went up in 1917, if I remember, to 400/- a doz. (a ludicrous price), we may be glad to be well stocked with what we can probably sell at a handsome profit. On the other hand we were short of ordinary High Table claret and thought it well to buy a little more while we could; so unless the cellars are bombed we can now carry on for a year or so. These problems have taxed the brain rather than the stomach, and as I myself seldom drink champagne and never port, I hope I brought a judicially impartial mind to bear on them.

What with one thing and another I have been dreadfully busy, and A.R.P. fills all the interstices — so if you think, as you well may, that it occupies too much space in the P.M., reflect that it does the like in my time and thoughts. I had scarcely got the term started when a series of long Alerts made it necessary to find sleeping quarters for the First Aid Party, eject two undergraduates from their rooms, and fit the rooms out for the purpose. Latterly I have been busy with an Observation Post on the top of St John's Chapel tower. This was an idea of mine, because we were uneasy at the possibility of incendiaries falling unnoticed in some corner of the College. We have no vantage point from which the whole can be properly surveyed, and as I vainly and painfully hoisted my creaking joints to summit after summit I was always conscious of being dominated by that tower. Consequently the two Colleges have combined to construct on it a gazebo fitted with bunks, lighting, heating, and a telephone, to be manned three days a week by each College, and on one by Caius. Magdalene and Sidney refused to cooperate, for which I give them a black mark for they stand to gain more than Caius (since their ground is better commanded from the tower), and they know very well that if we observe them on fire we shall tell them all the same. The College A.R.P. services had the other day a spirited exercise for all arms, organised by an ex-kitchen-man who is now a highly efficient Ambulance Sergeant. What he called the Grand Fine Ale was: oil bombs on the Great Gate and Chapel, both in flames: all casualties (by this time numerous) to be evacuated from the dressing station; several firemen overcome by fumes and requiring resuscitation. It was an ambitious scheme, and the parties really put up a very creditable show, though I didn't see much of it myself as I was impersonating the Warden on duty and sending the parties into action to deal with each successive disaster. The firemen indeed created a mild panic in Trinity Street by the brio and élan with which they advanced on an imaginary fire in Whewell's Ct. I blush, however, to confess that the First Aid party were flummoxed by a case of hysterical stupor included among the casualties. There was one real casualty, for Q., returning in the dark from a sherry party in the Old Combination Room, fell heavily over a hose pipe, suffering slight shock and abrasions and serious loss of equanimity.

The *Picture Post* of Dec. 7 contains some good photographs of the Master's admission, and the text (particularly the statement that the Master promises to observe the Protestant Faith, to maintain the Royal Prerogative, and to accept the Scriptures) does great credit to the author's imagination.

Contrary to my usual practice there will be an interval between the duplication and the dispatch of this P.M., for I have to spend some days in London clearing up and emptying out my mother's house. It would at any time be a weary and dreary business and I am not looking forward to it, though there will be alleviations as I shall stay at Eton. I expect however to be back for Christmas, and to send this out, if not in time to reach you with Christmas greetings, at least in time for New Year's. A year ago I said I hoped it would be a happier year than the last, but 1940 has been black indeed, and there are dark days and months ahead. Still, just now the clouds seem less uniformly black than they were six months ago, so let us hope for brighter horizons before the year is out. And in the meantime remember that I think of you all a good deal and really enjoy your letters when they come.

SEVENTEENTH LETTER

My Christmas vac. has been largely spent, as I said it would be, in clearing out my mother's house in Hampstead. It would at any time have been a laborious and disagreeable job, and every circumstance has conspired to make it worse — the war, the time of year, the absence of people who at other times would have helped, the impossibility of storing things, the difficulty of moving them, the unfavourable time for selling them. However, thanks to help from others and in particular to the Herculean labours of a cousin living in London, it is now nearly done. I didn't stay in London having nowhere in particular to stay and not fancying solitary evenings at my club or in a hotel, but I went up several times from here (a bore when days are so short) and for five days made a pleasant and much more convenient base at Eton. In the intervals I have been largely occupied with papers and so forth which I brought away with me. If one lives in College rooms one is apt to repine at the limitations they impose on one's acquisitiveness. No doubt one could collect stamps, or coins, or Japanese sword-mountings, but I feel little temptation to form collections which must be got out to be seen, and anything much larger is out of the question. Nor can one buy any object with the comforting reflexion that if one tires of it it will do very well in the spare bedroom or the servants' hall. Hence one's possessions must be comparatively few, and since one lives with them every day and all day, one must, if sensitive to one's surroundings, be sure that one likes them before one acquires them. Usually I am somewhat irked by these restrictions. At the moment, fresh from dealing with twenty years' accumulations in a fair sized house, I am prepared to regard them as blessings, and have been fired by my exploits in London to purge also my own more modest magpie's nest; whereby the nation's waste paper has been materially increased, the drains enlivened by a rich mixture of specifics for unidentifiable ailments, and a lot of old clothes dispatched to the relief of bombed areas — though, as perhaps you have observed, clothes must be old indeed before I discard them, and they may be rejected with contumely by the prospective beneficiaries who tend to be more fussy about their own appearances than I and my like.

Being occupied during daylight hours in Hampstead I had no opportunity of sightseeing in London, and have hardly been south of Oxford St. Of the arc north of that defined by Liverpool St, Hampstead, and Paddington I did, however, see a good deal for I traversed it often and by various routes; and for the benefit of parishioners who have not been in London lately (especially those in foreign parts) I put down some impressions. On the whole I was encouraged by what I saw. There are many nasty scars of course, but it is possible in many parts to go for a long way without seeing anything worse than broken windows, and for a considerable way without seeing so much; nor, when one has a distant view (as from parts of Hampstead), does one notice gaps in the skyline — though since the incendiary raid of Dec. 29 I fear this may no longer be true. Of course the districts I traversed have suffered much less than some others, but my impression is of a London scratched and dishevelled, yet still London and far from a ruin. The temper of its inhabitants is sufficiently plain by now, and I have nothing to add for I was not there at night, and by day everyone goes about his business exactly as usual. I chanced, however, to arrive at Liverpool St. about 10.30 yesterday (Dec. 30) when City traffic was still badly disorganised by the damage of the night and the crowds of people trying to get to their work were enormous. I made my way to Hampstead through them and was amazed at the universal cheerfulness, patience, and good humour with which they were supporting their various inconveniences. In a mild way it was my most heartening experience of the war.

For the benefit of Etonian parishioners I add that the damage at Eton, of which pictures have appeared in the papers, is infuriating: but that Savile House and Upper School can be restored to approximately their old appearance, whereas (and this is the silver lining to the cloud) the windows on the north side of Chapel cannot. That nobody was hurt is little short of a miracle. I heard some lively tales of an earlier shower of incendiaries there, from which it appears that a burning sofa is far harder to extinguish than a bomb. It is suggested by the principal victim that a retaliatory shower of incendiary sofas might well be dropped on Berlin.

Christmas here passed off quietly and pleasantly, and our Christmas Feast, if shorn of oysters in deference to economy, and of barons of beef in subservience to the food-controller, was enlivened by a number of undergraduates for I had a party of stalwart firemen staying up. Unfortunately the shortage of lecturers has made it necessary for me to examine again in the University Scholarships, and (with more nobility) to offer an extra course of lectures next term to which I ought to have been devoting more attention than my other preoccupations have allowed. However the subject, though it is long since I discoursed on it, is not new, and I hope by sweating next term to get through without disgrace.

17.1.41

Having nothing more momentous to write about, I shall now answer three questions addressed to me; and the first two together since they concern financial matters. The first was about the suspension of professorships mentioned in no. 15; the second about a statement on University finance which appeared in the papers. This I did not see, but I have no doubt that it was the summary of a report of the Financial Board which was published last term and gave a general prospect and retrospect of University finance in war time. On the first of these subjects I said something in no. 7. Since the war began, as teaching offices became vacant by death, resignation, or retirement on reaching 65, the vacancies have not been filled unless, in a particular case, an urgent necessity has been shown. Sometimes, for instance in scientific professorships, it would be difficult or impossible to fill them now since the best men are engaged on war-work, but in general the suspension is a measure of economy designed to help in meeting our dwindling income. At present five Chairs, and perhaps twice as many lesser posts, are vacant, and the number will increase. Our other chief economy is, of course, in the stipends of men away on war service. In neither case is the whole stipend necessarily saved since absentees who are earning less than they did will, so long as we can afford it, have their stipends made up. Herein we are often directly subsidising a Govt. Department, for when we are urgently asked for the release of somebody with a special qualification (e.g., a knowledge of colloquial Japanese) but, as sometimes happens, less than half the man's ordinary salary is offered, the man may have a family to consider and be unable to accept unless his income is guaranteed. Also when we release somebody we may have to pay a substitute to provide essential courses of lectures. Still, the total economies effected by these and other means are substantial. In no. 7 I said that the reduction of our income in fees looked then as though it might be of the order of £50,000 for the last academic year. Fortunately it has proved to be only about half that amount. Of course the barometer will go on falling and there are stormy times ahead, but at present the ship is still afloat and as yet not quite down to the Plimsoll-line. Naturally the situation might change in the twinkling of an eye, but on the present showing we should weather this year all right. What comes after I shall not attempt to guess, both for other reasons and because, having no head or taste for finance, I keep my nose as remote from University and College accounts as I may. The recent entrance scholarship examination was not very cheering, for the candidates were down both in numbers and quality, particularly in the humaner subjects. I don't altogether understand this, for though no doubt many parents may have decided that they cannot afford a University education for their children scholarship or no, I should have expected schoolmasters, wanting the réclame, to have insisted on the boys going in. A good many schools, however, have had their work much interfered with either by bombing or by evacuation, and this has no doubt had some effect on the entry.

(You consider this boring? You do — and one of you complained most acrimoniously of the statistics of numbers contained in no. 15. You have my sympathy; but the Parish Magazine should be, inter alia, a record of Cambridge in War-Time, and with that object in view I am determined to spare you nothing.)

The third question related to the Septemviri to which one of you noticed that the Master had been appointed; and this answer may well form *The Mysterious University: lesson 6*. Know, then, that the Septemviri and the Court of Discipline are disciplinary bodies, the second having jurisdiction over members of the University *in statu pupillari*, the first over senior members. The second meets but rarely, usually at the instance of the Proctors, but I have twice supported a pupil summoned before it; the first, owing to the exemplary behaviour of senior members of the University, hardly meets at all. It has been convened, I think, three times in the last fifteen years, but on one of those occasions it was because a man imaginatively charged various high University officials with defrauding him of his degrees. A pedant might even say that the Septemviri have met but once, for on the two other occasions they were only six in number. Q. Why was their number increased to seven? A. Why, largely because our cultured journalists, hearing that the Sexviri had been convened, immediately assumed that the charge into which they were enquiring was of a sexual character. (You may not believe this, but it is nevertheless perfectly true.)

Term began again on Jan. 14 but its suggestions have not as yet acquired that mellow maturity which the P.M. requires and must keep for another number — not that at present there is much to keep.

EIGHTEENTH LETTER

2.2.41

My impressions of the new term have now ripened sufficiently to be placed in the cold storage of the P.M., but they don't amount to very much and one of you at least will be glad to hear that they don't include any very elaborate statistics. I see that nearly 200 men matriculated in January but I have no means of telling how many vanished in the vac. If Trinity is a criterion the University should be larger than last term for we are about 20 up in numbers. On my own Side two men went down, seven freshmen arrived, and two aliens returned from internment in Canada, with their studies somewhat less prejudiced than they might have been owing to the fact that their supervisor was interned with them — a stroke of luck for them though the supervisor, I dare say, did not appreciate it. He was Friedlander, about whom there was a good deal of fuss in the papers some time before Christmas, some saying (truly enough) that he was being very stupidly treated by the authorities, and others adding (with less truth) that the College had displayed a fine spirit in electing somebody to a Fellowship while he was in an internment camp. I wasn't electing myself, but having had a good deal of experience of Fellowship elections I should think it unlikely that any elector gave a moment's thought to the matter, and absolutely certain that if it was mentioned at the meetings of electors at all it was immediately dismissed as irrelevant.

The inclusive price of undergraduate meals has gone up 2/6 a week owing to increased costs, and catering, I gather from the Kitchen Manager, who wears a harassed look, has become difficult — certainly some strange dishes have appeared at the High Table, which, for the first time (and several others) in my knowledge of it, has been outraged with rabbit. That eminent gastronome Brillat-Savarin, who observed 'Dis-moi ce que tu manges: je te dirai ce que tu es', would be hard put to it to place us just now. I hope the K.M.'s eye was not caught, as mine was, by a letter in the *Times* last May which began 'I hope you will spare me space to say, as an advocate for the consumption of grass-mowings, that I have eaten them regularly for over three years and off many lawns. The example I am eating at present comes off a golf course on Mitcham Common'. Now I come to think of it, however, this dish may perhaps have appeared in Trinity already. At least, I remember an impecunious contemporary of mine who, faced with the necessity of entertaining to lunch an aunt from whom he had expectations, thought of hard-boiled eggs, and was inspired by the sound of the lawn-mower, then opportunely cutting the New Ct in which he lived, to bed them on the products of that process — or so it was alleged. There is nothing improbable in this story, for he was a man of originality and resource, but I will not conceal from you that he had two friends, subsequently promoted to deserved eminence in their professions, who employed their fertile imaginations in weaving a kind of saga about him, and I cannot positively assert that this incident was not an element of the saga rather than of history. I fancy the K.M's difficulties are more due to distribution problems than to shortage, and may be ascribed, at least in part, to the greatly increased population of Cambridge. I have amused myself for some time past by contemplating the local butchers', grocers', and pastry-cooks' windows (endeavouring, I trust successfully, not to assume an 'Ah, Bisto' expression while doing so), and certainly they are worse off than even small shops in quite dingy London districts, where cakes, fruit, and so on don't seem rare. Nor had I any difficulty in getting in London some chocolate for two members of my Fire Party who complained bitterly that they could not satisfy their appetite for it here. The only shortages which much affect me personally are of edible apples (but those who belong, as I do, to the Cox aut praeterea nihil school are accustomed to a hiatus in the supply), and of cheese. The second touches me nearly for I often lunch, and normally depend a good deal, on it (further apophthegm of Brillat-Savarin: Un dessert sans fromage est une belle à qui il manque un oeil); however rationing leaves me wholly indifferent (as I have said before) and I count myself lucky after eighteen months of war to be suffering no worse deprivations than this. I dare say my pupils don't think much the worse of me if I am sometimes seen carrying home a paper bag containing something I have noticed in the window of an unfamiliar shop but cannot get in those I usually deal with.

You haven't had any literary tittle-tattle for four months. It will perhaps surprise some of you to hear that more has been asked for, but even those to whom it is least welcome can hardly have been so optimistic as to cherish the belief that I had forgotten this method of filling a paragraph.

My usual device for supplying myself with bedside books is to keep an eye on the tray in the University Library where accessions are displayed week by week, and to make a note of anything which looks likely to be interesting. Lately, however, I have been too busy to go there regularly, and, besides, the books have been few and boring for they have not been coming in as regularly as in peace-time and, when they come, take longer to catalogue and reach the tray owing to the depletion of the Library staff. Another device is to buy books that I want to read in the autumn and to read them before giving them away for Christmas presents; but Christmas presents have, I am sorry to say, been among my war economies. Consequently my reading has been more than usually desultory of late, but here is some of it. *I was Stalin's Agent*, by Krivitsky; *Last Days of Paris* by A. Werth (the second more interesting and probably truer than the first; neither cheerful) — and since both bear on the war I interpose here the observation that *Blackwood*, at which I usually look, has had during the last six months some interesting articles on various aspects of it. E. Lorimer, *Language Hunting in the Karakoram* (a very pleasant book); *A Forgotten River* (in Peru) by C. Sandeman, *Three Acres and a Mill* by R. Gathorne Hardy (both about travel and botany, and too much of the latter for my comprehension); C. Scott, *Lions on Trust* (about keeping lions as pets — not that I contemplate it); A. Polovtsoff, *The Call of the Siren* (this I insert not because I found it interesting but in the hope that you will assume it to be about A.R.P.: in fact it is about Naples, and the siren in question is known to those who have had the benefit of a Classical education as Parthenope, a name to which the more pedantic among them allot four syllables). H. Sutherland, *Hebridean Journey*, F. Darling, *Island Years* (both readable, but I wish my fellow Scots could write about their native country without being so sentimental. An exception — at least comparatively — is H. G. Graham whose *Social Life in Scotland in the 18th Century* I have, at odd moments, been re-reading; an interesting and entertaining book). *Kilvert's Diary* — another sad sentimentalist, though no Scot but a parson on the Welsh border in the 1870's. This has been creating a stir, at least among reviewers, probably because it is placid and escapist (horrid word); still he has an eye for the picturesque of various sorts, writes agreeably, and does well enough for bed, though I may excuse myself his third volume. T. Firbank, *I bought a Mountain* (a bad title but a pleasant book by a Canadian about sheep-farming in Snowdonia: contains, however, too much about the merits of his wife). E. F. Benson, *Final Edition* (amusing and well written though perhaps more amusing if you happen to have known the three Benson brothers). V. Woolf, *Life of Roger Fry* (again much puffed by reviewers, which, since it is Bloomsburian on both sides of the family, was to be expected. I did not think it interesting, or even a very agreeable picture of that attractive but exasperating man). No fiction? Well, yes; Somerset Maugham's newish volume of short stories called *The Mixture as Before* (rather below par I think), and Rose Macaulay's *Told by an Idiot* (Penguin; amusing).

And (while I am about it) I noticed some time ago that there was a batch of new volumes in the Everyman Library, and as they included one great favourite of mine which, if it had then been out, I should certainly have included in the list provided in no. 4 for those who wanted cheap books to read over camp-fires, I shall mention it here — W. H. Hudson's *Far Away and Long Ago*. It is about his early life in the Argentine; the subject matter, which is a good deal concerned with natural history, is interesting, and the style of extraordinary beauty. In no. 5 I used the word 'competent' of Somerset Maugham and had subsequently to explain that it was not a criticism. What I meant was that when one reads S.M. one thinks (or I think), no doubt wrongly, that given the element of luck necessary to all such enterprises one could, with sufficient expenditure of blood and tears, reduce one's own paragraphs to the same shipshape efficiency. I shouldn't ever entertain the delusion that I could write like Hudson, and if I were told to try I shouldn't have the faintest idea how to begin. Possibly Hudson hadn't either: *Far Away and Long Ago* is, I think, much his best book though he wrote other good ones (*A Shepherd's Life*, about Wiltshire, is perhaps no. 2), but he was capable of English which would do no credit to a scullery-maid. Anyhow, whether his limpid prose is a native wood-note or not, I admire and envy it very much; and if you don't know the book I commend it to your attention.

For information: 'Lady Benn writes from Limpsfield, Surrey, to ask why mid-wives are still without steel helmets, which she considers are a most necessary protection for them' (*Times*, Feb. 5).

I HAVE been taken to task, quite properly, for using Cambs. as an abbreviation not for Cambridgeshire but for Cambridge, and, as you shall see, am resolved to mend my ways. I do so the more willingly because I have never written the peccant letters without hesitating whether or not to put a full-stop after them. This question often troubles me, for the only rule I know — that when the word is curtailed it should, and when it is syncopated it should not, have the stop (as Bart.'s for St Bartholomew's, but Bart for Baronet) — produces some repellant results and I often reject its promptings even where they are applicable, as in Cambs(.) for Cambridge they are not. I fear, therefore, that the future Ph.D. candidate who attempts to discover from the P.M. my principles in this matter will reach the conclusion that I am unprincipled — a result perhaps not less important than that of many Ph.D. dissertations. I remember an early American pupil of mine setting the Registrary, who is a stickler in orthographical matters, a nice problem in this field. His name was (let us say) William K. Peabody, but when asked what K stood for, he replied that it stood for nothing but that he had it because everybody in America had an initial between his Christian and his surname. Problem: since K was not an abbreviation, could it, when printed in the list of men matriculated, properly have a full-stop after it?

Term ended yesterday and on the whole it hasn't been very agreeable — the Lent term seldom is — and it was enlivened with epidemics of measles and chickenpox. At the beginning we had a week or ten days of very cold weather with the concomitant, as last year, of frozen pipes; and though on this occasion my own didn't burst, by way of compensation the melting snow came through my bedroom ceiling. As recorded also a year ago, the cold was accompanied by seagulls on the Backs and by chilblains on my person though by both in smaller numbers. I fear that, whatever the seagulls may intend, the chilblains have formed a habit. I have reverted to bedsocks, abandoned nearly fifty years ago, and I dare say that if I survive so long another winter or two will see me night-capped. Cold weather returned towards the end of last month and again in this and it has cramped the style of the crocuses which are only now reaching their best, but there was before that a fine show of aconites and snowdrops, and on sunny days our Fellows' Garden and the John's Wilderness have had a golden carpet of aconites such as I haven't seen in either place before.

I have been revoltingly busy. University machinery has by now got fairly well into its war-time rhythm, and its larger bodies — the Council and the General Board — have been a little less occupied than they were — that is to say their meetings tend to last an hour and three quarters rather than two hours and a bit; but their committees, which apply general rules to particular cases, have not had appreciably less to do. The University Scholarships and some prizes in which I was awarding (or more commonly failing to award) took up a good deal of time but less than last year as there were fewer candidates. This carried with it, however, the disadvantage that the paid examiners (some are *ex officio*) felt under an obligation in the University's straitened circumstances to demand less pay. Tutors were given a good deal of trouble by the registration of the 1921 class on Feb. 22, for the rules drawn up for the older classes did not apply, and we were deluged with obscure and contradictory instructions from various quarters and were hard put to it to say what undergraduates ought to do. I had also on my hands the extra course of lectures mentioned in no. 17. It was on the *Persae* of Aeschylus which, though it was not chosen for that purpose and had in fact been announced before Greece was invaded, is in places startlingly apposite to the times; and if Mussolini's mother does not, like Atossa at the tomb of Darius in the central scene of the play, perform necromantic rites at her husband's grave, it is perhaps partly because she is already dead. When my boots pinch, as sometimes they do, I derive considerable comfort from the reflexion that Mussolini's must be far and away the most uncomfortable pair in Europe. I laughed also at the picture in the papers of the rock on the road to Sollum[1] with his pompous portrait and, of all unluckily chosen slogans, the words *Chi si ferma è perduto* — and to do the Italians justice I expect some of them saw the joke as they passed it on their westward journey. As to the registration of the younger classes a good many details are unsettled and the effect on us is not yet fully plain; and since I am not sure how much of what I know about the position is still confidential I had better postpone my observations to a later number.

Cambridge had its first showers of incendiaries during the term, and in the first of them University and College buildings were hit for the

---

[1] Sollum had been taken on Dec. 16 during General Wavell's advance.

first time. They came to no serious harm, and so far as I know the only bomb which went through a roof crossed the floor diagonally, leapt into a sink, and fizzled to its end in happy and undetected privacy. A pity that not more are house-trained. A couple of small fires were caused in the town (one has been mentioned in the papers), and the poor display the Borough Fire Services were reported to have put up contributed to an access of stirrup-pump-consciousness which would have occurred in any case. S.-p.'s are hard to get but our orders come in bit by bit, and we shall soon have one to every two staircases besides others at strategic points, and I have been organising demonstrations by professionals and gingering up practices among the laity. The incidents referred to also stimulated our nerves, already a little frayed, about the area between Trinity St and the Great Ct which is troublesome by reason both of its complication and of the ramshackle nature of some of the buildings it contains. The occupants watch this themselves, but I spent some gloomy hours crawling about on roofs to decide where they had better watch from — gloomy because, though my figure is now better adapted than it was to trapdoors and garret windows, my joints increasingly rebel at such exercises. Bombs in this neighbourhood have so far tended, whether by accident or design, to fall somewhere near a railway — and as they have usually fallen only somewhere near, and Cambridge is surrounded by railways on all sides but the west, I do not think this is indiscreetly precise. Anyhow we may have cause to be more grateful to those who kept the railways at a distance from the centre of the town; still more grateful I should say myself, for except when starting early or returning late I have not been unappreciative hitherto. I do not know who these benefactors may have been, but I guess they were the University authorities of the day, who were not by way of standing any nonsense from Railway Companies. The Railway Act of 1844 which authorised the construction of the railway to Cambridge provided that Proctors and Tutors (poor souls) might frequent the station at the arrival and departure of trains, interrogate the staff about passengers whom they suspected of being *in statu pupillari*, and prohibit the Co. from carrying them even though they had paid for their tickets; and I have long treasured as a model epistolary rebuke the letter written to the Manager of the Gt Eastern in 1851 by Dr. Corrie, Master of Jesus, and Vice-Chancellor at the time. And since you have probably never read the *Memorials* of that worthy man (which are, indeed, as dull as ditchwater) I shall here transcribe it for your edification:

Sir,

I am sorry to find that the Directors of the Eastern Counties Railway have made arrangements for conveying foreigners and others to Cambridge on *Sundays* at such fares as may be likely to tempt persons, who, having no regard for Sunday themselves, would inflict their presence on this University on that day of rest. I should be obliged, therefore, by your making it known to the Directors that such arrangements as those contemplated by them are as distasteful to the authorities of the University as they must be offensive to Almighty God and to all right-minded Christians.

I have the honour to be, Sir,

Your obedient servant

G. E. CORRIE

Vice-Chancellor of Cambridge.

The suppression of the *Daily Worker* naturally elicited shrill screams from our advanced undergraduate thinkers and their kindred in evacuated institutions, with which were mingled a bellow from the biochemical department and its political neighbourhood (I have never understood the link between biochemistry and communism but in Cambridge it is close) and a genteel yelp from the Girton High Table. The undergraduates no doubt screamed the shriller because they were aware that the Proctors were contemplating an edict requiring them to put their names to their publications and to obtain permission for their public meetings. As a matter of fact I regret all these things myself, holding that air, even if hot or deleterious, is usually best allowed to escape, but I don't regard them as among the major horrors of war, and I should have more sympathy with these advocates of freedom of speech if freedom of speech were really what they wanted; but the most vociferous of them, so far I know, bore with silent fortitude the suppression of the Fascist organ and the more candid do not conceal that all they really want is freedom to speak themselves. However I am told they are secretly delighted because the martyrdom of the *D.W.* brings the revolutionary millennium appreciably nearer.

Answers to correspondents (H.C., H.J. and others): No, Squirrel Pie has not yet been served at the High Table.

TWENTIETH LETTER

23.3.41

My somewhat discursive impressions of last term ceased rather because I had completed my tale of bricks than because I couldn't find any more straws, and as vacation brick-making is hard work I shall now rake the residue together.

The Master got into his Lodge early in the term except for the drawing-room and the dining-room which were in workmen's hands. The latter is so still for we have had a great bit of luck over it. In no. 16 I said it was a terror of a room, and so it was. It is panelled, and so far as living memory extends the panelling had been covered with that most hideous of all decoration, a bogus oak-grain in brown and yellow paint. The panelling has now proved to be real oak of very fine quality, and, as sometimes happens, the better for having been painted; for instead of being black it is of a lovely cool brown tone. It will be the making of the room. It isn't quite perfect, for it is patched here and there with pine, and there is reason to think that it was transferred from some other place, and that the patching and first painting date from the time when it was put in its present position. The patches, and some Victorian deal in the oriels (which were built by Whewell), are now being replaced by oak, and the whole will make a very fine room. I shan't get any credit for this transformation, and may have already got some discredit (for the Master is naturally anxious to get into the room and mending the panelling takes longer than painting it would have done), but I shall here stake out a firm claim since it was my importunate curiosity which led to the discovery. I had, it is true, no real hope that the panelling would prove to be oak (having been told repeatedly that it was pine), but I could think of no paint which would look nice and wondered whether the pine, if stripped, might not look better than any. But I did, too, for various reasons, cherish a doubt about its being really pine.

I have also had a certain amount to do with rehanging pictures in the Lodge. Given a free hand and plenty of time to experiment hanging pictures rather amuses me, for even if the results are not all one wishes one can satisfy oneself that one has done one's best with the available material. Here, however, I have had neither, and though the drawing-room is a good deal better than it was, it is not as I should like it and I have therefore rather grudged the time I have spent upon it.

Items of A.R.P. news (in case you should think there couldn't be any more) are that some University buildings and Colleges now receive the form of private warning, known as Rainbow, which is issued to factories and indicates the near neighbourhood of hostile aircraft. We have been rather puzzled to know what use to make of it. On the one hand it is useful to be told during a long Alert which are dangerous periods: on the other a long series of brief Rainbows with no Alert is rather troublesome, particularly for College Wardens as at night they must go to the post. In practice it will probably mean that I, at any rate, during my week of duty, sleep regularly in the Porters' Lodge; and since one must in any case sleep in one's clothes this is no great hardship, though the sleep I get there on my pallet is not of the grade guaranteed to regular consumers of Horlick's Malted Milk. We thought, when the Rainbow system was installed, that it would enable us to dispense with Hall Observers and empty Hall at once on receipt of the warning, but experience showed that if we did that a single meal might sometimes be interrupted three times, so we still have a man on guard though his task in deciding whether to empty Hall is eased by knowing whether a Rainbow is on or not. As a matter of fact it hasn't been emptied very often. Last term, for instance, I cleared it once during dinner when flares were dropping pretty near, and an undergraduate cleared it at lunch when a Dornier came over low apparently firing machine-guns. So far as I know this was the only Hun machine yet seen by me except in fragments on a lorry. A woman was hit in the arm by a spent bullet (the only casualty), but I suspect she owed it rather to the misplaced enthusiasm of an H.G. in the neighbourhood than to the Dornier.

We had towards the end of term a fairly elaborate fire practice with an A.F.S. critic, and the Fire Party put up a show much inferior to that of last term. This was partly bad luck, for the engine gave unexpected trouble, and partly slackness on the part of one squad, and I don't really regret it. For one thing I would sooner put up a bad show at a practice than in the event; for another, the trouble here, as no doubt elsewhere, is to keep people up to the scratch after months and months of Alerts without incident. I hope that this failure will provide a stimulus, and it has certainly enabled me to reconstitute the idle squad. The First Aid Party would also be the better for a jolt, but all they have so far had was the case of a young gentleman who at the party after Commemoration (held in a very chastened form on March 16) became insensible. This phenomenon was ascribed by impartial observers to alcoholic excess, and by the victim to a surfeit of chocolate éclairs taken immediately before dinner (though whence obtained he did not say). The F.A.P. hurried round in their shirt-sleeves with a stretcher, but stomach-pumps are among the few articles of medical equipment which they have not demanded of me, and it is perhaps as well that nature rapidly supplied their absence, for the F.A.P., whose party was interrupted, looked to me in the mood to see what could be done with a stirrup-pump.

The Fire Party has suffered a casualty by just such another sudden blow of fate as I described in no. 6. A man was found dead in bed from some obscure haemorrhage in the spine. He was a Chinaman, not my pupil though I knew and liked him, and he was one of my stoutest firemen.

12.4.41

I have been away for the inside of a week, to Oxford, Eton, and London — not a long holiday and largely concerned with business, but at least a pleasant change. I really need a more extended vacation but have little inclination to take one even if I could. I don't know that I found much to report in any of these places. Oxford seems to have benefited more than Cambridge by the scrapping of superfluous railings, perhaps because it had more to scrap. I am not an anti-railings man myself; I think, for instance, that this College did ill some years ago to remove them from the shapeless grass-plot at the east end of Chapel, and proposals to scrap those round the Senate House, where the railings themselves have some dignity, have now, I hope, been defeated. Those that have so far been scrapped here haven't made much difference though some might think the front of Emmanuel is better without them. In Oxford I noticed one or two places where they seemed better away, and the removal of those opposite Magdalen in front of the Botanic Garden looked, at any rate at first sight, a marked improvement.

The Eton scene changes but little. School Yard is encumbered with piles of bricks saved from the wreckage of Upper School for use when the time comes to rebuild. Apart from that I noticed only a large coal-dump on Agar's Plough, the origin and purpose of which seem as mysterious as those of the latrines mentioned in no. 8. A good deal of allotment-digging is going on, and one boys' house has been closed owing to a fall in numbers. It has been taken over by the Office of Works though its new occupants haven't arrived yet. Masters continue to disappear, and I hear rumours that, as in the last war, the era of the comics has begun though not as yet that of the aged crocks; no doubt all schools are facing the same predicament.

As to London, I visited a few galleries and may write about them later. I saw also rather more of its central parts than I had done at Christmas but found little there to modify the impressions which I gave in no. 17. Dishevelment proceeds of course, but not apace, and though here and there a big shop has been replaced not by a pile of rubbish but by holes in the ground, solid buildings take a good deal of battering and leave no such area of desolation as a slum street. My club, for instance, has had bombs in the road within a few feet of three of its four sides but apart from glass is little the worse. Even round St. Paul's, where the damage has been very severe, the scene that meets the eye is less horrific than the photographs had led me to expect — though it should be said that I didn't explore, and that when the immediate mess has been cleared up one cannot appraise the real state of affairs without doing so. I am glad, by the way, to notice that pictures of ruins are becoming a little less frequent in the weeklies and shouldn't mind if they ceased altogether, for we most of us know by now what a wrecked church or shop looks like and continual reminders are not only dispiriting but also boring.

The chief local event of the vacation has been the burning of Pembroke in the worst College fire in my memory. It was on March 21, and was caused, ironically enough, not by enemy action but, as the occupants (who were not members of the University) assert, by a fault in the electric wiring, or, as the College authorities maintain, by the occupants' frivolity with their cigarette-ends. It has left their new buildings on Downing Street roofless for about eighty yards. However, if you must have a fire, better there than in a lot of buildings I can think of. (Conversation between W. E. Heitland and his wife on seeing from afar a fire at Fulbourn: *Mrs H.* Oh, I *do* hope it isn't the Asylum. *Mr H.* What would you prefer, my dear?) And there is further faint irony in the fact that the Master of Pembroke, who is chairman of the University A.R.P. committee, has for some time past been enlivening the Council with weekly eloquence on the importance of fire-watching.

20.4.41

I MEANT to say in my last letter, but had no room, that I read lately in a book called *Road through Kurdistan* (by A. M. Hamilton, an engineer who built roads in those parts) that when the R.A.F. had occasion during the Kurdish revolt (in 1930 I think) to bomb Kurdish villages, not wishing to kill anybody, they gave notice of their intention by loud-speakers. The notice was in the form 'In the name of God, the merciful, the compassionate, we are going to drop bombs upon you.' The wording provokes reflections of various kinds, but at least the intention was humane, and I prefer it to the totalitarian method of bombing first and making sanctimonious speeches afterwards.

And, talking of the R.A.F., I meant also to say that I hope you have bought (for 3d.) and read the official pamphlet called *The Battle of Britain*. I would not at the time trust myself to write about that resounding victory, which cost most of us, I imagine, some friends, nor will I now. But here is an account as intelligible to the layman as is likely to be written and it is well worth reading. I used to wait impatiently for the successive volumes of the *History of the (last) War in the Air* (of which the first was by Walter Raleigh and the remaining five by H. A. Jones), for if one skipped judiciously it was an enthralling narrative. A corresponding history of this war, when it comes to be written, will, I suppose, be so technical that nobody but experts will read it.

17.5.41

Term began again on April 18, but the transition was less marked than any I have known except perhaps October 1939 for we were unusually populous in the vac. Besides the College Fire Party there were under-graduates (male and female though not, I believe, simultaneously) fire-watching on University buildings, members of the S.T.C. performing tactical exercises, linguists attending a French course, Evangelicals attending a conference, and communists (possibly also some others) attending a congress of the National Union of Students, though the last were mostly from other Universities. I gather from the papers that they were debating how best 'to implement their responsibilities to the community' (whatever that may mean), and that they decided the proper way would be for them to continue their studies at the Universities (while the less intelligent were conscripted) and, *en passant*, to reform those effete institutions. The N.U.S. has been coming in for some acid criticism in the *Cambridge Review*, which points out, among other things, that though it is no doubt very nice and high-minded to proclaim that there is no quarrel between the Youth of England and the Youth of Germany, the Y. of G. is ostensibly 'striving unceasingly to be worthy of the greatest German of all time' as the leader of the Hitlerjugend bids it, and it might be well to find out if they are feeling as matey as the N.U.S.

Term, I repeat, is a month old, but it has produced precious little for me to write about, since I take it that you will not want to be told again that I have been very busy, nor why, nor how. Numbers are perhaps a trifle up — my own tutorial side, at any rate, lost five but gained seven. What we shall be like next year I still cannot tell you, for though the Board of Education has issued its instructions to headmasters, that pudding is still to be eaten. The instructions arrange for medical, scientific, and technical students to go on much as before, and they also provide for the arrival of some exponents of humaner subjects provided that 'they show exceptional promise as potential officers, or intellectual ability above the average, or evidence of a balanced combination of the two.' It is pretty plain, I think, that the authorities would like to see a good many Arts students here, both as a reservoir of potential officers and as leaven for the somewhat indigestible lump of scientists. Meanwhile headmasters are no doubt scratching their heads over their instructions, and parents over their income-tax returns, and the results remain problematic, though we shall probably ease the problem of some parents by extending the terms on which scholars can receive the titular values of their emoluments. Why Oxford should expect, as it is said to do, to have about as many men up next year as they have now is more than I can guess — though it should perhaps be remembered that the motto of that University is *Dominus illuminatio mea*.

The Fitzwilliam now has five rooms open, which is more than it has had since the beginning of the war. The big room contains miscellaneous pictures and furniture, two others pictures and objects of a (somewhat vaguely) baroque character, a fourth French furniture and engravings, a fifth mezzotints and medals of British admirals. Most of this comes from bits of the Museum collections not important enough to have been removed to safer places, but some things have been lent by various folk, myself among them. The present Director has a great talent for arranging an amusing show out of unpromising materials, and I dare say the Fitzw. at the moment offers more entertainment than any other gallery still open. The Ashmolean has (or had) on loan a flash set of Boucher tapestries and furniture to match but not much else of interest. In London there was at Christmas an excellent show of Augustus John's drawings in the National Gallery to which I hope some of you went. I could only spare half an hour then and was annoyed to find it over last vac. The drawings were of very various merit, but few artists have been more versatile with pen and pencil, and though J. is not (for me at any rate) of that very select company who will sometimes make one catch one's breath with delight by the sheer magic of a single line, it is at least hard to think of a British draughtsman whose best drawings have been better. The N.G. now has a loan exhibition which I haven't seen: when I was last there it was exhibiting only the war artists, who improve a bit I think; but the rooms are dominated and obsessed by Eric Kennington's over-life-size heads in pastel which (though I wouldn't deny them a certain horrid ability) give me the creeps. Dealers in London naturally keep little on view and that little not their best, so that one's Bond St crawl (if one is given to Bond St crawling) is a dull affair. What is at the Tate I know not; the British Museum (rather discreditably I think) has only a couple of rooms of miscellaneous junk to show, and S. Kensington, though more extensively open, is not vastly more exciting in contents except that it has a small Memorial Exhibition of Eric Gill's work — quite good though short of sculpture and recent drawings.

I was sorry for Gill's death last November. He was, may be, no genius, but he had a very refined and original talent, and I admire a great deal of his work. Also, in spite of his contrarieties, I liked him as a man. I didn't know him well, but, surprisingly enough considering how little interest Cambridge takes in the arts, there is a fair amount of his work here, so that his cassock and beret were seen about the place from time to time; and I used sometimes to call on him at his hill-top farm near High Wycombe, where a picturesque square of black barns had been converted into workshops in which he, his sons-in-law, and pupils sculpted, lettered, printed, and woodcut, while their wives and pullulating infants sewed and sprawled (respectively) on the lawn in the middle — a pleasingly patriarchal scene. I wish I had seen him in his earlier establishment four miles beyond the ruins of Llanthony Abbey up the narrow and solitary Ewyas valley in the Black Mountains, but he had left those parts before I reached them. I have lately been reading his *Autobiography*, which is a queer compost of modesty and assurance, religion and sex, Ruskinian socialism, mysticism, and what not. For all the confidence with which these themes are handled it is engagingly unpretentious, claiming to be no more than an unvarnished account of Gill's own spiritual Odyssey. I wouldn't say it had no longueurs, but in the main I found it extremely interesting — though if you think of trying it on my recommendation remember that I probably started with more interest in the author than you, and better prepared for the sort of thing I was in for.

I have been lecturing on Herodotus, and though I have been more concerned with the author and composition of the book than with its historical contents, here too, as last term in the *Persae*, are tracts for the times. Let me translate for you the reply made by the Athenians in 479 B.C. to Alexander the First of Macedon when he brought overtures from Mardonius who was in command of the Persian army in Thessaly. They said: "Even of ourselves we know that the forces of Persia are many times greater than our own; there is no need to cast that in our teeth. Nevertheless, since we earnestly desire to be free, we shall defend ourselves as best we may. Do not try to persuade us to come to an agreement with the barbarian; we shall not be persuaded. And now carry back to Mardonius this message from the Athenians: 'So long as the sun traverses the same course he traverses now we shall never make terms with Xerxes. We shall go forth to defend ourselves against him trusting to find at our side the gods and heroes whose dwellings and images he has impiously burnt.' And as for yourself, appear no more at Athens with such messages as these, nor advise us to take unlawful courses thinking to do us a service thereby. You are our friend and we would not have you come to any hurt at Athenian hands."

TWENTY-SECOND LETTER

1.6.41

You would have been surprised if you had walked through the College one radiant Sunday afternoon last month. You would have found by the Bridge the College fire-pump and an enormous Dennis engine supplying water by lines of hose through the New Ct and Hostel to five more pumps in the Great Ct; also a large fire-float moored under the wall of the Bowling Green with a line running up the Bowling Green and Great Ct to another enormous engine outside the Great Gate which was supplying two lines of hose in Whewell's Ct and a third held by a man poised above the Chapel at the top of an immense steel ladder. The occasion of these unwonted phenomena was a grandiose practice for which the whole Borough A.F.S. turned out. The battle-orders, in skeleton, were: 14.30 Incendiaries dropped on College. 14.45 Fire in Whewell's Ct out of control; all mains useless; immediate assistance required. 14.55 Chapel on fire and out of control. 15.00 Area bounded by Trinity St, Trinity Lane, and the river on fire and out of control. From the Borough point of view it was an exercise in seeing what could be done by relaying water from the river, the new Borough inspector (who seems to be a good man) having found in various attacks he has been through elsewhere that the mains invariably get put out of action. It appears to have been a success, since we were told that the area could have been controlled with fewer engines. From our point of view it was mainly an exercise in co-operation and in using our engine to boost others; and we didn't do at all badly in detecting and extinguishing the incendiaries which started the show and later when the inspector took command. These affairs, however, take up a good deal of time, for there is planning to be done in advance and tidying up to be done afterwards. Also a certain amount of minor damage is apt to result, and as that admirable man the Clerk of the Works looks rather sourly upon the pranks of the College Fire Party I prefer as a matter of tactics to point out to him the broken tiles and leaking roofs for which we are responsible before he comes and reports them to me. The College Fire Party have now compiled, and I have had printed for them, a brief manual of drill suited to their special circumstances.

Perhaps you would not have been less surprised to find me, one night shortly after this practice, rolling hoses in Nevile's Ct at 11 p.m. To tell the truth I was surprised at this myself for I do not count rolling hoses part of a Warden's duties and I lent a feeble hand and foot only because the Fire Party, with Triposes staring them in the face, were backward with corvées of the sort. Less unusual, though perhaps as surprising to you, would be to find me in the small hours perched (commonly with company) on the ridge of the Library roof. The explanation would be that if, when I am not on duty, I am roused by explosions in what seems indecent proximity, or by other untoward sounds, I am apt to go the rounds and, if the night is fine, to ascend one of the local summits to brood on the prospect, somewhat (but only somewhat) like stout Cortez upon a peak in Darien. I do not much enjoy these exercises, and the Library roof is a hard, cold, seat for the arthritic, but in moonlight Cambridge is very lovely from aloft, and one night in particular when, under a full moon, the sky was patterned with exhaust-trails and searchlights, I should have been sorry to miss. I think, however, of patenting some form of pyjama trousers which can be guaranteed not to come down when their occupant is halfway up a ladder. Mine have so far withstood the demands made upon them, but they add to my anxieties.

Trinity and St John's had one day a joint gas exercise conducted in their New Ct under the auspices of the R.A.F. I do not know how many of our flock attended but I did not see much of them at the finale in the Magdalene baths, where a long-suffering airman was stripped naked and pitilessly scrubbed before an assembled multitude. It is no exaggeration to say that this spectacle drew tears from every eye though they were perhaps elicited less by compassion than by the considerable concentration of tear-gas introduced into the bathroom on the clothes of the spectators. The sequel to this display was a morning spent with the Divisional Gas-officer in considering how, if we must, we might convert the Great Ct baths into a decontamination station — a pretty occupation for an elderly philologist even in the bedlam in which we are at present compelled to exist.

Last week the Emergency Blood Transfusion Service, with whom I registered in August 1939, awoke again to my existence and bade me come and be bled. I was somewhat amused to notice that I surrendered a pint of the turbid and stagnating fluid which fills my system with much less commotion than several hale and hearty young things of both sexes whose veins should pulse with much nimbler fires than mine. On the other hand the cup of black kitchen tea with which our losses were consoled probably did them less harm than it did me.

14.6.41

Term ended on June 9, and I add some further random impressions to those which precede. It has been very cold with persistent north winds, and I have had a fire almost continuously into the first week of this month. Consequently, though there were in various parts of the Backs some lovely drifts of daffodils, anemones, and hyacinths, spring has been very backward and blossom long behind its usual date. The wistaria in the Great Ct, for instance, was only just starting on May 20, the chestnuts, so far from casting their flambeaux by the end of May, had hardly lit them, and the may did little more to deserve its name. For the information of those interested in phenology I add that I saw a couple of swifts on May 12 which is only two days behind the right time (see no. 9), but I saw little more of them for another fortnight, though as an amenity of Nevile's Ct they were partly replaced by a pair of mallard that took to spending the day there. Also that I heard a cuckoo, which should have been here in April, on May 6; but I shouldn't have done so if I had not chanced to be awake during what ornithologists romantically call the Dawn Chorus, and it was long before I heard another. However I can do without cuckoos myself, and though Housman used to commend them on the ground that alone of feathered creation they use the diatonic scale, except as a symbol I do not admire their voices much more than their morals. I turned the pages not long ago of a work by E. P. Chance called *The Truth about the Cuckoo* in which their iniquities are fully exposed — not a very readable book for the laity, but a good bit of sleuthing, for the author knew his cuckoo so well that he could tell in whose nest it was going to lay on what day.

Term was a little complicated for me by the fact that the Classical faculty, like some others, partially combined their Tripos and Preliminary examinations, thereby economising papers and examiner-power but also curtailing my lectures to Preliminary candidates by about a week and obliging me to recast a good deal of them. On the other hand my serious teaching for the term ended a week the sooner and during the last month I have begun to think again of that immortal work which has lain untouched since last September; not much more than think, however, for there have been many oddments to clear up, some regular at this time of year, others incidental to the times. Among the latter was the composition of an inscription for a memorial brass for Sir James Frazer who died last month. My lapidary style is a halting thing and I am glad I have seldom been asked to trot it out — four times in all, so far as I remember, but once was for a Fellow long dead whom I had never even seen, and I merely undertook to construct some Latin if two contemporaries would tell me what it ought to mean. One said the man would have done better to marry, and the other that he had never heard a worse lecturer; and as these facts didn't lend themselves to a memorial inscription in any language and no others were forthcoming I held myself excused from proceeding. My other subjects are at least distinguished, for Frazer had an O.M., Housman belonged to the much selecter class of those who have refused one, and the third was an Eton pupil who earned a posthumous V.C. on the N.W. Frontier. Do not ask me the Latin for O.M. and V.C. for I do not know it.

The successive deaths of Rutherford, the late Master, and Frazer have rather stripped the College hand of O.M.'s which was of recent years spectacular; still, even now, of the thirteen non-military members three, if you include the Master, are Fellows, two are honorary Fellows, and one an ex-Fellow — facts I hope you will remember when next tempted to make a mock of the venerable figures who used to dine above you on the dais.

Some of you will have received ere now a circular signed by the Praelector (though penned by Another Hand) about taking your degrees in virtue of allowances for national service. On the similar occasion last year I wearied those not in that position by estimating the pros and cons of this proposition. Not wishing to weary them still further I shall merely say here that the terms are generous and I do not see that you can lose anything by accepting them.

TWENTY-THIRD LETTER

12.7.41

SINCE I last wrote I have been away for the inside of a week — to Wigan and, on the way back, to Stone in Staffordshire. A long and weary journey, you will say: and neither Wigan nor the Potteries a very suitable place for a brief villegiatura. True. But at Wigan, or rather on a neighbouring hill, lives an old friend whom I have hardly seen since the war began. Moreover Wigan, despite its music-hall reputation, is not so large as to be a gross blot on the landscape, and when distance and haze have added enchantment to the view chimneys and factories differ little from more noble buildings. Hence with but little effort of the imagination you might fancy yourself surveying the dreaming spires of Oxford or, as chimneys are more like towers than spires, that spiky townlet San Gimignano so much admired by the romantic traveller in Tuscany. Also the rhododendrons, though past their best, were still making a good show, and there were pictures to look at — a great refreshment in these days. Stone too, or the house in which I was staying, is pleasantly rural on the banks of the Trent. My Wedgwood cousin there took me over the new

Wedgwood factory which is both interesting and impressive — mainly occupied at present with china for sale to America, which clamours, among other things, more loudly than you would, or I, for expensive sets of dolls' tea-things. I was also taken for a good walk in Dovedale, a district I haven't touched since I was a boy and lived in Nottingham.

I went away reluctantly and should probably not have gone at all if I had not had a pretext of business to transact in Wigan, for fire precautions have been more than usually troublesome lately. The Fire Party had its quarters in the New Ct commandeered at 24 hours notice, whereby the defences of the College were wrecked and much expenditure of time, trouble, and money rendered of no avail. Temporary arrangements have been made, and ultimately the party will be housed in the Judge's Kitchen in the Lodge. The Judge, it is thought, will not want, or be able, to give large parties in wartime, and his kitchen, though less convenient than the old quarters, will do well enough when various alterations have been made. But strutting, building blast-walls, and laying telephones take time, and the last, which are the most essential, are very hard to get put in, and very expensive. (The College A.R.P. bill since the war began is already nearer three than two thousand pounds.) Besides this crisis it has been more difficult than usual to make vacation arrangements, partly because people were reluctant to say precisely when they would or could be up, partly because the squad-leader responsible for the gap between the Easter and the Long Vac. terms is very stale and has consequently been idle and unreliable. However Herr Goering seems not to have heard of this, and I am glad I went away for I wanted a brief respite; and though the hot weather when at last it came (as it did quite suddenly on June 16) was very welcome, it grew into a sultriness common here in August but quite unusual in June; whereas in Lancashire the air held a breath of sea and hill.

I came back from this jaunt on July 3. The Long Vac. term began nominally on the 4th but most people came up at the beginning of this week as lectures set in then for those that have them. As a matter of fact the College has been far from empty in the interval for the S.T.C. has been running courses preparatory to Certificate B and there have also been members of the Air Squadron about, and my tutorial hours have been about as busy as in term-time for some of the other Tutors have been away. For the Long Vac. term there are, or will be, about 130 men in residence, which would be quite a lot in peace-time and is phenomenal in view of our present numbers; but medicals, engineers, and scientists have nowadays to get on with their programmes as fast as they can. I found a welter of stuff awaiting me on my return, and have immersed myself in it again reluctantly enough. I dare say you will guess that a good deal of it concerns A.R.P. but for once I have decided to spare you details.

Though the prospects for next year clear but slowly, it is pretty plain that there will be a decline in numbers, and as four Tutors even with our present establishment are something of a luxury I shall absorb none of October's freshmen though I shall continue to be Tutor to survivors from this year. Thus having ceased to be Tutor in June 1939 by the sudden blast which usually extinguishes Tutors I shall now (unless a sudden blast of another kind intervenes) experience a second extinction by slow gradations of decay. It is a reasonable solution of the problem and on the whole I do not regret it. In June 1939, though sorry in some ways, in others I was glad; and when in September I was called on to resume office it was a little like setting out again after having just come in from a long walk; one could have prolonged the walk for a mile or two with pleasure but, having once sat down, didn't want to put on one's boots again. Truth to tell, tutoring is an odd and in some ways an unsatisfactory occupation. In peace-time much of it is sheer drudgery; one is tied by the leg for two hours a day, and during them one is subjected to too many interruptions to get down to any serious work; and much of one's life is occupied with writing dreary letters, making out dreary lists, entering people for examinations, and signing exeats, absits, and late-leaves. One hopes that one discharges the last function in a sufficiently sympathetic manner to encourage one's pupils to consult one on more important matters if they are in difficulties. And, naturally, some do and some don't. The advantage and reward of the position are that it brings one into contact with people one would otherwise not have known and enables one to make friends; and they are sufficient. But again official interviews are no passports to intimacy, and whether one makes friends or merely acquaintances of given pupils is largely a matter of chance, for one is usually dependent upon some accident to reveal common ties or sympathy or liking. I suppose that most Tutors, when in normal times they take leave of their pupils after three years, feel of some that here are men they would like to have known better. But A's and B's and C's University careers have produced no episode which has helped to set relations on a less formal footing; they may have come to lunch or dinner and have been shy or tongue-tied; you may have been worried, or preoccupied with other matters, when they came on business, or may have, as I am reputed to have, a forbidding manner; and the three years have slipped away with only the surface of the ice thawed. Of course Tutors in this College see more of their pupils, and do, or try to do, more for them than they used. My own Tutor I happened to know quite well for he was also my Supervisor, but I should have been surprised if he had asked me to a meal, and if, when I chanced to be ill, he had come to see me I should have been astonished. Fifteen years earlier than that I know of a Tutor who saw his pupils only when they came for terminal exeats, and urged them to send their gyps even for those. We do better I hope, but there are limits not only to what a Tutor can, but also to what he should, do. The University is, or ought to be, where one learns to stand on one's own feet; and Tutors who keep their pupils in leading strings (if they can) and Colleges which hardly differ in kind from public schools seem to me to misconceive their functions. But a Tutor who is anxious not to butt in where he isn't needed requires, in the matter of friendships, some encouragement from the other side. He makes them (as I hope the P.M. proves) but not quite as many as he would like.

Since the war began the job has changed a little, and in this respect for the worse. A good deal of the drudgery has gone, for exeats etc. are in less demand and one has fewer pupils. On the other hand much that was routine has, owing to constantly changing regulations, become a serious tax on the mind; and both Tutors and pupils have been busier — I with the things I write about with such pitiless prolixity in the P.M., they with courses speeded up, military training, and so on. Entertaining, owing to lack of time, rationing, and reduced staff, has become next to impossible. And, more than all these things, very few men are here for three years and many for only one; and in conditions where friendship must needs ripen slowly the third year is important. During the last year the undergraduates I have got to know best have not been (except by accident) my own pupils, whom I see on an average perhaps half a dozen times a term, but the members of the College A.R.P. parties, with some of whom I have been of necessity in constant contact. Decidedly tutoring has less attraction than it had.

And there is another reason why, regret it or no, I think it about time my spell came to an end. Youth is in any case apt to exaggerate the gap between itself and even early middle age — I remember at Eton being asked by a boy perhaps twelve years younger than I whether I had taught his grandfather, and undergraduates, unless they have changed more in thirty years than I think, no doubt regard most Dons over thirty as senile if not actually moribund. Still, as one's hair greys and the gap widens, the harder it is for one's pupils to believe that one is not so far gone in dotage that it would be useless to bring one their problems. It is even possible (horrid thought) that their doubts may be well founded. Anyhow if I last out until June 1942 I shall have been Tutor thirteen years as near as makes no matter; that is three years more than the normal span in this College, and I think it is enough. You need not, by the way, on reading this *confessio tutoris*, tell me my principles are all wrong, for it is too late to change them; nor enumerate the pupils to whom I have been a bad Tutor, for all Tutors have, and are aware of, their failures. That is one of the penalties of the profession.

TWENTY-FOURTH LETTER

16.8.41

No. 24 concludes the second year of the Parish Magazine and, as in no 12, I record a few details of its progress. Parishioners are slightly fewer than they were, fallings-off not having been quite balanced by replacements, and an average issue lately has gone to one or two less, not to one or two more, than a hundred. I am very glad to say that not many of the lapses are due to casualties; most are represented by those who, without an adequate reason, let three or four months go by without writing and show that they no longer want the P.M. enough to comply with my modest conditions. I am sorry to lose touch with any parishioner, but as I am under no illusions as to the entertainment I have to offer, such lapses neither vex nor surprise me; and since the dispatch of an issue is a really burdensome job at busy times I do not altogether regret a slight decrease in its circulation. Engagements and marriages, I have noted, have a very deleterious effect on my correspondence if not on my correspondents.

Some more countries have been brought within my ambit since last year but except for Malta and Turkey I cannot enumerate them, for addresses in Africa and the Middle East seldom indicate where their owners are, and though I may hear that a parishioner has received one copy in Palestine or Abyssinia I cannot guess where he will be when the next reaches him. Twice I have fallen foul of censors, single copies of nos.

19 and 20 destined for the Mediterranean having been returned with a leaflet of regulations they were said to infringe. As they obviously didn't, they were re-posted and I presume got through. However I make no complaint for my heart bleeds for those whose task it is to sit all day censoring letters. Military and naval censors, unless they have intercepted whole letters (which I think improbable for my parishioners are painfully discreet), have troubled me little, but a few place-names, probably in Italian Somaliland, were neatly snipped from a letter from those parts. I have had one or two airgraphs (or -grams), and though they have one advantage over letters, which now take 2-3 months from most places, as vehicles for feasts of reason or flows of soul I think poorly of them.

I read lately in an American work on business methods that 'the large lower right hand drawer could be made to accommodate a quick refer-ence work file including a tickler file with wobble blocks between the sections', and though, having no large lower right-hand drawer, I have not yet risen to these heights for the P.M., I have gradually evolved a fairly efficient system for recording the receipt of letters and keeping those received since the last issue within reach when I send out the next. I will not say that it is infallible, but when I tax you with not having written for x months do not suppose that the figure is a random guess. A tickler file, by the way, I understand to be one which tickles or stimu-lates the memory.

Now that the P.M. has tottered to the end of its second year I have an announcement to make — namely that I shall not in future feel obliged to aim at four pages (or, if you must be precise, at three and a bit). As I have said before, neither the daily life of a Don, nor, now the war-rhythm here is established, the changing face of Cambridge, provides enough material for an indefinite series on this scale, and whereas I got through the first year without much trouble, during the last six months or so I have often been very hard put to it to think of things to write about. That must necessarily have been as obvious to you as it was to me, for hard writing of this sort makes weary reading. Take note, therefore, that though in future I shall write four pages if the spirit moves, I shall also on occasion write three, or two, or one, without apology or further excuse. Let those that dole me out three measly octavo sides every three months reflect that a close-spaced quarto of typescript takes a deal of filling, and remember that the P.M. now nears its 100th page and has probably passed its 40,000th word — and then let them cast a stone if they dare.

Twenty or more years ago a friend in Pekin sent me a small metal bar engraved with Chinese characters, which, as it was a Christmas present, I assumed at the time wished me a happy Christmas or its Chinese equivalent. I used, and use, it fitfully as a paper-weight, and as it chanced long after to catch my eye while I was talking to the one and only pupil I have ever had who could read Chinese, I bade him translate it, which he did readily enough. The inscription means 'In the book called *The Yellow Hall* there are few characters'. After long rumination on this somewhat indigestible aphorism I take it to enjoin conciseness and to mean that if so weighty a work as the *Y.H.* (which is a Taoist book) can be written in a small number of words there is no excuse for verbosity. This is not normally an injunction of which I stand in need, for, to say nothing of a natural leaning towards brevity, the journals which publish my important works are usually short of space and might forgo that privilege if I spread myself too luxuriantly. But the P.M. is quite a different kettle of fish, and the prospect of having to conjure three or four pages of it out of nothing is a wicked temptation to be wordy which I fear I have not always resisted as I should. I had thought of bestowing the Chinese bar on a colleague who never uses one word where ten will serve, but it is plain in the light of the past two years that I ought to keep it in a conspicuous place on my own writing table. And when in future you get shorter numbers of the P.M. you must remember that in addition to the cause set out above the tattered remains of my literary conscience are also involved.

It is a very long time — six months in fact — since you had a turn in the Literary Corner, but that is easily explained. For one thing the prospect of three vacation numbers to fill caused me to hold it in reserve so long as term-time issues could, by hook or by crook, be filled. For another I have increasing difficulty in finding new books to read and have been falling back on old friends. I see, by the way, that the late Lord Montagu of Beaulieu was never without a Bradshaw to read at odd moments, but Mogg's *Ten Thousand Cabfares* as used by Mr Soapy Sponge (older parishioners see no. 8) suggests to me a cosier bed-book. Anyhow, my Mogg of late has been Lamb's *Letters* in a completer edition than heretofore, and while it lasted it did very well. He is the most engaging of correspondents, and I thought as I read that the P.M. would be vastly more entertaining if some of its unimpeachable veracity could be exchanged for

Lamb's soaring flights of fancy. I have also re-read a good deal of Norman Douglas who is a favourite writer of mine — not *South Wind* which I think overrated (if one must read about goings-on at Capri Compton Mackenzie's *Vestal Fires* amuses me more), but the discursive travel-essays. If you don't know them you might give *Old Calabria* a trial. My more modern reading, so far as I can recollect it, seems to have been mostly biographical. *H. L. Piozzi* by an American named Clifford is a full-dressed biography of Johnson's friend Mrs Thrale with much new material — perhaps fuller than any but enthusiastic Johnsonians require but very well done and producing a more sympathetic picture than my previous knowledge of the lady (which was not inconsiderable) led me to expect. John Buchan's autobiography called *Memory Hold-the-door* on the other hand left a faintly disagreeable impression and I think his undeniable talent was better employed on fiction. I have skimmed in recent times two novels — *Sick-heart River* and *Castle Gay*. The first is a poor, the second not a very good, story, but both contain pages of excellent descriptive writing. In the biographical line I have also read a slight but quite amusing life of Erasmus Darwin by H. Pearson, a competent sketch of Capt. Marriott by D. Hannay (by mistake for some other recommended by one of you), *Low Company* by M. Benney (an ex-burglar who writes well), *Wide Seas and Many Lands* by A. Mason (readable), and two Penguins — *The Quest for Corvo*, by A. J. A. Symons, about that singularly disagreeable character, the novelist Rolfe, and *Siamese White*, by M. Collis, a very interesting account of an English adventurer in Siam in the 17th cent. To these might be added the correspondence of Robert Bridges and Henry Bradley, though unless you are more interested than I am in spelling reform (and I notice that one or two parishioners are at any rate unorthodox in the matter) or accentual verse I don't recommend it, for these two bees hived in both those eminent bonnets.

Travel books are represented by *Libyan Sands*, by H. Bagnold, who was, I suspect, largely responsible for the rapidity of our advance in Libya last year, *Asian Odyssey*, by D. Alioshin (a White Russian adventurer; too sensational to be credible though it may be true), *My African Neighbours*, by H. Coudenhove (interesting), *Assam Adventure*, by Kingdon Ward (too botanical for me), and two sixpennies (or the first may be a shilling) which pass the time but have no literary pretentions — *Slaves and Ivory*, by H. Darley (informative on Abyssinia), and *Ju-ju and Justice in Nigeria*, by F. Hives. Fiction is, as usual, very poorly represented.

I have read *Gallions Reach*, by H. Tomlinson (Penguin: a goodish story rather foppishly written), but otherwise only a little Balzac. Besides these I can think only of *Purbeck Shop*, by E. Benfield, a quarryman who writes interestingly but assumes too much knowledge in his readers (or at any rate in one of them), *Inside the Whale*, leftish literary criticism by G. Orwell, an ex-pupil whom I have mentioned before in the P.M., and two large volumes by L. Venturi called *Archives de l'Impressionnisme* which contain the correspondence and other records of Durand Ruel, the dealer who backed most of the Impressionists in early days. This is important for earnest students of the subject but it is not in the main very bright reading and I did little more than pass my eye over it.

I fear this isn't a very helpful list, but several of you have asked in recent months for one so I supply the best I can leaving myself no room for the meagre incidents of the Long Vac. term now drawing to a close. However with two vacation nos. still to go I dare say more than justice will be done them in the end.

TWENTY-FIFTH LETTER

29.8.41

I turn back to consider the events of the Long Vac. term which got squeezed out of the last number, but I don't find much to consider beyond the fact, already recorded, that unwonted numbers of men were up. The usual committees held their usual Long Vac. meetings and mostly had so much to do that they took two bites to their cherry. The Council of the Senate, whose cherry had swollen to the size of a small melon, even took three, but I do not think its business was of much public interest. There was a question whether coupons would be required for gowns (hoods had already been deemed to be hats, which indeed they are though seldom worn as such), and, if so, whether we could insist on their being worn. However we learnt that coupons would not be required, and that, though the manufacture of the stuff was illegal, the hosiers had plenty in stock. You will therefore hear with relief that the freshmen of this October (at any rate) will not be born naked into the academic world.

Of the unusual committees the National Service Committee spent a good deal of time over people graduating in August by virtue of war allowances, but though there are a few difficult cases the business of this committee is largely created by inefficient Tutors who do not supply adequate evidence. (I need hardly say, therefore, that none of you who took degrees then occupied its attention.) The College had, and has, a committee sitting on the finances of the kitchens but I have had enough of this perennial theme and declined to serve on it. The University had another, which I could not escape, on the Govt. requirement that all undergraduates shall undertake some form of national service. This is a very troublesome matter, one problem being to fit in the programmes of the S.T.C., C.U.A.S., or H.G. with lectures and labs., another to safe-guard College and University A.R.P. services. The difficulty is that all these forces are part of the H.G., and if the H.G. were ever called out (I hope they won't be) almost all the members of our Fire and First Aid parties would have to be with them. There seems to be no satisfactory solution of this problem but the details are still under discussion. In the meantime I am glad that I have lately reinforced the Fire Party, which was already highly polyglot, with an Indian, a Lithuanian, a Rumanian, and a brace of Turks, for these, not being liable to national service, can stay behind and put the Library out.

Naturally A.R.P. business supplied me with a background to these activities — completing the new quarters for the Fire Party, painting, numbering, and distributing tin hats of which we have at last a sufficiency (Victorian sun-bonnet pattern), organising services for the end of August and September, attempt to get gas-masks and a second fire-pump, revised edition of the College Fire-drill, erection of telephone line between St John's Chapel tower and our Wardens' Post, apparatus for drying and winding hoses, etc., etc. Still, I have been less busy since the end of the Summer term, have made some progress with the immortal work, which lay unregarded from September until June, and have even composed two papers for learned journals, though I admit that one was provoked by what seemed to me some ill-considered observations proceeding from the sister University.

In normal times I should not allow myself to become so entangled in affairs that I had no time for my own work, for nobody, I am sure, ought to teach in a University unless he is also engaged on research even though his research may not be very fruitful or important. For a schoolmaster it matters much less — up to a point it matters not at all — but a University is an institution for the advancement of learning, and its teachers ought to have towards their subjects the attitude of mind which regards them as alive and in need of advancement. Obviously that will not in itself make them competent teachers but without it they will be, at any rate for the best men, incompetent. Therefore I am shocked by the policy of certain Colleges which buy up able boys by lavish expenditure on scholarships, yet make no corresponding provision by means of Fellowships to secure that they shall be properly taught; and I remember that when I was called on to decide whether I should return to Cambridge a question which caused me very serious anxiety was whether after twelve years disuse I could recover a taste for research.

The greater part of research, in all subjects I imagine, is drudgery. Mine, which is concerned with determining what precisely a Greek poet said and meant, consists for the most part in detailed investigations of language and usage. But in practice one drudges happily enough, learning by the way odd things which bear upon one's teaching, and pondering one's problems as one walks abroad or lies awake in bed; and when, as sometimes happens, one has a bright idea, the chase, if you have that sort of mind, becomes exciting. Similarly one acquires in one's teaching facts which bear on one's research, and the two occupations complement one another very aptly. Of course a Tutor has a good deal less time for research than others, but still, up to the war, I used to get through a substantial amount during the year. In war-time however one drudges less happily. For one thing the war, however little one is consciously thinking of it, forms a dark background in the mind against which it is very hard to keep scholarly problems in sharp or continuous focus. For another, your research, at any rate in the humaner subjects, looks less important. It is, as Housman once said, the common end of research in every field 'to set back the frontier of darkness', and it is not obvious whether it is ultimately more important to clarify the observations of a Greek poet or to discover a means of locating aeroplanes in the dark. But whichever of these problems is ultimately the more important, there is no doubt which is at present the more urgent; and with such inky clouds ringing the horizon the task of kindling farthing dips on my tiny sector of the darkness front must needs be less engrossing. Hence I have not been very impatient at my inability to get on with my work during the last academic year, though to get back to it for a couple of months was a pleasant change even though the stretch I am on at present happens to be a dull one.

14.9.41

The above I wrote in Wales, having taken a fortnight's holiday; but as the holiday repeated exactly the programme of last year's which occupied some space in no. 13 it will not supply me with much material for this letter—a night near Pershore and the rest spent on my favourite green hills in Radnorshire and Montgomeryshire. I was not lucky in the weather, which for the most part continued as cold and wet as it had been here for the previous month and added a tempestuous quality which made walking on the heights a labour. Herein the holiday differed from last year's; also, the season being much later and I a week earlier, the bracken was still green and still patched here and there with the gold and purple of gorse and heather. Otherwise there was little change, for these uplands can happily never be anything but sheepwalks. There is a lot of new ploughland about the countryside but cultivation lays only a gingerly hand on the hills; and if here and there a plantation is missing from its place, or a field of oats has climbed beyond the wonted level, it is only the eye of old acquaintance that notices. And, wet or fine, it was good to get away for a breathing space out of sound of siren and almost of aeroplane; and besides doing a little work I took a good deal of air and walked a fair amount despite a mild attack of lumbago, due in part to falling heavily down a slippery staircase — a foolish action, and undignified. I would gladly have stayed longer, for when I came away the weather was turning fine in time for the harvest, and the prospect of sleeping for a week in my clothes on Warden's duty and fussing round the Fire Party (which, though fairly constant in numbers, varies in composition from week to week and requires a good deal of attention) was uninviting. I returned on Sept. 5 and found my sitting room looking a deal cleaner than I left it, for, after much havering, I had decided to have it redecorated. This was perhaps naughty since one is bidden to avoid expense; and was certainly tempting Providence since a bomb may fall on it. But, as to expense, my room, as you may have noticed, is neither Blenheim nor Chatsworth; and, as to bombs, I am told that after the war we shall be unable to get such work done for love or (if we have any) for money. Since, therefore, my fire, which smoked venomously throughout the winter, had added heavily to ten years' normal accumulation of dirt, I decided to risk the bomb rather than endure indefinitely a squalor which was already beginning to be oppressive.

In my review of the P.M.'s history during the last year I should have mentioned, if I had then known it, that one copy, unless it has been devoured by sharks, now floats the China Seas — blown overboard from a launch by the negligence of the British Resident in a Federated Malay State to whom a parishioner had lent it on hearing that the Resident and I had known each other as undergraduates — 'Fly, white butterflies, out to sea, Frail pale wings for the wind to try. . . .'

TWENTY-SIXTH LETTER

28.9.41

My increasing difficulty in filling the P.M. has sometimes caused me in recent months to consider wistfully the stopgaps employed by other journals when they are short of material. I could not, I decided, follow the example of the Oxford gentlemen who write the *Times* and keep standing in type a paragraph enumerating the contents of the last issue of the quarterly called *Oxford*; and I have no mind (in any sense of those words) to write you a serial, or to compose crosswords, acrostics, or quizzes. So my blanks, as I said in no. 24, will remain blank. One night in bed, however, I did, before falling asleep, adumbrate part of a quiz, and as this is likely to be a desultory issue I shall put the result down here. Indeed it may almost, by virtue of *Qu.* 1, be called *The Mysterious University: lesson 7*, for your instruction in that obscure subject has been too long intermitted: —

> *Qu.* 1. Who are at present High Steward, Deputy High Steward, and Commissary, of the University? What are their respective duties and stipends?
> *Qu.* 2. What University worthy of modern times has: *a.* Been obliged to make public apology to the proprietors of Keiller's marmalade, *b.* Prosecuted his neighbour for erecting an electrical appliance which caused him to hear abusive language on getting into bed, *c.* Been miraculously transported from one side of the Senate House railings to the other?
> *Qu.* 3. Where in Cambridge are the following inscriptions and what is their significance? *a.* A.S.P. *b.* Henslow Common Informer. *c.* Cambridge Bolo Otto.

Not to keep you in undue suspense the answers are given at the end of this number.

This is the season at which there are usually changes in the outward appearance of the town to chronicle, but this year, not unnaturally, there are practically none. An enormous building resembling a hangar (it isn't a hangar, but as I do not know what it is I can betray no secrets) is going up between the Observatory and the Coton footpath and will spoil some amenities the Cambridge Preservation Society has been at much trouble to protect. However in these times such sacrifices must be endured. Inside the town Pembroke has begun repairing the damage caused by the fire mentioned in no. 20, and a few more railings have disappeared, but I know of no other changes. The John's new building still in part hides coyly behind hoardings because it can't get, or has not the face to put up, new railings just now. It has, however, put up an iron gate guarded by two pompous stone eagles, and through it I catch glimpses of promising beds of onions; and from some irregularly shaped parterres, open to the street and no doubt destined for grass, a nice crop of potatoes has just been lifted. This, however, is not the first time that vegetables have squeaked and gibbered in the Cambridge streets, for when St Catharine's, about twenty years ago, cut down the elms which stood in front of their court and laid out the rectangular grassplots which are there now, some enemy, as rumour said from across the street, sowed them with swedes and carrots which presently did very well — not in the best of taste perhaps, but I confess to having been amused at the time. Vegetables grow in certain other unwonted though more secluded spots (the lawn in the Botanic Garden for instance), but they have not as yet invaded our gardens, and the grass in our courts, unusually green for the time of year, is kept in order mostly by Besicovitch, who may be seen daily taking exercise in a pyjama jacket behind a man-power mowing-machine. We have on the Madingley Road some allotments for undergraduates but I have not visited them.

How have I spent my time since I returned from Wales? Well, I went over to Oxford for two nights, partly to see my mother and partly to acquire some archaeological information from the learned Professor with whom I stay there; and to Eton for two more to see some old friends; but I have written about both these places before and don't bring back much news from either. At Oxford I learnt that the women's Colleges were fuller than usual, and that the town, already crowded with evacuees, had been told to expect another two thousand inhabitants. At Eton I noticed the disappearance of the mysterious latrines on Agar's Plough mentioned in earlier P.M.'s, observed some strange — very strange — faces on the staff, and heard that the school had gone up in numbers — good news which rather surprised me.

Apart from that week-end I have been busy here over various odds and ends. Two days I spent presiding over a board to recommend R.A.F. Cadets for commissions at the end of their six months' course. This was neither so boring nor so useless as my previous experience of such interviews in other connexions had led me to expect; and, though I do not know who originally selected these men for the course, I thought he had picked a very good lot. If they had turned up any October in the last twelve years as my consignment of freshmen I should have considered myself to have done well. At odd moments I read the MS of a book at the request of the University Press who had been asked to publish it. This is a corvée which befalls one from time to time and is usually tedious. However this was not a long book; nor hard to decide whether or no it should be published. Another occasional corvée which happened to coincide with this was the composition for the *Times* of what that journal elegantly calls a stock obit. — that is to say an obituary notice of one of your distinguished friends (at present in robust health) which they put away in a pigeonhole, perhaps revise from time to time, and ultimately extract from their columbarium when they hear that he is dead. I dislike the task very much but this was one I could not well refuse. I have also been busy with the committee mentioned in no. 25 on the requirement of national service for all undergraduates, and have, after much labour, joined in issuing a kind of vade-mecum on the subject for Tutors. It might seem simple but is not so at all, and the vade-mecum fills five folio pages of typescript without, I dare say, envisaging all the cases which will arise. I have also tidied up and put away two years' accumulation of pamphlets and offprints, and this too is a more serious job than you might suppose. Those on one's own immediate subject are easy, for the collection is homogeneous and not too large to keep in working order, but friends, and scholars whom one knows by correspondence, are apt to send one their writings on other subjects, and sometimes entirely unknown scholars send theirs too — in recent years, for some unknown reason, the Swedes (who since the eclipse of learning in Germany have become the best Classical scholars in Europe) have taken to sending me their works in some profusion. Thus, what with one thing and another, one collects a mass of heterogeneous papers and pamphlets hard to classify or keep so arranged that one can lay hands on them if need be. I can't say that I have ever solved this problem and I sometimes contemplate calling in an expert to catalogue and arrange them; but for the moment the pile which has pricked my conscience for months is out of sight and mind; and with the continent beyond reach the new pile will grow slowly.

Answers to Quiz. (1) The Duke of Devonshire, Lord Wright, Sir Malcolm Macnaghten. The Commissary certifies that charges brought before the Septemviri are properly so brought (no laborious occupation as you learnt in Lesson 6); the other two have no duties. The Deputy High Steward receives £4 per annum; the other two have no stipends. (The modern statutes discreetly say that the duties of the High Steward and his Deputy 'shall be as heretofore customary', but as they and the Commissary sat as Judges in the University Courts which have long ceased to exist they have in fact no duties).

(2) *a.* Rev. J. E. B. Mayor, Prof. of Latin (d. 1910). He was philanthropically anxious to set up a relative of his bedmaker in a small shop and provided her with a recipe for making marmalade at a penny or two a pot and a supply of Keiller's pots collected from undergraduates to put it in. *b.* Rev. Dr. J. Mayo (d. about 1920). He lived in Cambridge and spent his declining years in taking various Specials with the ambition of getting a first. The late Master was subpoenaed to bear witness that such an apparatus was not beyond the resources of science. *c.* Solomon Schiller-Szinessy, Reader in Talmudic (d. 1890). He claimed to know the correct vocalisation of the Hebrew name of God, and to have pronounced it with this result when accidentally locked inside the railings—but I do not vouch for his veracity.

(3) *a.* On a pillar of our Library (and elsewhere). All Saints Parish (boundary). *b.* Stencilled on the wall of Corpus, but now growing very faint. Henslow was Professor of Botany; he, in 1835, took steps to eliminate bribery in parliamentary elections and incurred the displeasure of those who expected to receive the bribes. *c.* On the wall of the Old Schools (at least it used to be but I failed to find it recently). It reflected, no doubt libellously, on the loyalty of a Cambridge tradesman during the last war. Bolo was a French traitor whose execution caused a stir as he had a brother highly placed in the church; he lives in my memory, however, rather by reason of his profession, which was that of a traveller in lobsters and communion wine.

TWENTY-SEVENTH LETTER

Term began on October 7 — eight days, in fact, before the date on my last letter. But I had been looking ahead, and seeing that its first week would be a nightmare in which I should have no time for parish affairs, I finished scribbling my airy nothings just before it began, and dated them for the day on which I thought I might be able to begin dispatching them.

Nightmare indeed it proved, and my estimate was a day or two over-optimistic. The fact is that the last few months have been calculated to turn any Tutor's hair grey by reason of the shower of bewildering and conflicting paper which descends on him from four or five different sources, as Dante says, like snowflakes on the Alps when there is no wind. Most notices have more than one theme, and any theme may be handled in the notices from each source; and I, at any rate, have found no means of filing them accessibly and sigh for tickler files and wobble blocks. The notices which grey the hair mostly deal with the liabilities of under-graduates in this that and the other category, and, to say nothing of R.A.F. Cadets, R.E. Cadets, Radio Bursars, Chemistry Bursars, or Engineering Bursars (who are probably unknown to you and don't much concern me as I have no freshmen pupils), there are far too many categories of ordinary undergraduates. Some have not registered, some of the registered are attested and some not, some are attested but not registered; some (medicals and theologians) are in reserved classes; some (mostly scientists and engineers) have been recommended by technical committees of the Joint Recruiting Board to continue their studies, some have been allowed to do so by the War Office, others by a Hardship Committee, others by a Conscientious Objectors' Tribunal. Those attested are under the War Office; the rest under the Ministry of Labour. Some classes are under an obligation to do part-time national service while in residence, others are not; similarly with duties under the Civil Defence (Compulsory Enrol-ment) Order. Part-time national service may be undertaken in the S.T.C., C.U.A.S., H.G. (with three different battalions of slightly varying charac-ter), or in Civil Defence Services (Fire or First Aid). One of these fits in with one man's programme of lectures, another with another's, and not all can accommodate as many as wish to join them. All this, and more which I omit, the unfortunate Tutor is supposed to have at his finger-tips, and, in short, circumstances conspire to endorse the view expressed in no. 23 that it was high time I retired into private life. It is some measure of the fuss that my introductory address to pupils, which for the last twelve years has been steadily decreasing in length (owing to a growing conviction that the less I said the less absurd it would be to hope that the audience might favour it with their attention) and had latterly got down to about ten minutes, on this occasion lasted forty. I need hardly add that the task of collecting for College A.R.P. purposes a Fire Party, a First Aid Party, St John's Tower Observers, Fire-Watchers, Hall Observers, Messengers, and Staircase Marshals (all of which has to be done over again at the beginning of the Michaelmas Term and involves more than a hundred men) was not eased by these further demands on men's time; and the prospect of this year's A.R.P. was in any case blackened by the loss of my principal N.C.O., who, in the disguise of Organising Secretary to the Fire Party, really kept an eye on much else besides and was quite invaluable throughout last year. However, thanks largely to his labours, the machine is much better oiled than it was twelve months ago, and as I have competent heads for the Fire and First Aid Parties I am hoping that it may run for another year at any rate without a major breakdown.

The November issue of the Parish Magazine is Our Statistics Number, and despite an advance protest from one parishioner who says he would sooner endure more quizzes than learn the number of theological students in Downing (information which I should not impart even if I possessed it), so far from sparing you I shall even repeat for the benefit of new parishioners some information from no. 15. In the Octobers of 1938/39/ 40/41 respectively the numbers in residence have been: Men, 5491/4353/ 2908/2756: Women, 513/465/497/515. This year's total among the men is composed of: B.A.'s and advanced students, 181: 4th year, 20: 3rd, 394: 2nd, 891: 1st, 1270.

These figures are highly surprising to me, and I think to most people, for I expected the lowering of the registration age to 19 to result in a heavy fall in numbers; and if I had had to guess six months ago how many men would be up, I should, though having little or nothing to go upon, have thought 2000 an optimistic estimate. Two years of the last war reduced the University to under 500. The number of freshmen is actually higher (by 146) than last October, and though they are swollen by nearly 400 of the above-mentioned cadets and bursars (of whom perhaps two thirds would not have come up except as such), I am still surprised at the numbers of ordinary freshmen. The big drop is of course in the 2nd year (283), but I should have expected the earlier registration to make it much bigger. That it is not so is partly, I suppose, due to the fact that many more men now come up before they are 18, and partly to the fact that a much larger proportion of the population are now scientists and technicians who have been recommended by Technical Committees to continue their studies. The last fact no doubt accounts entirely for the numbers of third year men, which are practically unchanged. There are no figures available (perhaps you will be glad to hear) to show the distribution of men among subjects, but I know that among the freshmen at any rate there are more studying the humaner subjects than we looked for, since Sandbach, Rattenbury and I, who have on our hands all the Classical teaching of Trinity, Clare, Corpus, Pembroke, and Sidney, were expecting to have less work than last year and are in fact doing almost exactly the same amount. I know, too, that there are fewer medicals than was expected, for some Govt. Department (probably the Ministry of Labour), thinking, I suppose, that some would-be *embusqués* might suddenly experience a call to the subject, rationed Universities in medicals on the basis of their average intake in the last three years. Our ration was 188 and we took some laborious steps to see that it was not exceeded; but we might have spared ourselves the pains for the freshmen were some 50 short of that number. A few more will presumably come up in January, but it seems plain that a good many people have judged this no moment for embarking on a course which takes at least five years.

I add, to keep this number in line with nos. 3 and 15, that this College has 321 men in residence (B.A.'s etc. 22: 3rd yr., 33: 2nd, 123: 1st, 143) against 334 last October: and that the number of students in institutions evacuated to Cambridge, in spite of a decline in males, has increased by about 250 — and so to other news.

15.11.41

— or so I intended a fortnight ago, but since then I have been rather harassed. In the first place my Bedmaker and Help were suddenly reft from me. My Bedmaker, who was a jewel, is a real loss, and though I part from the Help without regrets, to lose both at once is a bore. Owing to the Sidney St Hostel having been commandeered I have come by its personnel — a Bedmaker who seems competent and pleasant, and a Help who is so retiring that I have only once set eye on her — but there has been a tiresome interval in which they have been learning my routine and I have been unable to assume that anything was where I expected it to be. Secondly, the Committee on Resident Students' National Service has discovered, as last month I predicted it would, that its vade-mecum doesn't cover all the cases, and it has been obliged to deliberate over the residue. The freak cases are of no public interest and mostly arise from confusions elsewhere which have resulted in odd men being simultaneously in two or even three mutually exclusive categories; but they are wearing to disentangle. Thirdly, my autumn cold, no doubt inevitable as everybody else has one, set in too soon, and, fostered by cold weather and by an anxiety about coal supplies which has limited me hitherto to an electric radiator, has been unduly heavy and has made teaching a burden. Normally, provided I have, or believe myself to have, something to say, I do not at all dislike lecturing; but even when one is fit it is tiring, and when one is not, and particularly if one has to husband one's voice, the effort required to put one's stuff across is exhausting. Hence I haven't been feeling very spry or observant, and if there is any further local news to report (I doubt if there is much) I shall leave it to be swept up in the next number and now give shelter to some waifs and strays.

Will those of you who wear uniform of whatever colour please make a point of telling me in your next if your envelopes are not properly addressed? I have been meaning to say this for some time for I am painfully aware that each issue insults quite a number of you; but I know no means of calculating your rank, and I haven't liked to guess. However, shaken by the discovery that one whom I have been addressing as 2nd/Lt. is really a Major, I have decided to transfer the weight of blood-guilt to your own heads.

I have culled, from a rather amusing volume of essays by J. B. Atkins, called *Side Shows*, a small bouquet which I present to all parishioners who graduated this summer — 'Her father had been a B.A. and so was her husband; so she was fortified with intellectual connexions.'

Mr Hore-Belisha at Devonport: 'Whether or not amphibious — or rather triphibious — raids ... would seriously distract the enemy was doubtful' (*Times*, Nov. 4). I learn from *Who's Who* that Mr Hore-Belisha was educated at Clifton College, Paris, Heidelberg, and St John's College, Oxford.

TWENTY-EIGHTH LETTER

7.12.41

I TURN back to consider the term which ended on Dec. 5, and indeed go back a little beyond term, for the weather, which, without ever being bitter, was disagreeably chilly throughout the early autumn and produced some unseasonable snow-showers in October, really set in early in September. I suppose it to be responsible for some unwonted botanical phenomena. First, that hideous vegetable Opuntia Cantabrigiensis — a form of prickly pear which owes its name to the fact that its original habitat (I believe Texas) was lost and it was for some time known to grow only in our Botanic Garden — suddenly studded the edges of its revolting slabby stems with a wealth of cream-coloured blossoms like those of water-lilies, and for the first time in my memory did its fosterparent some credit. Secondly, the fig-trees in the College Bowling Green produced an unparalleled crop of figs which made some amends for the complete failure of the peaches and nectarines on the same wall. (In peace-time, when only two or three are here in mid-September, a bonus of these fruits was a welcome reward for one's assiduity, but now, when almost everybody is up, there aren't enough to go round). Thirdly, the trees have behaved oddly. Some lost their leaves quite early when they were still green but the majority held them very late. I keep a daily eye on their proceedings while shaving, for my bedroom window commands a very attractive view of the river and the John's Backs, this year somewhat distorted by a coating of cellophane lacquer. There and elsewhere I have noticed great discrepancies among trees of the same species, and even on the same tree one branch with only a golden leaf left here and there and another still fully covered with leaves which had hardly begun to turn colour by mid-November; but it was only the last week of that month which really stripped the Backs. As to the cellophane lacquer, I had all my windows coated with it a year ago and wish I had not, for experiments which I made (with a hammer) on some control pieces lacquered at the same time suggest that it is no great protection, and in my sitting room, where the lacquer became black with smoke, I have had it taken off. There at your next visit you will find me cooped in chicken-wire which lets in much more light and hardly obstructs the view.

Term has had a slightly Balkan flavour, for the King of Yugoslavia, having been generously excused the Little-go by the Council, matriculated as an undergraduate of Clare; and in November the King of Greece was given an Honorary Degree. I haven't, so far as I know, seen the first, but the second is a distinguished figure, and made, in the proceedings which followed the degree ceremony, a brief and dignified speech in very much better English than his Prime Minister who subsequently addressed us more expansively on the virtues of democracy. It was a fine afternoon, and having little taste for such ceremonies I attended less from inclination than from a feeling that the P.M. should be represented. I meant to creep in unobtrusively with the crowd but found on arrival that, as I had omitted to equip myself with a ticket, my only available method of entry was by joining a procession of Eminent Persons. Senate House Yard was stiff with cinematograph cameras, so if anybody has detected me in a news-reel let him note that I was there not from love of pomp but in search of copy. After the proceedings in the Senate House there was a service in King's Chapel conducted jointly by the Bishop of Lincoln and the Exarch of Thyateira, a prelate whom I was once privileged to meet at lunch. But by this time the claims of the fine afternoon had asserted themselves, and, feeling some need to digest the virtues of democracy, I had retired towards Coton; so I cannot do more than record that the service took place.

Apart from this incident term has been very uneventful and I think of nothing to record except that the Fitzwilliam has shifted the contents of three of the five rooms it keeps open, and now has in one a collection of modern pictures lent by the Artists' International Association (rather dreary, but that is their fault not ours), and in two others an assembly of architectural models and drawings which would be remarkable even in peace-time. The Museum has been in luck's way lately, for Oscar Raphael, who died recently, left his very fine collection of oriental things for us to divide with the British Museum, and from another bequest we got, besides a few decent pictures, one or two choice Chinese bronzes, so our Far Eastern Department, which was very weak, has looked up a lot. As I have said before, I think we deserve to be favoured too, for we have done more since the war began to keep things going than most museums. The Ashmolean when I was there last was still subsisting on the Boucher tapestries mentioned in no. 21, and I haven't of late found much to look at in London except the Sickert exhibition at the National Gallery, to which I hope some of you went. I read recently, in an article by a friend of mine, that there could be no disputing the fact that Sickert was the most considerable English painter alive to-day, and I felt tempted to send the writer a postcard to say that, if provoked, I could easily dispute it. Still, if not there he is thereabouts, and though a better exhibition could be collected in peace-time, the hundred paintings and odd drawings which were on view included some lovely things.

Nor do I think that much has happened in the College. We elected four new Fellows in October, but none of them are here now; and three Honorary Fellows — W. W. Greg, Sir J. Jeans, and A. V. Hill — in November. The two first, who are a good deal older, I expect we ought to have elected before, but our methods in this matter are rather haphazard and unsatisfactory. I record for legal parishioners who may have sat at his feet that Hamson, who was taken prisoner in Crete, is now in Germany and writes cheerfully from his camp.

My own occupations during the period closely resemble those of a year ago. Examiners for the Seatonian Prize (see no. 14) normally go on for three years, so the opening week of term was embittered by some execrable poems on Henry VI to which we declined to award a prize. I have also, for the fourth year in succession, been setting papers for the University Scholarships. This is far from normal, but there is such a shortage of Classical Dons that even by turning on the whole lot we can barely muster the examining-power necessary for the year and I shall have to do a bit in the Tripos as well. The same shortage obliged me to put together a paper for the Philological Society of which I chance at the moment to be president. Apart from these distractions I have trodden the usual round of teaching, committees, and A.R.P. but shall not trouble you with details. It hasn't been a very agreeable term. For one thing the obligation of part-time national service for undergraduates complicates the lives of their pastors. Classical students, for instance, do their weekly morning parades on Saturday, which must therefore be left clear of lectures. Consequently all who lecture three times a week must lecture on Monday, Wednesday and Friday; and I, since I decline to lecture at 9 and must be at the Council from 11 to 1 on Mondays, am pinned to 10 on those days. Moreover, since a good many people lecture three times a week, the three days are crowded with lectures, and one has therefore to fit most of one's supervision into Tuesdays and Thursdays. The result is an easy day on Saturday, which has some advantages, especially if there is a P.M. to send out, but a disagreeably-spaced week which leaves one somewhat worn by the time one gets to the free day. Besides this I have been rather below the weather. Cambridge, though in general I think its climate maligned, is certainly no place to cast off one's ailments, and the cold mentioned in my last has hung about, vexing me with neuralgia and other discontents which blighted my *joie de vivre* — no very sturdy plant at its best — and I have been glad for that as well as for other reasons that we have been very little troubled with sirens and other such disturbances. My only diversions, I believe, have been that a pupil took me to see *Target for Tonight*, which I thought interesting but less so than *Bomber Command* which I hope you have read; and a parishioner to see Cambridge beat Oxford at rugger. These events are more portentous than you might suppose, for it is some years since I have been to a rugger match on Grange Road, and I shouldn't like to guess how many since I have been to a Cambridge cinema.

The Philological Society? (*The Mysterious University: lesson* 8 perhaps.) It is composed of Classical Dons and some others who normally meet on Thursdays two or three times a term, indulge in tea and tittle-tattle for a quarter of an hour, and then compose themselves to be entertained (or otherwise) by a paper or papers on learned themes, abstracts of which are presently published in an annual volume of Proceedings. Like the beverage which should introduce them these gatherings may sometimes cheer but do not often inebriate, though they have their uses. Tea, however, is now off owing to the difficulty of providing it, and with half the members away and the rest unusually busy the entertainment (or otherwise) is also getting rather hard to supply.

This number must carry my wishes for a Happy Christmas and New Year; and if they reach some of you ten days before, and others ten weeks after, the appropriate date, they are none the less warm for that. Twelve months ago I said that my hopes for 1940 had miscarried, but that some lightening of the darkness seemed to promise better for 1941 — and it has proved a less gloomy year than its predecessor. As I write (some days before the date of dispatching my letter) the outcome of various important events is still uncertain, and I add only that I hold to a sober hope that the improvement will continue in 1942. And I repeat here what I said last year — that I think of you all a good deal and that it is a real pleasure to hear from you.

TWENTY-NINTH LETTER

25.12.41

I WROTE the last paragraph of no. 28 on Sunday Dec. 7, knowing I shouldn't be able to get it off for a week, sent it to be typed, and fell heavily into my bed having no idea that before I got out of it next morning I should have read that we were at war with Japan. Consequently that was not one of the important events envisaged in the paragraph. The P.M. of set purpose avoids the war, and I mention this fact now only because the paragraph may have seemed a little odd if you did not notice the date. Of the event itself I say only that I am sorry more millions should be dragged into this filthy mess; but, if they must be, then I am glad that the English-speaking peoples should stand side by side in it, and that the circumstances of America's entry should be such as to set her long and very natural doubts and hesitations at rest.

The reason I fell into bed more heavily than usual was because the military, the Home Guard, and the Civil Defence Services had been conducting a joint invasion exercise over the eastern counties, and I had been on duty from 14.30 hours on Saturday until 17.00 hrs. on Sunday. The only incident in College — a H.E. in the Great Ct at 01.30 — since it did no damage and caused no casualties, incommoded nobody but the Warden on duty (myself naturally); but there was a good deal of *va* and *vient* during the night, with thunder flashes (whatever they may be) going off in the streets, continual telephoned reports from the observers on St John's Chapel, H.G.'s sleeping in one of our shelters, people popping in and out to use the telephone, etc. etc., and I got little or no sleep. The exercise, if it was to be of any use, had to be taken seriously even though by the time there is really a battle going on at Newmarket the C.D.S. are likely to have declared their innings closed. Seriously, anyhow, we took it, keeping Fire and First Aid Parties on duty, closing the College, scrutinising identity cards, mistaking scholarship-candidates for fifth columnists, and generally inconveniencing ourselves and others; so I hope that in course of time we shall hear the results. One very unfortunate one was that the Master of Pembroke, who is also Mayor, was run over and badly hurt while visiting C.D.S. posts.

I knew I shouldn't be able to dispatch the letter for a week because it takes three or four days to get the copies, and I was due to spend

Wednesday revising University Scholarship papers, and was going to London for two nights on Thursday, partly to see various friends, partly to try and shake off my various ailments by a brief change of air and a Turkish bath. Turkish baths are not what they were for my regular haunt was long since blown to bits, though the curious wayfarer in Jermyn St may still discern through a Moorish arch the circle of marble slabs on which our perspiring forms used to be pounded and pummelled. However one can sweat, if less luxuriously, elsewhere, and the holiday certainly refreshed me a bit.

I have been in London for the day several times in the last eighteen months but I hadn't slept there; and on the whole, unless one is staying with friends (as for one night of the two I was), it didn't seem a very good thing to do in the winter. I am told the place is very gay if dances and night-clubs are your idea of gaiety; but they are not mine, and the trouble of getting about after nightfall is considerable unless there is a moon or you enjoy falling over kerbstones. Perhaps I should eat more carrots to improve my night-vision, but it seems to me that I eat at least as many as is reasonable or palatable already. I don't think I observed any very remarkable changes since last Christmas when I reported impressions. On the whole the life of the streets struck me as more normal, and they were a lot tidier — as they might be after a long lull in destruction. There is a noticeable decrease in railings, which makes some of the squares look rather out-at-heel, and a noticeable increase in supplies of static water for fire-fighting, including large concrete reservoirs in the basements of demolished houses. I noticed, too, that most shops close early, and some, art-dealers for instance, are tending not to open at all on Saturdays (very sensibly, for if you want a picture you ought to be able to control your passion until Monday). Still, it is a good deal easier to buy things in London than in Cambridge, and, I am told, easier in Cambridge than in Oxford.

Here we have shortages of various kinds, but not many of them affect me. Matthew's provides its regular customers with a shopping card and puts up each week a list of goods in short supply which it will part with only to the elect. You may picture me, then, perusing the list, not, I hope, greedily, but with a certain interest, week by week. Often it contains nothing I want, but I contrive by this device to keep myself going in biscuits, occasionally to get some potted meat for my modest lunch (in London this would present no difficulty), and sometimes a box of matches. This last shortage, which set in very suddenly in September, promised at one time to vex me considerably. However by dint of research I acquired a table lighter which represented neither a lamppost nor a yacht nor a man in armour nor a young woman out of it, and now with the aid of spills (for I have not yet acquired a taste for petrol in my pipe) I am virtually emancipated from matches. Queues are in fair evidence, particularly for cigarettes, which I get without difficulty from my London tobacconist — and as I never smoke one myself I shall bear even his default with some stoicism. Tobacco would try me harder, but again my weekly allowance has so far arrived without interruption. Some people, I am sure, enjoy and join queues for their own sake. A crocodile outside Marks and Spencer's which reached to the end of Petty Cury I discovered one day to be crawling towards acid drops, but I am sure its hinder parts did not know what prey they were stalking; and a lady of my acquaintance whom I encountered queued up outside a butcher's replied to my commiserations that she quite liked the excitement of seeing what you could have when you got in. A wireless neurosis was one of the earliest diseases of the war, and I suppose a queue neurosis is now being formed. I am in no danger of suffering from the first, and I am inclined to hope that I shall sooner go without most things than acquire the second.

We were threatened with a serious coal shortage, or rather a difficulty in getting supplies delivered, and the Junior Bursar issued such sinister warnings that I was really rather alarmed, for my rooms are bitterly cold. However the Clerk of the Works urged me to buy an electric radiator which he chanced to be able to supply at the moment, and with that I have done well enough — so well in fact that I have not lighted my fire since June. It looks like a chimney-pot, is hideously ugly, and no doubt costs rather more than a fire, but it keeps my room at a bearable temperature, and moreover warms the parts round the desks at which I work better than the fire ever did — though it is to be noted that the weather hasn't really tested it severely, and on the table as I write a rosebud surreptitiously removed from the row of trees outside the New Ct is slowly unfolding.

15.1.42

Christmas passed off quietly and was shorn of some of its usual ritual, for the side-table, which should groan from Christmas to Epiphany with boar's head, game pies, and the like, for the Fellows' lunches, and the

sideboard, which should hold a display of College plate, were both bare —
the latter because, owing to shortage of staff in the plate-room, we have
put most of our silver away. Still, we had a tolerable Christmas dinner,
enlivened, as last year, by the Fire-Party, which included three Siamese
(since Thai, I understand, means 'free' I shall no longer obtemper to their
whim and call them so), a German, a Russian, and a Lithuanian. They
might have included also two Estonians, a Hungarian, a Rumanian, a
Chinese, an Indian, and perhaps a Malay, but these went off to heathenish
celebrations elsewhere, and for a while caused me some anxiety by doing
so, for at this season it is not easy to keep the party up to strength.

I have been hard at work throughout the vac., for I have a new course
of lectures to deliver this term on a subject in which I am not really at
home. It is a set book in Part 2 of the Tripos which would naturally fall
to the Professor of Latin, but the subject normally runs for two years
and, as the Professor is due to retire next October, I generously but
imprudently said in pre-war days that I would hold the fort. I did a little
preliminary work on the subject two years ago (and even mentioned it
in no. 4), but, what with lack of time and doubts whether there would
be any candidates, had done nothing since. There will in fact be five candidates: and as lecturing on the subject involves also setting a Tripos paper
both on it and on another unfamiliar topic, I thought I had better get
those done too, for they make a heavy job of work, and as I have, in addition to the new course, the two short courses I usually give in the Lent
term, I am not looking forward to much leisure.

On Christmas Day itself I did remove my nose from the grindstone and
spent some time, as you see, in writing to you. On looking at the result
I fear that much of it will not be news to those of you who are still in
this country, for most towns, at any rate in reception areas, are probably
much like Cambridge. I was thinking as I wrote rather of parishioners
overseas. However when Malone, calling on Dr. Johnson, found him
roasting apples and reading the *History of Birmingham*, and remarked that
local histories were usually dull, Johnson replied 'It is true, Sir; but this
has a peculiar merit with me for I passed some of my early years there';
and unless those whose apples still sizzle on English hobs find the same
excuse for me I must now be incurring my twenty-ninth distinct
damnation.

THIRTIETH LETTER

1.2.42

Term began on Jan. 13, a day or two before I sent out my last letter, but having been somewhat borne forward on Christmas Day, I said there nothing about the tail end of the vac. There was, it is true, little to say, but after two and a half years of the P.M. it takes more than that to deter me, and I shall remorselessly say that little now. Let me tell you, then, that I took another night off and went to London again, mainly on business, but that I found little there except exhibitions at the Warburg Institute of photographs illustrating the influence of Mediterranean art on England (quite interesting): and at the National Gallery of Jack Yeats and Nicholson. Yeats has nothing to say to me, nor much, I should suppose, to anyone; and though Nicholson certainly has a pretty talent for the laying on of paint, he doesn't really excite me very much. Still, there are some agreeable pictures there and he went up a bit in my estimation. For the rest, when not occupied with preparing lectures, I attended a meeting or two, presided over a board appointed by the Air Ministry to consider adverse reports on R.A.F. Cadets (it hadn't had occasion to meet before, and though the particular case was plain sailing, the procedure required careful consideration), and looked over some University Scholarship papers. This was no great labour, for there were only five candidates and none up to standard for an award. I think we shall have to consider whether we ought not to suspend this examination for the present. Hitherto, unlike Oxford which suspended practically all University prizes and emoluments on the outbreak of war, we have withheld hardly any open to men in their first three years; but it is not usual for a man to get one of these scholarships in his second year, and very rare to get one in the first, there aren't likely to be any second or third year Classics here next year, and the examination is troublesome. The papers are laborious to set, and there must be five examiners, of whom, as I have said before, we begin to be short; and even when, as in the last two years, they voluntarily forgo a substantial fraction of their stipends, the expense is worth considering.

As to the Term, not far from two hundred and fifty freshmen have come up, of whom twenty-four to this College. This is rather more than the January entry last year in both cases, and, though I do not know how many went down, I should guess that we were rather above than below our October numbers. Eighteen of the newcomers were medicals, but that, as medical parishioners will be pleased to note, still leaves us a long way below the ration mentioned in no. 27.

I ought, by the way, to have said before now that the numbers which adorn (or, as some hold, disfigure) that and previous statistical issues, though presented by me in a slightly different form, are derived from the *Cambridge Review*, which collects them from Colleges. Since they are asked for before the Colleges can be quite sure who will and who will not be up, they probably include some who do not come, and are therefore a little in excess of the truth. Some other figures, based on returns of men attending lectures, were circulated last term to some body or other of which I am a member, and, though hard to reconcile or even compare with the other set, they suggested that the estimates I have supplied have not been very far out. The new figures are interesting because they show the distribution of men among subjects. It seems that scientists (including medicals) number a little over 800, and engineers a little over 450. The most numerous faculties after these are, in that order, History, Modern Languages, Law, and Classics, who number collectively not quite 650; and only these six faculties have as many as a hundred men up. It is too early to say how the new registrations will affect us, but they can hardly fail to mean a heavy drop in the Arts faculties next year, and few of the Arts students who have come up this January can expect to be here for more than two terms.

Another problem which is at present perplexing us is posed by the progressive raising of the age of reservation for University teachers which set in in January, and we are now trying to determine which of the men affected is so indispensable that we must ask for postponement of his calling-up. This is a very difficult enquiry, not only because of the uncertainty as to the numbers of undergraduates to be catered for next year, but also because, in addition to University teaching, there are the needs of Colleges both for supervision and administration to be taken into account, and a man who in any one of these three capacities might in extremity be spared, may well be deemed indispensable if all three are considered together. However my own impression is that nearly all the faculties are now so near the bone in the matter of teaching that if, as we are told, the essential minimum must be kept up, we shall have in the great majority of cases to ask for postponement for at least the next academic year.

And, while on such themes as these, I may mention that I saw in the

Oxford Magazine last term that Oxford had 2059 men and 814 women in residence, which is rather more than they had had a year ago and justifies their optimistic predictions which were puzzling me last May. They have reorganised their examination system much more drastically than we have, and (so far as I understand the matter) now hold terminal examinations. Thus an undergraduate can score up something to his examination record for each term he resides, whereas here a man called up, say, at Christmas will have residence in the Michaelmas term to his credit but no examination to show for that fraction of the academic year. Their system has certain obvious advantages, and I think it has attracted a certain number of people away from us, but I am glad that we did not follow suit, for the coupon system is not really appropriate to a commodity of which the price is above rubies, and, apart from the burden of examining it must entail, I do not think it sound educational policy to examine at a University in this piecemeal fashion.

14.2.42

Further impressions of the term had better stand over until my next, and I will fill up this with oddments. And first a recantation which should have been made long ago.

In no. 16 I made mock of the ridiculous eight-inch mace carried by the Head Porter at the Master's admission. I said, and say again, that we had better lose it before it is next wanted: but I also guessed that we had invented it for an admission in the early 19th century, and for some months I have had it on my conscience to withdraw this foul aspersion. My attention having been drawn to the thing I have since found a good many like it, some in curiosity shops, others in the Folk Museum here; and I suppose that a century ago such an object was easily come by. Its proper name is a tipstaff, and it was a badge of office carried by bailiffs, Bow-street Runners, and such. Probably its size was so designed that they could produce it disconcertingly from their pockets when arresting you for debt, sheep-stealing, or what not: but it seems to have been carried also by more exalted personages, and one of those in the Museum is said to have been used by the Mayor on the occasion of Queen Victoria's visit to Cambridge in 1847.

The account of Cambridge shops in my last might well have mentioned one golden day when two grocers at least were plentifully supplied with salami — that admirable Italian sausage made of raw ham and garlic which in England one mostly meets as a hors d'œuvre. They were alleged to come from a captured Italian ship, and, being apparently caviare to the general, were sold without restriction. I had not hoped to look on them again during the war and they enlivened my lunch for many days. I chanced at the time to be re-reading over that meal *Le Memorie di un Pittore di Quadri Antichi*, an amusing, malicious, and probably untrustworthy, volume of reminiscences by I. F. Ioni, a well-known restorer and forger of Sienese pictures (there is a translation called, I think, *Affairs of a Painter*). It went well with the salami, but together they infected me with some nostalgia for Italy and particularly for Siena which is a favourite resort of mine. Most central Italian hill-towns command finer prospects, and many are more attractively situated, for the landscape in Umbria and the Marches is greener and less austere than the waterless hills of central Tuscany: but there is incomparably more to see in Siena than in any other, and two or three times I have spent there a fortnight or more in August and September, working at the pictures and motoring about the surrounding villages and townlets — and shall again if it is ever possible, for as much as most things in these cribbing and confining times I resent being cut off from Italy.

And while on the theme of lunch, I will add that that meal has been complicated for me, and my shopping robbed of some of its more poignant interest, by the extension of the points system to tinned fruit and vegetables, for the College kitchens, requiring these things for meals in Hall, have taken away my book of points. This threatens to make lunch in my rooms difficult, and, besides, I shall now never savour the strange American meats with which the Cambridge counters have lately been laden. This latter blow has moved me to an Elegy (or, as Wordsworth would no doubt have said, an Extempore Effusion) on Being Deprived of a Pink Ration Book. Its opening lines, which I think very affecting, are as follows:

> When shops of late the praises sang
> Of Prem and Mor and Spam and Tang,
> I lunched in dreams beside the Cam
> On Tang and Prem and Mor and Spam;
> But Spam and Tang and Prem and Mor
> Must dreams remain as heretofore,
> Since Mor and Spam and Tang and Prem
> Cost Points to those that purchase them.

THIRTY-FIRST LETTER

13.3.42

Term ends on the above-mentioned date (at which I hope to loose this number on the Parish), and as I write, on March 8, it is drawing to an unlamented close. Cold weather, attended by seagulls and chilblains, returned in company with the undergraduate population and appears likely to keep the term with it. At the beginning of this month the wind seemed at last to have moved with some resolution to the south, but after three days it repented, and until today it has been as cold as ever, with a sprinkling of fresh snow; and we have had alternations of snow and rain, thaw and frost, throughout the two months. The heaviest fall of snow fortunately turned to rain and so left no great depth on the ground; but if it has never frozen hard enough to ice the river over, equally it has never thawed hard enough to melt any thickness of ice or to soften the earth; and it has nearly always frozen at night. Consequently rain and melted snow lay about in pools, or in sheets of ice which covered grass-plots in an extraordinary way long after the snow was gone. The only people I saw on skates were disporting themselves on such sheets in the middle of our, and the John's, tennis courts, and had I been so minded I could have emulated them myself in Nevile's Ct. I should doubt if any games were played before March, and my fire-party had the greatest difficulty in holding practices. Aconites and snowdrops, which may sometimes be seen before the end of the year, scarcely appeared before the second half of February, and even now not a crocus is to be found. It has all been very cheerless, and though the College plumbing suffered only minor damage, the heating system of Hall broke down, and for some days we fed in arctic discomfort. Most people had colds, and I started a bad one on the first day of term and have been struggling with a second lately. This is my third of the winter and infuriates me, for, though I expect one, I have not of late had more than one; but I suppose one's resistance must needs be lowered by the various inconveniences of wartime. The second I treated by swallowing large quantities of the popular nostrum of the moment (which is called serocalcin) and by drinking more Madeira than I should normally consider good for me, and between them they tamed its worst fury in about a week. I am at the moment subjecting the third to the same mass-attack. I am rather a believer in paper handkerchiefs on these occasions, and have so brought to light another wartime shortage, for they are no more to be come by. Necessity, however, is the mother of invention, and another form of paper which it is still not illegal to destroy, though packets of it on the writing table may look odd, serves the purpose well enough — a discovery which I make public gratis, *urbi et orbi, pro bono publico*, and (in case you should think I didn't know the language) *ne quid detrimenti capiat respublica*. In my room the temperature has rarely been above 50, and I have spent most of the time shivering over my desk with numbed brain and fingers. Compared with the hardships which many of you, and millions, I fear, on the continent, have been enduring this grim winter, these discomforts are nought; but they have combined with bad news and anxieties public and private to make a very disagreeable term, and I have not been sorry to be a good deal overworked.

University business has on the whole been slack, and the meetings of the Council and the General Board have been shorter than in recent terms. My only special corvée, except the University Scholarships mentioned in my last, has been the Porson Prize, which is for a translation (usually from Shakespeare) into Greek Iambics. I dislike having to place translations in order of merit, for there are too many qualities to balance against each other — is the Greek or Latin accurate? does it fully represent the English? does it read like the work of an ancient writer? And where, as here, there are a good many competitors (even in war-time) and the best much of a muchness, one is apt to feel doubtful at the end and to change one's mind as to the order every time one reads the stuff again. However there are three examiners, and, as on this occasion, they usually reach an agreed result with some confidence that it is the right one. Apart from these examining jobs, urgent private affairs, which took me to Oxford for three days in mid-February, gave me a good deal to do thereafter, but my main preoccupation has been with the unfamiliar course of lectures mentioned in no. 29. It is true that in this course I was only pontificating twice a week, but I had to lecture for an hour and a half each time to cover the ground, and since the subject required that I should know precisely both what I was going to say and how I was going to say it, it has demanded a lot of work betweentimes. Lecturing when one is below par, as I have said before, is a weariness both of flesh and spirit, but I was somewhat fortified by a conversation which I overheard when emerging in the dark behind two undergraduates who had been attending me on another theme. — *A.* 'Damned uncomfortable seats.' *B.* (after some mental calculation) 'Yes; but it was worth it.' This I take to be an appreciably warmer testimonial than that overheard by A. D. Godley in similar circumstances. — A. 'Bloody rot.' B. 'Yes; but no bloodier than usual.'

I cannot think of any University news of importance, but record here that the Fitzwilliam, having got rid of the International Artists mentioned in no. 28, has put on a very lively and entertaining show of French coloured lithographs, mostly by Bonnard and Vuillard. We had planned to flank them with a room of recently acquired Japanese prints, but the Ministry of Information (Local Branch) vetoed this project. I suppose the public might have learned from it (if they didn't know already) that a century ago the Japanese were still living in the Middle Ages, and that some of them had a nice sense of design; and I have sufficient confidence in my countrymen to believe that their morale would have withstood this subtle attack — but the M.O.I., as you know, is a cautious body. At present, having a vacant room, we have accommodated a show of Yugo-slav Art in connection with a local Yugoslav Week. This, however, is to be of brief duration; and fortunately, for the exhibition, not organised by us, is hardly likely to enhance the prestige of that gallant nation.

There has been some clamour in the Parish of late for a further contri-bution from Our Literary Correspondent, and as the next number is a vacation issue, he is quite likely to be let loose, and to tell you there at some length what he has been reading in bed during the last six months. In the meantime he reports that he has lately been engaged upon *Forging Ahead*, by W. Partington, a life of T. J. Wise, which, though not a good book, throws some light on that very puzzling affair. Wise was a business man who was, or became, rich, formed a very remarkable library of rare editions of English classics, and printed elaborately annotated catalogues of it which are generally considered standard works of reference. He had unquestionably a great flair as a collector, and his library was bought for the British Museum after his death for what rumour reported to be the bargain price of £60,000. As a bibliographer he received an honorary degree and an honorary Fellowship at Oxford, and though these gestures may not have been unconnected with the idea of securing the library for Oxford, the first at any rate was not absurd. In 1934, however, two young bibliographers named Carter and Pollard published a highly ingenious piece of bibliographical sleuthing called *An Enquiry into the Nature of Certain XIXth Century Pamphlets*, which examined some fifty booklets purporting to be first editions of single works by such writers as Browning, Tennyson, Ruskin, privately printed for the authors before the pieces were published. These pamphlets were coveted by collectors of first editions (a foolish tribe) and fetched high prices. Carter and Pollard showed (by such means as typographical minutiae, chemical analysis of paper, and so on) that some of them could not have been printed until long after the dates on their title pages, and that the rest were under grave suspicion. They also showed that where it could be discovered how copies had come into the market all had come either from Wise or from somebody with whom he was known to be in touch. The inference, though they carefully refrained from drawing it, was quite unmistakeably that they were forgeries which had been printed for Wise, who had had, as they also showed, good opportunities for getting such work done. There followed a hullabaloo. Wise made a feeble attempt to hand the baby to somebody else; and, on its prompt refutation, relapsed into silence under a plea of failing health, and died in 1937. It is a very odd story, for W. really was a great collector, and also, though I believe inaccurate, a keen and industrious bibliographical scholar; and yet it is quite plain that he had planted these forged rarities on the market, and, knowing them to be his own forgeries, had nevertheless included some of them with learned commentaries in the catalogues of his own library. Odd it remains; but Carter and Pollard left it inexplicable, for the prices W. had received for the copies they traced to him were quite small. Partington, however, besides filling in some other details and drawing a highly disagreeable picture of W., shows that he was a dealer on a considerable scale, and that after he had artificially forced up the auction prices of the pamphlets he sold copies privately to American collectors — so here is, if not a complete explanation, at least a partial motive, for it is now plain that he may have made quite a good thing out of them.

THIRTY-SECOND LETTER

14.3.42

THIS is Our Literary Corner, and this is Our Literary Correspondent got loose and writing it.

And first, a parishioner who has trailed through Eritrea and Abyssinia and is now in Libya taxes me, unjustly as I think on looking back, with not disclosing which books can be had in cheap editions. To pacify him I have in this instalment prefixed an asterisk to such as may without undue extravagance be abandoned in the great open spaces among the camels' bones and petrol tins. They aren't all Penguins or Pelicans, partly because the paper shortage has had a bad effect on these, and, while the older tend to be out of print, the younger are printed in a type which I can no longer read with comfort. Consequently when in need of literature for casual occasions I am sometimes driven to the Evergreen, Guild, or some similar series which cost a shilling. I don't distinguish here the one class from the other, both for other reasons and because some weeks ago I handed over all such books as I possessed to the depot which collects literature for the Forces and I can no more remember which was which.

My recent reading seems again to have been largely biographical. Chronologically it begins with *Challenge to the Highlander*, by A. A. W. Ramsay, which contains studies of some 17th cent. Scots written by a Scot who can write without sentimentality even about Montrose — a rare phenomenon, and a readable book. Next would be *Admiral's Wife*, which contains the letters and journals of Fanny Boscawen, 1719-1761 (attractive); and the *Diaries* of W. J. Temple. Temple excites curiosity not because he was the ancestor of two archbishops (though he was) but by reason of the astounding letters Boswell used to write him. He proves, however, to have been a futile and querulous man whose diaries are mostly about trifles — the state of his inside or the difficulty of beginning the important work which he decided yesterday should begin today; so unless incited by Boswell you can safely let him be. I have also skimmed the third volume of *Kilvert's Diary* mentioned in no. 18, but though it has the same qualities as the first two, the sentiment, which was already oppressive there, has by now become nauseous. From more modern times I have read the *Life and Opinions of W. R. Sickert* by R. Emmons which, if you are interested in such matters, is well worth while by reason of the extensive extracts from S.'s controversial writings which it contains, for he had much worth saying to say and said it with admirable point and precision. (S., by the way, since I wrote of him in no. 28, is dead at something over eighty, having lived to see this book and an exhibition of his work at the National Gallery — *felix opportunitate mortis*, therefore. But his death, and more recently Wilson Steer's, mark the end of a not unimportant episode in the history of English painting.) *E. P. Warren*, by Burdett and Goddard, is an account of an American who collected, both for himself and for the Boston Museum, antiquities of the very finest quality, and maintained a very odd ménage at Lewes in Sussex; I don't know that it would entertain the Parish, but it was of some interest to me because I used to know W. Besides these I have read a slight but diverting life of Ouida by Y. ffrench; *Harpooner*, by R. Ferguson, and *A Pot of Smoke*, by D. Owain (unvarnished but quite readable records of adventurous lives); *Father was a Handful* (an amusing and attractive sketch of a New England childhood by R. Y. Williams); *The Forge*, by A. Barea (Spanish childhood, neither amusing nor attractive but quite interesting); *Fragments from my Diary*, by Gorki (queer, like most Russian books, but readable); *I found no Peace*, by W. Millar, an American journalist (also readable, and contains a good deal about Abyssinia). Here I may put down four books about country life since all but the third are of an autobiographical character — *Lark Rise*, and *Over to Candleford*, both by Flora Thompson; *Portrait of a Village*, by F. B. Young; *The Farm by Lough Gur*, by M. Carbery. The first two are about the Cotswolds, the third a bit to the west of that, the fourth Irish, and all are attractive in a placid sort of way. I shouldn't say so much of *Good-bye West Country*, a desultory Devonshire diary by H. Williamson who wrote rather a good book called *Tarka the Otter*. This does to read but it does not, as a good diary should, make me wish to know the author, who has almost (but not quite) convinced me that A. Hitler and *Tarka the Otter* are the noblest works of God and man respectively.

Travel is not largely represented but I have read Arthur Young's *Travels in France in* 1787-9. Y. was more interested in turnips than I but he did notice also that a revolution was then going on and has some interesting things to say about the state of France. *Orchid Hunters*, by N. Macdonald, is about Central America, *The Wild Asses*, by W. V. Emanuel, about a tour in Persia and Afghanistan. Neither is very exciting, and better is W. Seabrook's *Adventures in Arabia*. Finally in this section two books recommended by parishioners, both having some bearing on the war — *Desert Encounter*, by K. Holmboe, a Dane turned Moslem, with gloomy pictures of Graziani's administration of Cyrenaica; and *Into China*, by E. Bigland, a lively but not reassuring account of the Burma road.

More miscellaneous works include Sir A. Sherington's *Man on his Nature* which I thought very interesting. It is about the light thrown by advances in physiology upon the nature of existence; but I warn you that it is not light reading especially for the layman. More mildly scientific is *Watching Birds*, by J. Fisher (good). *Inside Italy* by C. Franzero is a slight but readable account of opinions in Italy just before the outbreak of war; *An Epic of the Gestapo*, by Sir P. Dukes, is titled and written like a detective story but is an account of an enquiry into the disappearance of a Czech industrialist and is not uninstructive. *Notions in Garrison* is a very minor work by that admirable writer E. Œ. Somerville. Novels? Very few I fear. *All Passion Spent*, by V. Sackville West, *Go She Must*, by D. Garnett, *Tampico*, by J. Hergesheimer: none have left much imprint on my mind (perhaps because I read them in trains or Turkish baths) but I recall that they all did to pass the time and that the first had considerable charm.

12.4.42

Term ended, as predicted, on the day no. 31 went out, and that same evening we celebrated a frugal Commemoration with only one speech and no guests, except that a parishioner who chanced to be staying with me was squeezed in on the ground that if he had not been in the army but in residence he would have been invited anyhow. Two days at the beginning of the following week I spent recommending R.A.F. Cadets for commissions (see no. 26), and again, though not quite all could be recommended, and though the original selectors had tapped a somewhat different stratum, I thought they had done their work very well. Five hours interviewing a day, however, is hard work, and I look forward with some apprehension to a large increase in the number of these cadets which is at present in contemplation.

This duty discharged, I betook myself to London where I had a good deal of business to attend to. I shall have to go there again when I have finished the week on Warden's duty which holds me here now, and as this no. falls a little awkwardly in date I think I had better consolidate my vacation experiences (not that they promise to be very exciting) in the next issue and fill this one up with scraps of social intelligence.

First, then, the Pitt Club has been commandeered, and its eponymous hero looks down from the pediment, with a nose visibly tiptilted in disgust, upon an enormous notice displaying the legend 'British Restaurant'. I hope Mutton Pies (Bellamy's recipe) will sometimes be on the menu, but when curiosity took me in the other day I found that for a shilling I should have cold meat and vegetables followed by date pudding.

I resisted the temptation because at present only the dining room is in use, and as there are over three hundred lunchers daily there is rather a jamboree. When the other room is available I shall perhaps experiment. The seizing of the club inflicts no hardship on the members for at the beginning of the war its premises were closed and let to Jesus, who used them for I know not what purpose behind closed doors. I endured this calmly myself for though I sometimes dined or lunched there as a guest, I should think that if I went in once in two years in my own right it was as much as I did. The rump of the club, on whom the closure bore more hardly, established itself as the Interim Club in the premises over the shop opposite the Great Gate from the window of which the Athenaeum were once wont to contemplate the public *de haut en bas* (in more than one sense) — a nice room which I never was in until the other day when A.R.P. duties caused me to nose round those labyrinthine purlieus. It is still adorned with the Athenaeum's owls, but I suppose will not be so much longer for the leases on that side of the street have fallen in and we had begun before the war to contemplate a kind of annexe of Whewell's Ct which should keep the frontage with shops on the ground floor but connect the rooms above them with the Court. And while on the subject of undergraduate clubs, I may as well conclude this paragraph and issue by recording that the Hawks was open and in use until it was taken over about eight months ago, and that the Union, though partially in alien hands, still retains its library and a room or two besides but no longer provides meals.

THIRTY-THIRD LETTER

19.4.42

My last no., which was sent out ten days before term began and written a bit earlier, left the vac. for further consideration, but there is not very much to record about it. I was away rather more nights than usual as I had business in Oxford and London and sandwiched a week-end at Eton between two visits to town. It is a misfortune, though unavoidable, that my wartime vacations, such as they are, tread always the same round for they produce little new copy for the P.M. and on this occasion I brought none from Eton or Oxford. In London my business, which was legal, took me into some devastated streets in the Gray's Inn area, which I had not seen before, but my general impressions remain what they were.

In the hideous welter of ruin in which we live destruction nauseates the more in proportion as it is aimless and useless, and none that I have seen serves any end whatever. But the proportion of buildings and objects destroyed which had any intrinsic merit or interest is so far quite small, and there is some consolation in the thought that most of what is gone is, and will ultimately seem, better away; and, in the City, there is some immediate compensation in the noble prospects of St Paul's which the clearance of wreckage has disclosed. For the rest, when not engaged on business, I took the opportunity of seeing a number of friends, and of trying, without much success, to unstiffen my creaking limbs in Turkish baths; but I also made a fairly thorough survey of picture-galleries though without much profit. There are a good many English pictures (mostly modern) on view — the best, as is proper, among the recent acquisitions of the Tate, now exhibited at the National Gallery — but there is precious little else. The shuttles which shift the stock of the international dealers between Paris, London, and New York came to a stop long since, and what was not left in Paris is probably in America with its owners, or if in England is not to be seen. Hence when decent French pictures appear in the sale room (there were some at Christie's on · March 27) they fetch starvation prices. So far as I am concerned perhaps this is as well, for if I had seen anything I much wanted I was in the mood for an extravagance which I should have justified, or at least defended, by the excuse that picture-dealers must live. But I didn't see anything, and the continued purchase of bits of guns, tanks, and battleships, if less amusing, is no doubt more meritorious.

Among other exhibitions I went to one at the National Portrait Gallery of works by members of the Forces in the London District, a show I should normally have excused myself since it contained near three thousand exhibits ranging from statuary to pillow-cases and called for a more ostrich-like artistic digestion than I command. I went wishing to find the works of a parishioner who told me that he was exhibiting there, and this proved a more formidable undertaking than I had anticipated, for they had been omitted from the catalogue, and as I did not know what to look for, I was perceptibly wilting by the time I had run them to earth. The moral is that though I hope parishioners will tell me when they are contributing to such shows, they might chance to save me a good deal of time if they told me what they had sent and where it was to be found.

Apart from these excursions I have been here, and occupied much as usual with odd jobs of work, a few committees, and A.R.P. If I had followed my inclination I should have cast care aside and stayed in bed for a day or two, for war and worry and work and winter have left me a bit battered. However one cannot very well stay in bed in College rooms, nor should I be very comfortable in mine if I did; and though I have thoroughly enjoyed my brief and infrequent occupations of the Evelyn Nursing Home, I haven't quite brought myself yet to the point of going there merely for a rest. I shall come to it; but in the meantime I contented myself with sleeping rather more than usual, neglecting jobs which were not urgent, and watching the spring advance, which it did in a very leisurely manner. The crocuses were very late and had a much curtailed season for when they did venture out they got a rough reception from the wind; but they were good while they lasted, and on Palm Sunday, which chanced to be fine, the Avenue was looking very gay — though I never see it without regretting that the crocuses were planted carpet-wise and not in irregular clumps about the boles of the limes. Daffodils in these parts, though they come before the swallow dares, seldom take the winds of March with beauty, and naturally did not in this backward season; but by the second week of April they were beginning to make a show among the squills and anemones in the Roundabout. Trees have been very slow to move, and though at that time almonds and willows, which always do well in Cambridge, were wearing their pink and green, one had to look closely at the others to notice that their buds were beginning to unfold. In London they were much further forward, but here they had their excuses, for though the wind shifted after term was over to west and south it remained on the whole decidedly chill. However this last week we have had a day or two of real spring sunshine and there is now a faint mist of green over most of the Backs.

16.5.42

Term began on April 20, and on the following day I delivered what was in all probability my last Speech from the Throne to my assembled pupils. While turning over notes of previous harangues and collecting suitable matter for this I came on a correspondence of the year 1757 between Stephen Whisson, then Tutor, and an infuriated parent. I used sometimes to read this in my address to those in their ninth term as an example of the sort of reply I might make if any of their parents showed similar dissatisfaction with their sons' academic careers. I haven't done so, however, for a long while now, and though Winstanley, who originally supplied me with a copy, has since printed it, I do not suppose many parishioners know it. I shall therefore put it down here, leaving impressions of the term to mature a bit. The parent's letter was as follows:

> I received my sons from you in so wretched a condition that I am afraid of sending them again. However that the younger may not lose his degrees, I have ventured him for the remaining part of this term. The elder I dare not trust with you until I have untaught him his University accomplishments. I don't wonder now our polite gentlemen are so extravagant and prophane, since they suck in so much poison in a place where we only can expect a foundation of virtue and good principles. But I must be dumb — my only hopes are now from the restraints and instructions they have had, and are to have, from me. I have sent you the demand to Michl. by my servant, and am
>
> your most obedient,
I wish I could say
obliged, servant
Andrw Hackett

Whisson's reply to this attack seems to me admirable in every way:

> Your last gave me great concern as it represented your sons in a light so very unfavourable, and you must pardon me for adding that it greatly surprized me also. For I did not suspect that my conduct would be so severely censured, nor could I imagine that their extravagance or prophaneness (if they are prophane) would have been, even in the most distant manner, imputed to my sufferance or negligence. I have, what every honest man ought to have, a great regard for reputation which, hitherto, I have had the happiness to support without blemish; and if I was to say I had done everything in my power to promote the true advantage of your sons by inculcating on all occasions virtue and good principles, it would be no more than truth. But I leave this to them. Let them declare what has passed between us, they will, I think, do me justice, and more I do not desire. The young gent, whom you dare trust a little longer with us, may still depend upon my utmost care, and I wish my advice may have as good an effect on him as your instructions and restraints will doubtless have upon his elder brother.

These letters, I say, I used sometimes to read at my last interview with third-year men. At my first with freshmen, I used sometimes to think of reading a letter written by Dame Agnes Paston in 1458 asking someone to tell her son Clement's Tutor to write and let her know if he was industrious: 'And if he hath not done well nor will nought amend, pray him that he will truly belash him till he will amend, and so did the last Master and the best that ever he had at Cambridge'. However Clement Paston was not at Trinity (a contributory reason being that it did not yet exist) and, belashing for undergraduates being out of fashion, I forbore. Another academic fashion unhappily fallen into equal desuetude I was reminded of just now when looking up the date of Whisson's letter — that of deceased Tutors lying in state in Hall in order that their sorrowing pupils may attach copies of verses to their coffins. I think of reviving this.

THIRTY-FOURTH LETTER

14.6.42

I HAD barely posted no. 33 when zero hour for an invasion exercise struck — and these affairs, though plainly necessary, are also a nuisance, for it takes some time to arrange that the various parties with the proper reliefs shall be on duty throughout, and the exercises are usually announced at short notice by a series of only partially intelligible orders from the Borough A.R.P. authorities. This particular exercise produced no incident in College and our personnel for the most part had a fairly restful night, but this was of little profit to me as I had handed over the routine wardening to the other Wardens and spent the small hours on the top of St John's Chapel Tower wishing to find out what could be seen and heard from there — a good deal as it proved, though the night was dark. Bangs and flashes, being mere tokens of incidents, were not very informative from aloft, but one could hear, and approximately locate, fire-engines being started up, and just below me there was a spirited staccato on gas-rattles which fancy placed in the hands of Kitson Clark and the Matron who are wardens in the Trinity St area — fondly as it later appeared, for the gas was in the next sector.

For the rest, I do not think the term has produced very much incident. The weather up to the middle of May was brilliantly fine, and though the drought was unwelcome to farmers, and the searing north-easters (which blew almost without intermission) to me, blue skies and sunlit blossom made substantial amends. And it has been a good year for blossom — chestnut, cherry, lilac, laburnum, Judas-trees, and wistaria at any rate; for I have not been able to go further afield or see more than an occasional fruit-tree. The wistaria in the Great Ct has been about up to its usual mark, but it is growing old, I fancy, and those much younger in Whewell's Ct and the Hostel are, as I noticed this year for the first time, becoming its serious rivals. The season, too, after a late start, caught up a good deal and was much less backward than last year. The wistaria was well on its way by the first week of May; I heard a cuckoo on the first, saw the first convoy of ducklings on the Backs the day before, and swifts on May 10. The last I think I heard from my bedroom a day or two earlier, but this year, for some reason, they have been using the interior of this court as a speed-track much less than their wont and I have seen and heard less of them than usual and than I could wish. And while on such themes I shall record here that I have not, I think since the war began, heard curlews overhead at night; and this is sad, for that elfin piping used not seldom to delight me when I chanced to lie sleepless in spring or autumn, and I count it, with the bubbling spring-call of the curlew, among the most magical of bird-notes. I have been told that its absence is due to the black-out because lighted towns draw passing migrants towards them and bring them down to lower levels, but perhaps one of the Parish ornithologists will provide me with another explanation.[1]

Before leaving botany and zoology I may say that I have been taken to task for criticising our crocuses in the last number, but that I am quite unrepentant. Regiment your geraniums, tulips, and other professional beauties in geometrically shaped beds if you wish, but flowers of the more artless sort — crocuses, daffodils, primroses, for instance — should preserve at least an appearance of nature in their growth — or so I hold, and so you tacitly admit when you plant them not in beds but in turf. If I had my way with the Avenue the crocuses where they grew should grow no less thickly, but it would be in irregular semicircles round the roots of the trees with intervals between the clumps. I myself should keep the colours separate, or at least not mix yellow with the blue and white, but on that point I do not feel so strongly. Their present disposition in a rectangular carpet, however, offends me — I think it, in fact, an error of taste, from which academic societies are no more immune than other corporate bodies. Queens' have committed a similar one on the peninsula which

[1] See p. 250.

extends in front of King's, for they have planted their daffodils so lavishly that instead of looking like drifts of flowers in a wood they look like a horticulturalist's seedbeds invaded by trees — two of which, by the way, were blown down by the above mentioned searing north-easters.

Problems of supply continue to be difficult and the High Table dinner has been cut down to three courses, a matter of small moment to me for as it was I seldom ate more and often less. Undergraduates sometimes complain that they do not get enough to eat in Hall, and I think there is substance in the complaint, for they are of an age when they might well be thought to need extra rations which the rules do not allow them. Apart from that, however, our particular difficulties arise rather from shortage of staff than from insufficient food to sustain life, and I have had, for that reason, to default on the dinner which I should have given this term to the dining club to which I belong. This, by name The Family, consists when full, as at present it is not, of twelve members who dine with each other in turn each fortnight in Full Term. Since the war began it has contrived to carry on, though its menus have naturally been mere skeletons of their former portly selves, but this time the kitchens said flatly they were too short-handed either to cook or to serve a meal of any kind and I was reduced to holding a postprandial party over some decanters (which have not yet run dry). Though the first to default I have since been followed by another member who provided the same substitute, and I hope we may prolong this ghostly existence for some time, for the Club, which has a historical existence of well over a hundred years and a legendary of considerably greater length, makes a pleasant interlude in a busy week, and such things once discontinued are hard to get going again. As for the waiting in Hall I shall say only that the diners do a good deal in another sense of the word, and that though I do not know to what trade the majority of the waiters were brought up I know that it was not waiting. To judge from the din they contrive to make I should suppose it to have had something to do with pneumatic drills.

Nor is it only in the Kitchens that shortage of staff is beginning to be seriously felt. The Matron has for some time been in considerable difficulties which are likely to increase as the enrolment of women proceeds. My Bedmaker has been without a Help all this term, and no doubt there lies before us a mounting prospect of such small inconveniences. One large one is staring me in the face for my Gyp has announced his intention of abandoning me. I must not complain, for he is beginning to feel his years and the Observer Corps takes up a good deal of his time and energy; but he has minded my affairs since I came back to Cambridge in 1925, and though on ceasing to be Tutor I shall have less need of a general factotum I shall miss his other ministrations a lot. The difficulties of the College have been augmented by accident as well as by war, for the Manciple is in a nursing home with a bad heart-attack, and the College porters, a decrepit band of veterans for the most part, have suffered two more casualties, one from calling-up but the other from illness. It is mainly owing to shortage here that if you should stray into the Backs on a fine afternoon they would remind you less of the shady groves of Academe than of Hampstead Heath on a Bank Holiday or sometimes (I blush to say) of the beach at Margate. This is partly attributable, however, to the crowded state of the town, and as a rule the public behaves with reasonable decorum; but its continued intrusion at all hours is beginning to be a serious problem.

Classical examinations began on May 25, and my lecturing and supervision for them therefore ceased at the end of the previous week — the season at which an elderly Don's fancy might be supposed to turn lightly to thoughts of research. And in fact I did get out my immortal work again and have given some fitful attention to it, but there have been oddments to distract me. I had two papers in Part 2 of the Tripos to assess, and though this was no great matter as there were only four candidates, the task of discovering the answers to your colleague's questions (to say nothing of your own) always takes some time. I also found myself delivering a short course of lectures to R.A.F. Cadets—to my considerable surprise and I dare say to yours. 'And on what subject, pray?' (*Risum teneatis, amici*) On Greek Art. I anticipate your objection that a knowledge of this subject is not essential for airmen. It is not: but we had to fix up at very short notice a course for Cadets who were to read humane subjects, and as it was based on existing courses for undergraduates it left a chasm between the end of University lectures and the Long Vac. Term into which I, with other Q.Curtii, was more or less forcibly precipitated. It is in fact no great trouble to me for one cannot adapt a course on the subject to any specific need of the Air Force; and if it is doing them no immediate good as airmen, it is, I hope, doing them no irreparable harm as citizens.

Term ended on June 24, and on that day I took down my tutorial shop-sign for the second and last time, put up the shutters, and retired into the comparatively private life of a University and College lecturer. When the time came for me to do this in June 1939 relief and regret stood fairly even in the balance, but this time I have few regrets. For one thing tutoring, for reasons which I set out a year ago, has lost a good deal of its attraction in present conditions. For another I am a lot more than three years older since 1939, and I am war-weary — not defeatist or down-hearted or anything of that sort, but jaded with war conditions and lack of respite from year's end to year's end from problems and responsibilities remote from my interests and from any aptitudes I may be supposed to possess. It is true that I have not lost interest in the problems which present themselves to a Tutor — many of them are more interesting than the administrative puzzles on which much of my time is spent — but I am conscious that for the present I cannot count on bringing to them the alertness and elasticity of mind which they require, and therefore I am not sorry to be relieved of them. I shall, though no longer Tutor, still have some tutorial duties to discharge, for the affairs of my pupils now out of residence but waiting for war allowances in order to graduate cannot well be handled by a Tutor who knows nothing of their careers. Therefore parishioners in this position had better address any enquiries they may wish to make to me, since to me they must come in the end. But these will involve but little trouble and no anxiety, and since for the most part any fool can deal with them if he has the facts, I shall do so no worse than another.

When I retired in 1939 I had intended to see my successor firmly into his seat and then to take a couple of terms off, for the University statutes allow a teaching officer one sabbatical term in seven, but I, owing to the fact that I was a Tutor, had never been in a position to avail myself of leave of absence. It will amuse some of you to hear that I meant to go to Egypt (not expecting much pleasure from the country, but there are things there I should like to see), and to come slowly home through Greece, where I have not been for many years, Sicily, and Italy. Such was the stuff of which dreams were being made three years ago before they were couponed and controlled, and now, if there ever comes a time when I can take sabbatical leave, which will not be before the end of the war, I suppose I am more likely to spend it in a bathchair at Buxton or Droit-wich (Vichy being somewhat out of fashion) — and may be I shall spend it not less contentedly, so do not suppose that I repine.

I have lately had a brief lecture on University finance from the Treasurer, and since its contents can be set down quite briefly and it is long since you had any news on this head, I shall now tell you roughly how we stand after three years of war. Counting summarily in thousands of pounds the University is about 80 down in fees of all kinds (matriculation, lecture, degree, etc.) on an average pre-war year. Against that deficit it is saving about 30 in stipends to absent teaching officers, 11 on vacant professor-ships, 19 on prizes and scholarships suspended or not awarded; and it receives about 13 in payments from institutions temporarily housed in Cambridge. That still leaves a deficit of about 7, but there is a good deal of peace-time expenditure (on research, for instance) which is not being incurred at present, and the ship is not only still afloat but labouring much less heavily than one had reason to fear two years ago.

As the result a mild agitation is now afoot to fill some of the vacant Chairs, and indeed there is something to be said for it. When, however, we decided to suspend in all cases unless a special reason was shown for not doing so, the financial argument was not the only one in view. There is also the difficulty in war-time of getting the proper field of candidates. People may miss the announcement of a vacancy, or be too busy with war-work to consider the step, or be unwilling in times of uncertainty to commit themselves to change and to new responsibilities. It is also pos-sible that in scientific and technical subjects the man who would now seem best, might, by the end of the war and before he was ready to take up his duties, have been passed by somebody else. In short there are real diffi-culties, and though, if other Universities are leaving Chairs vacant (I do not know if they are), there may well be an unseemly scramble when the time comes to fill them, that may seem the lesser of two evils.

16.7.42

Since the end of term I have composed for a learned journal a rather tiresome paper about some problems which I cannot solve, but for the most part my occupation might justifiably be called messing about — and for a month of gnawing anxiety such as this has been[1] miscellaneous

---

[1] The Allies were retreating in Libya and in Russia; Tobruk fell on June 21, Sevas-topol on July 1; the Battle of Egypt had opened on June 27.

occupation is perhaps the best. At this time of year A.R.P. is always a worry, for there is the Long Vac. to be provided for and one must also consider who shall take over key posts in October from those going down; and as people are mostly uncertain whether they will be up in the Long or in October it is hard to get anything fixed or definite. I have had a good many tutorial papers to go through and destroy, and I took the opportunity of committing some others to the salvage basket. I have also been in London for three nights in all. I thought I had better discover from an arthritis-expert whether my hip-joints were disintegrating as rapidly as their behaviour during the last nine months led me to suspect (it would seem that they are not), and I wanted to get some other business done and to see some friends. In the intervals I looked at some pictures, but there isn't much of interest to be seen. The National Gallery is exhibiting a lot of paintings of England done for a series called *Recording Britain* which is sponsored by the Pilgrim Trust. It is, I dare say, a good way of subsidising impoverished artists (which is perhaps its main object), but as I failed to recognise the two views of Cambridge it contains I feel less sure of its other uses. One was of Little St Mary's as viewed by a Peterhouse undergraduate out of his bedroom window; the other of King's Parade as viewed by a sparrow perched on the summit of Caius; and I think the recorders would do better to depict the objects as seen by less exclusive classes of observers. London is full of unfamiliar uniforms, Dominion, Colonial, and Allied, which you may see in force in Trafalgar Square where a military band is apt to play in the morning — when last I passed a Czech band was somewhat incongruously discoursing the Londonderry Air to them. It also grows slowly tidier as ruins are demolished; but if it looks tidier, in summer sunlight it looks increasingly shabby, and the painters and decorators will have their hands pretty full when the war is over and they start making up for all these years' neglect.

I have lately been looking through the first draft of a College War List (casualties and honours) which will in course of time be printed and sent out to you in the *Annual Record*. It is, I have no doubt, full of mistakes, and I hope you will let us know of any you detect, and not merely snort and consign it to the waste-paper basket. It has been compiled mainly in the College Office, where the Chief Clerk, robbed of all his underlings, is now supported only by young women and boys who come and go. (The best of the boys was in the A.T.C. and has lately been killed in a flying accident.) I do not suppose that the young woman who goes through the lists in the papers and compares them with the College registers does it very well, but even if she did there are bound to be many mistakes and omissions, for where you see such a name as J. Smith there is no means of telling whether he is the J. Smith who matriculated in such and such a year unless his Tutor or another happens to have private information, and that is comparatively seldom the case. Perhaps it is unwise to try and make a list at all in present circumstances, but the College really does take an interest in its members, so, as I say, I hope you will collaborate. I will pass on any correction or additions you send to me.

Among the tutorial papers which I turned out I came upon a long letter from a landlady whom I had reprimanded for refusing to take in a lodger who came up a day or two before the beginning of Full Term. One of its many paragraphs reveals a chapter of accidents so moving that it deserves a wider public than it has hitherto reached:

> As you have asked the reason about this we should like to say that 3 very important reasons greatly hindered us in the vac. First we both (my brother & self) have been under the dentist which took a lot of valuable time. Secondly my brother was troubled with gastric for a time which all helped to hinder & then thirdly we have had to spend a good deal of time at the cemetary as our grave stone has caused us trouble leaning forward and becoming dangerous, so we saw Mr Hibbet & made full arrangements with him which meant taking everything off the grave and replaceing them all again which took more of our time. The Vac. is short if everything goes as usual, but when they do not it cannot be surprising getting behind hand a few days especially when one arrives extra early.

THIRTY-SIXTH LETTER

14.8.42

No. 36 brings the P.M. to the end of its third year, and, as on two earlier anniversaries, I begin with a brief retrospect. During the year the Parish has shrunk both geographically and numerically. Geographically Tokyo, Hongkong, and Malaya have been cut from its boundaries by force; Cyprus by the local parishioner's retirement to Palestine; Gibraltar by his return to England. Against these losses the only additions are the Transvaal (where I do not chance to have had a correspondent before),

Palestine, and Irak. America was nearly engulfed in outer darkness also, for my one surviving American parishioner is now serving with an American hospital much nearer at hand. His place in the U.S.A., however, has been taken by an English medical student who is pursuing clinical studies there with a Rockefeller grant. I was amused, by the way, to learn from a parishioner who has withdrawn to the remotest parts of the Sudan that his P.M. is apt to reach him borne in a cleft stick by a naked Nuer. Numbers have fallen by about a dozen, of whom half are accounted for by events in the Far East. Three of them I have reason to think safe; of two I have no news; one, I am very sorry to say, was killed when the *Dorsetshire* was sunk. Besides these, there have, of course, been defaulters, who have succumbed (like the late William Shakespeare) to a surfeit of cold small-beer, aggravated in some cases by matrimony, which, as I have said before, has a detrimental effect on my correspondence. I regret them, for the main object of these letters is to try and keep in touch; but I am neither surprised nor shocked, for the beer, I know, grows, and must grow, less and less exhilarating as the months go by. Hitherto such defections have mostly been made good by the enrolment of new parishioners, but of late men have been up for so short a time, and I have been so busy, that I have got to know few well enough to add them to the Parish. My recent issues have been going to between eighty and ninety.

The true circulation is larger than this, for some copies are passed on by their recipients, and some, I understand, are read even by people who know neither Cambridge nor me. I sometimes wonder a little apprehensively what they make of them. I hope I usually contrive to make my general meaning plain, but in such letters as these something depends on undertones, which are hard to catch unless one knows the writer; and my writing, as I have lately been reminded, even when it is more careful than it can or should be here, seems to convey varied impressions. A writer in the *Spectator* lately called an essay of mine 'marmoreal'; an American reviewer once called the same essay (whether in praise or disprise I hardly know) 'port-wine-flavoured'. It is not for me to say which it is, or whether it is either (except that, as I do not drink port, if it is the latter the flavour must be faint); but I assert with confidence that both it cannot be, and that never in the history of the world has a writer, searching for the *mot juste*, stood poised between these two epithets. And, as I say, I wonder a little apprehensively what revisions of judgment I may cause if I ever meet my unknown parishioners face to face.

A year ago I announced that I should not thenceforward aim at writing four pages a month. Of those who deigned to comment on this announcement a few received it with resignation, and one with positive enthusiasm, but more expressed regret; and in fact the last twelve numbers have all been of standard length. Nevertheless the time will come, and I think before long, when you get something shorter. For one thing, as I said in my last, I am thoroughly jaded; for another I am no longer a Tutor. And if as a member of the Council of the Senate and of the General Board I am still well-placed for knowing what is going on in the administration of the University, I shall (thank goodness) no longer have to master the interminable circulars about the conditions under which men are allowed to continue their studies; nor shall I hear nearly so much of the joys and sorrows of undergraduates — and these are perhaps more important, and certainly more interesting to you, than problems of academic administration.

I have lately been reading the records of two University scandals. The first concerns this College and Bertrand Russell, who was dismissed from a lectureship by the College Council in 1916 after having been fined £100 for making in print statements 'likely to prejudice recruiting and discipline'. Russell had written a more or less innocuous leaflet about the treatment of a conscientious objector, but busybodies in various places had prosecuted people for distributing it, and when R. wrote to the *Times* to announce himself as its author a prosecution, and probably a conviction, were inevitable. However, though the pamphlet may have broken the law, R. had evidently done nothing disgraceful or dishonourable, and his dismissal by the Council caused a hullabaloo among the Fellows, for many of those who disagreed with his views (myself among them) strongly disapproved of the Council's action. Ultimately R. was reappointed to a lectureship in 1920 but resigned for private reasons before he ever took it up, having in the meantime somewhat complicated matters by making in 1918 a statement of a really harmful kind and being sent to gaol for six months. It is a story which does no great credit to either party, and G. H. Hardy, who has lately printed an account of it, might be thought to be washing dirty linen in public. However it is perhaps as well that the facts should be on record, for the outside world mostly knows only that R. was dismissed, not that his dismissal caused a rumpus, nor (since he never in fact came back) that he was reinstated. The College linen is therefore not as dirty as some suppose.

The second scandal is the strange case of Mr R. P. N. Downing of Emmanuel whose name did not appear in the Classical Tripos list of 1882. His answers to a philology paper had been missing from the examiner's room but had turned up again, and he was suspected of having removed them for improvement. However, evidence having been given that they were such as he might have been expected to write, it was supposed that the examiner had mislaid them, and the incident appeared to be closed. When, however, his name did not appear, enquiry was naturally made whether it was for this reason, and it became known that the examiners had other grounds for thinking that he had cheated. Thereupon his father printed a series of lengthy pamphlets asking that D. might be heard in his own defence, and, as the affair was by now notorious, the request for investigation was supported by numerous flysheets circulated by members of the University. Consequently in May 1883 the Council of the Senate invited five external referees to conduct an enquiry. The case against (complicated by numerous red herrings) was that in more than twenty out of twenty-eight passages set for unseen translation D.'s versions showed a verbal resemblance to cribs and commentaries which could not be accidental, and at some stage D.'s scripts and their alleged sources were actually printed. The defence consisted in showing how by a fortunate chance he had lately read each passage. The referees presently reported that they were not satisfied with the explanations, that D. had done something to lighten the weight of the case against him, and (by a majority) that if they had been examiners they would not have omitted his name — a verdict, in short, of Not Proven. The Council of the Senate thereupon put forward a Grace to insert D.'s name in the Tripos list, but at this some of the examiners rose up saying that the Tripos results were nobody's affair but theirs, that they saw no reason to change their opinion, that they had not been heard by the referees, and that they would be no party to these proceedings. A nice constitutional point was thus raised. Followed a storm of flysheets, some in favour of the Grace, some announcing an intention to non-placet it, another from an ex-Proctor proposing to vote placet to the Grace but to non-placet the Supplicat for D. to take a degree (on the ground of a much earlier row with the police). However in November 1883 the Grace was passed by 80 to 60 and the Supplicat by 66 to 47, and D. duly became a B.A. The affair interests me because my father, who had been some time out of residence and had lately ceased to be a Fellow of this College,[1] was

[1] See p. 157.

one of the referees (chosen, perhaps, because he had had legal training), and he used sometimes to talk of it. He believed, I do not know on what evidence, that many years afterwards a compositor of the University Press confessed that he had taken impressions of the references to the passages in the papers and sold them to Downing; I have also heard that D. on his deathbed denied that he had cheated; but of all this there is nothing in the dossiers I have been reading and the problem remains unsolved.

In my own tutorial experience I remember two charges of cheating brought against my pupils. One was where two men next each other in alphabetical order had produced identical answers and diagrams with identical mistakes. Fortunately, however, though alphabetically neighbours, they had been sitting at opposite sides of the room and could produce the notebook of a third party which they had borrowed and worked at together, so they left the court without stains on their characters. The other case was that of a candidate for the History Tripos under whose seat was found a sheaf of papers full of historical material which he was assumed to have brought in with him and used. Examination of the sheaf, however, made it perfectly plain to everybody except the Chairman of Examiners that what he had really done was to come in for the paper, write down all he knew (which, I may say, was little), and then see if any of it was relevant to the questions set. I do not recommend this procedure to intending examinees, but it is at least innocent, and I do not suppose this man ever knew that his honour had been impugned for I never told him.

THIRTY-SEVENTH LETTER

30.8.42

No. 36 was sent out towards the end of a week of Warden's duty and on the following Monday I shook off the dust of Cambridge and came down to Radnorshire as I regularly do at this time of year. I wasn't looking forward to the journey, which I usually make by car, for trains take much longer and promised to be uncomfortable; but in fact, though full, none of those I encountered was grossly overcrowded. Transport difficulties, however, have cramped my style and I have not been able to get to Montgomeryshire as is my wont. Was My Journey Really Necessary? Well, I consider that a journey, this or another, was, for I hadn't had a real holiday since last September, and Cambridge is no place to stay in from year's end to year's end. I have, besides, been growing short of sleep, for my subliminal self takes its (or my) A.R.P. responsibilities too seriously and wakes me at the first whisper of a sound which might call me out of bed. It is true that what it takes for the rising note of a siren often proceeds from a car, and that the aeroplanes it hears are usually friendly, but it hears one or other most nights and rouses me so sharply that I lie awake for an hour or more. Here in Wales it pays no heed to an occasional aeroplane by night. By day, too, the bark of a raven is commoner than the drone of engines overhead, and except for a mutter of guns from the Eppynt ranges near Brecon (not unknown, I think, to some parishioners) there is little to remind the ear of war; and this is a pleasant change, for the din in Cambridge skies both by day and by night is formidable. The eye would not have been reminded of war at all but for the fact that for two days a divisional exercise was going on, and a good many drivers, threading their way by narrow, tortuous, and unfrequented lanes, brought their trucks, bren-carriers, and what-nots up the dead-end which leads to the house in which I write. I remark in passing that hereabouts ravens seem to be increasing at the expense of buzzards which are to me the more attractive and used to be the commoner bird. Buzzards there still are, but I observed eight ravens apparently mobbing one of them, and I am afraid they will grow rarer unless the farmers, who complain of the ravens, come in on their side.

It has not been a very agreeable Long Vac. Early in June we had ten days of really fine hot weather which caused me to get into my tropical suiting, but I was quickly driven out of it, and since then I have oftener felt too cool than too hot. There hasn't been much sun and I do not remember a more continuously windy summer. I do not think it has produced much copy for the P.M. though it has been busier than usual. All the boards and committees on which I sit had more to do than they expect or desire at this time of year, and the National Service Committee in particular is confronted by some knotty problems posed by people who have been invalided out of the services. Fundamentally the difficulty is that though the University will allow a term's residence for illness, it does not, and obviously cannot, excuse an examination for that cause except on evidence that the man would have passed if he had been able to sit. For national service, on the other hand, it allows up to four terms' residence and a year's ration of examinations. But a man who has, let us say, served for two terms may be discharged and yet not be fit to return to Cambridge in the third term. Does he earn the allowance of examinations for the third term? The answer might seem to be that he does if the disability arose from the service, but apart from the difficulty of determining whether it did or no (and the actual cases so far are all of illness not of injury), there are also to be considered people who are engaged in work of national importance in civilian capacities, and conscientious objectors who are doing what their tribunals bade them. Do these, if absent from their work owing to illness, earn examination allowances which a resident undergraduate absent from Cambridge for the same reason would not earn? These nuts have been chewed but are now put by for further mastication. Naturally whatever rules are made will bear hardly on a few individuals, and no doubt there will be a general review of hard cases at the end of the war, but this point has now assumed some urgency as the men are returning into residence and must be told how they stand. Apart from matters of this kind my own Long Vac. was embittered by passages of arms with the Air Ministry, who made a blunder over their treatment of R.A.F. Cadets and attempted to hand the baby to a board of which I am president: and with the Chief A.R. Warden in the Borough, who was not sending to Colleges information of vital importance to them. However at the expense of a good deal of time and the composition of some acidulated letters these storms are now allayed.

17.9.42

I returned to Cambridge (reluctantly and much less comfortably than I went) on the day after I had written the above, much refreshed by a fortnight's almost complete idleness in weather which, if it might have been better, might also have been worse. September's news, if any, I shall leave until the next issue and abandon the remainder of this (by request) to Our Literary Correspondent who, as before, prefixes an asterisk to works which can be purchased for a shilling or less.

A good deal of my lighter reading is represented by *Thraliana*, the contents of six notebooks given to Mrs Thrale by her husband and used by her as a diary and commonplace book from 1776 to 1809. I suppose that since they knew it still existed all good Johnsonians have wanted to see this book, and all but the most inveterate have expected to find it boring; but it is not so. It contains too much moderate verse by herself and others (easily skipped), and too much about the end of the world (which was impending about 1800), but on the whole it does great credit both to her heart and to her head and I was sorry when I reached the last of its 1100 pages. Among the anecdotes, which are more entertaining than one had any right to anticipate, I encountered with surprise one about this College. The son of a Cambridge tradesman who wished to be ordained was asked by his examiners how many Persons there are in the Trinity and replied 'Indeed I can't justly say, Sir — though my father makes shoes for them all'. *Thraliana* caused me to read a somewhat similar work I have long had on my conscience — Spence's *Anecdotes* (of Pope, Bolingbroke, and other 17th-18th cent. worthies) which is also repaying. In the biographical line I have read also Henson's *Retrospect of an Unimportant Life*, the first volume of an autobiography too much occupied for my taste with ecclesiastical politics but interesting and, as was to be expected, very crisply written. (In case you should learn from it that I am, or was on one occasion, taciturn at table, I remark, without denying the charge, that H. is a talker whom one does not willingly interrupt, and that interruption might well be necessary if one wished to talk oneself.) J. W. Johnson's *Along this Way is the autobiography of a distinguished negro; Masefield's *In the Mill* an account of early experiences in an American carpet-factory — both quite readable, as are also three autobiographical books about country life: M. Leigh, *Harvest of the Moor* (farming in Cornwall: a better by the same about Scotland is called *Highland Homespun*), C. Porteous, *Farmer's Creed*, and *Teamsman*. Betwixt biography and art-criticism are *The Preraphaelite Tragedy* by W. Gaunt (too jauntily written), an almost unreadable book about Degas (for whom I have a passion) by Meier Graefe, and a readable one about Toulouse Lautrec (who repels me) by G. Mack. Betwixt autobiography and travel are two books about the war in Spain — *English Captain, by T. Wintringham, and *Secret Agent in Spain* by H. Greene (which left me with a disagreeable impression of the author) — and Somerset Maugham's *Strictly Personal*, an account of the fall of France and of his escape. This is a slight but interesting book and M. sees more future for France than I can. I hope he is right, for though Italy stands higher in my affections, I have enjoyed myself a good deal at one time or another in that varied and spacious country and would willingly go there again.

Of travel books I have read Ovington's *Voyage to Surat in 1689* lent me by a parishioner (quite interesting but rather too impersonal for my taste in travels), Mungo Park's *Travels* (in W. Africa 1795-9; more adventurous), *River of Golden Sand* by T. Woodrooffe (about the Yangtse; amusing), *Borneo Jungle* (essays by members of an Oxford expedition to Sarawak, marred, I regret to say, by the facetiousness of a Cambridge editor), *In Morocco*, by Mrs Wharton (readable), and *Unflinching*, by E. Christian (journal of a boy who froze and starved to death in the Canadian barren lands — a moving narrative).

Oddments include M. Friedländer's *On Art and Connoisseurship*, a collection of essays which I did not find very illuminating, G. M. Young's *Victorian England*, a good book which I should have enjoyed more if I knew more history, *The Screwtape Letters* by C. S. Lewis (a religious tract written with humour and insight), and two novels — E. M. Forster, *Howard's End* (good), and T. F. Powys, *Kindness in a Corner* (does to read).

THIRTY-EIGHTH LETTER

20.9.42

At this time of year I am apt to report any changes in the outward appearance of the town, but a mental tour of it discloses little to add to the reports in nos. 14 and 26. You would notice a large but not unsightly tank of static water on the grass at the east end of King's Chapel (and on one occasion you might have noticed punts and canoes laboriously transferred to it by some local humorist), and some unsightly but not dishonourable scars on the east front of Whewell's Ct. By poking about you might find some other wounds in that neighbourhood, and since both the B.B.C. and the papers, daily and illustrated, have disclosed that the Union was set on fire and glass in Whewell's Ct broken, I believe it will not be indiscreet to say that all our windows on Sidney St perished but that they were our only casualties. I know little about the damage at the Union but it is plainly not irreparable. Should your tour proceed round the corner into St John's St, you would see that St John's have erected two pompous yales on their new side-entrance to match the eagles on the new gate in Bridge St mentioned in no. 26; and that round the latter carrots now burgeon more gracefully than the potatoes of yesteryear. (What are yales? They are heraldic monsters with horns cocked in opposite directions fore and aft who support the arms of Lady Margaret Beaufort; and unless you are unobservant you should have caught them at it on the gates of St John's and Christ's. You may call them, if you wish, jails, or even eales.) Elsewhere a few more railings are missing, notably those round our Fellows' Garden which were luckily pinched just before it became illegal to replace them with split chestnut pales — luckily, I say, because during the three days the garden was unprotected thieves broke through and stole freely. Besides this the only changes that I can think of are that an eruption of small restaurants has broken out all over the place, to cater, I imagine, for evacuees; and that long queues, of which I once wrote, are hardly to be seen any more, whether because cigarettes and other such goods are more plentiful, or because they are in less demand owing to their price, or because the queuers have found some more entertaining pastime. When I am abroad in the busy shopping times (which is seldom) I see small numbers of people queued up at bakers and at vegetable stalls in the Market Place, but that is because there are many customers and few to serve, not because the goods are in short supply, and those who shop later in the day can usually get what they want. So much for changes in the town. What has happened outside it I know not, for I have not been there except so far as to notice that the wen on the Coton footpath, as wens will, has grown and swollen.

16.10.42

Term began on Oct. 7 but must keep until I have formed a more definite impression of it and have compiled those statistics to which you look forward with such insatiable avidity. Meanwhile I cast my eye back upon September.

As previously recorded I returned here on the 1st and filled in without regret my last tutorial return for the University Grants Committee (mentioned in no. 11), which reminds me to say that I think I may have been too plaintive during the last three years about the number of forms etc. which beset Tutors — at any rate having seen in Wales the supplies of such matter which confront those responsible for other forms of livestock, I began to doubt whether Tutors are much worse off than other folk except that it probably matters more to undergraduates than to the other forms whether the returns are accurate, and that Tutors have not dangling before their noses a bait of cream, butter, eggs, bacon, etc. Having done that I intended to get down to my own work for a good spell, and I did in fact have a sharp encounter with the Macedonian (Ptolemaic) calendar, which drives me nearly distracted whenever it crosses my path. (The poor fools had a lunar calendar which they corrected with intercalations on some unknown but visibly incompetent system. Consequently if you want to find out where at a given date some Macedonian month had got to in the solar year, you depend on those papyri which bear both a Macedonian and an Egyptian date. For the part of the 3rd cent. B.C. which concerns me there are a fair number of these, and, as the Egyptian calendar is known, a reliable double date skewers a Macedonian month for at any rate one year. On the other hand only those on official documents are reliable, for private people naturally could not cope with such a system and were apt to make shots or to put the same day of both months. Considering that, like everybody else in antiquity, they had no fixed divisions of the day — I think it is Seneca who says that there is about as much agreement among clocks as among philosophers — I sometimes wonder how they made or kept appointments; but the answer may be that they did not.) From this episode I emerged with head unbowed indeed but slightly bloody, and recollecting that the College A.R.P. literature would have to be overhauled before term began, took it up for a change. It proved a much heavier job than I had anticipated, and by the time I had written, or rewritten, manuals for College Wardens (now in its sixth edition), Fire-watchers, Hall Observers, Staircase-marshals, and Porters, a new proclamation about incendiary bombs, and a vade-mecum to the College water, gas, and electricity systems, and had seen that they were stuck up in the proper places, it was time for me to go to London for three nights as I had business there. There were indeed some other distractions besides A.R.P. literature, for I had very welcome visits from three parishioners, and spent two hard days interviewing R.A.F. cadets, a task not in itself disagreeable but exhausting. There were something over a hundred of them, and as at the next session there will be at least three hundred I do not look forward to it.

When in London I took the opportunity of spending something less than twenty-four hours at Eton, and the like with friends in Hertfordshire, but I brought no copy from either; nor much from London, a place which begins to trouble me, for buses and trains, being reduced in number, are apt to be unduly crowded; taxis are expensive and not always to be found; and nowadays two or three hours of pavement-padding reduce me to a painful limp. Still, in the intervals of odd jobs of business I saw a number of friends, some of them unexpectedly, and crawled round the galleries. And here I may record two remarkable events. One is that the National Gallery has acquired a small picture which, if not by Giotto, is at least much nearer to being so than anything it possessed or seemed likely to acquire, for such a thing, one would have said, no longer existed outside public collections. However here is an unknown work of considerable merit, belonging to a known series, bequeathed by a lady out of the blue, or (to be precise) out of Sevenoaks. The second event is that I came near to buying a very expensive work by Boudin; and though this may not cause the hair to bristle on your napes it did on mine for B. is by no means my ordinary cup of tea. Apart from these things London galleries were dullish, and, as I have said before, you will find more of interest in the Fitzwilliam than elsewhere in England. We have just rehung four galleries — two with watercolours of various dates from Cozens, through Turner and Cotman, to modern times; one with flower-pieces (we have a lot of various dates which make an unexpectedly attractive show); and one with English comic draughts-men (Keene, Beerbohm, and others). How long we shall be able to maintain our preeminence I do not know, for the hosts of Midian still prowl around casting covetous eyes on the premises, and even if we succeed in holding them at bay, shortage of staff makes the framing and hanging of new exhibitions increasingly difficult.

I got back to Cambridge on the 27th, by which time shades of the prison house in the shape of committee meetings and other preparations for term were beginning to close about me. In the intervals, besides correcting some proofs and doing a little of my own work, I have contemplated my Income Tax Assessment (not for the first time) with the emotions of a worm which has nowhere to turn; and my Fuel Target not with dismay (for my last year's arrow passed not so very far overhead) but with distaste; for if I have been miserably cold for the last two winters I shall no doubt be colder this. I shall, I see, have to cut out my bathroom, which consumes a good deal of gas, and bathe in the College baths or, more simply, go dirty. These reflexions led me to remember that I had a lot of clothing coupons which would soon be useless, and to expend a good many of them on warmer clothes. One further winter discontent to which I was looking forward will not occur, for my Gyp, who, as announced in no. 34, proposed to leave me, has relented and will discharge the much lighter duties which, being no longer Tutor, I shall still require of him. Since he now visits me at hours which suit his time-table he may sometimes be seen about the College in the dark beret and battle dress of Air Force blue worn by the Observer Corps.

Diversions have not been numerous, but as the paint laid on our Library roof two years ago by the College Fire Party is beginning to wear a bit thin, I got somebody to break the rules and fly me over the town to inspect it. I enjoyed this, for it was an afternoon of sun and big clouds when changing lights and shadows on the countryside make flying a pleasure, and it is long since I have been in the air and longer since I have flown over Cambridge. It took my memory back to the Long Vac. of 1930, for in the first year of my tutorship I had to sign a good many permits for pupils to have lessons at Marshall's Flying School, and being apprehensive about the risks to which I was thereby exposing them and also perhaps more conscientious than I should be now, I spent a month of the vacation in taking the course myself. As a matter of fact I did not dislike it, and the experience has more than once been useful to me since.

THIRTY-NINTH LETTER

14.11.42

THIS issue must consist of random jottings of various dates, and first for statistics. The number of men in residence is 2700, and of women 475. The figures from 1938 to 1941, which I repeat from no. 27 for comparison, were 5491, 4353, 2908, 2756; and 513, 465, 497, 515 respectively. This year's total of men is composed of 176 B.A.'s, Research Students, and 4th year; 218 3rd year; 780 2nd year; and 1526 freshmen. The numbers of freshmen in Oct. 1938 and the three subsequent years were 1839, 1624, 1124, 1270, but the present increase, though surprising and gratifying, is also a little misleading until it is explained that it is mainly due to an increase of the number of Cadets sent here for six-month courses. There are now over 400 of these as against about 200 last October. Still, they are fully matriculated undergraduates and outwardly indistinguishable from the rest. To these statistics I add some culled from the Vice-Chancellor's speech at the opening of the academic year. He gave the following figures for matriculations in 1939-40 and the two following academic years: 1923, 1513, 1759 — the average pre-war number being about 1800. And he contrasted them with those of the last war when the pre-war average was about 1200 and the matriculations in the first three years were 727, 344, 235. He also said that in October 1917 our numbers were reduced to 444, which was about an eighth of the then normal, whereas today we are a little over half strength. I add as a foot-note that the matriculations differ appreciably from my figures for October freshmen since, apart from inaccuracies in the latter due to the cause explained in no. 30, they include matriculations in the two subse-quent terms, and in particular a second batch of the six-months Cadets who replace in April the batch admitted in October. I add further (in case you have not yet had enough of this) that there are this term 289 men resident in this College, of whom 149 are freshmen; and that there are about 1900 members of evacuated institutions among us. Further still, that of 71 professorships 16 are vacant, and 16 more Professors are away; and of 370 Lecturers and Demonstrators only 143 are now in Cambridge. Of the vacant professorships I expect you may hear more, for, as recorded in no. 35, the policy of suspension is about to come up for discussion.

And the moral of all this? Well, one moral is that many Dons have too much to do; and this has a bearing on the question whether vacant professorships and other teaching posts should be filled, though the vacancies are mostly in faculties where there is also a shortage of students. The other is that we have so far survived the impact of war far better than anyone would have ventured to hope three years ago. I hear that townsfolk comment unfavourably on the number of able-bodied young men who are still at their books, but if anyone does so to me he will get a flea in his ear, for I have no patience with such stupid criticism. If you leave aliens out of account all undergraduates now in residence are at the disposal of the competent authorities if and when they want them; the great majority are technicians qualifying themselves as fast as they can to play their part in what is essentially a technicians' war; and the small fraction who are reading humane subjects have been certified to be of unusual ability, and they are devoting much of their time to military training. Precisely how small the fraction is I do not know, but in Classics I am lecturing to a class less than half the size even of last year, and more than half of those are female; and in the five colleges for whose super-vision Trinity is now responsible there are only thirteen Classics all told. Three years ago I should have predicted that if in October 1942 I was lecturing at all it would be to women only; and though I do not invite the nation to congratulate itself that a few men are still sitting at my feet, I think it may legitimately be pleased that a few can still be allowed to study non-technical subjects.

The most sensational piece of College news is that since the beginning of November British Restaurant lunches have been served in Hall. The immediate cause of this event was that the B.R. established in the Pitt Club (as reported in no. 32) found itself increasingly crowded by undergraduates from those Colleges which do not provide lunch and by students from evacuated institutions; and though the service was obviously not intended for such as these, it was not easy to see how the doors could be barred against them. The proposition that we should have a similar lunch open to undergraduates from King's, Clare, and London University reached us from the Regional Commissioner's office together with a mutter of compulsory powers vested in the R.C., so the College Council contented itself with drawing the line at the metropolitan females. May be it was not in any case inclined to do more, for in one respect at any rate the arrangement is advantageous to us. Since the food is provided by the B.R., College rations go further, and our undergraduates (who now pay 35/- a week for their board, as against the 30/- mentioned in November 1940) get a better breakfast than they have hitherto enjoyed—a definite gain, for, as I said in no. 34, I think rationing bears hardly on them and that they need more food than they are allowed. The arrangement is nominally for this term only, and it is possible that it may collapse sooner, for the visitors have to sign on for a week at a time, and presumably those who didn't like what they got one week would lunch elsewhere the next. The food, which I have seen but not eaten, looks sustaining rather than appetising, and though I have heard no complaints from Trinity undergraduates, the Steward doesn't seem too confident that it will be very popular. For the rest, to judge from the High Table dinner (as one may, since except on Sundays it is virtually the same as the undergraduates'), feeding has definitely improved in the last six months, though those who share my opinion that rabbit is unfit for human consumption must regret its too frequent appearance. If you insist on sherry, however, you must come on a Sunday, for our stocks are running low and we now confine it to that night in order to make them last longer. Claret still flows freely, but some similar measure is likely to be necessary there too before very long. Other amenities, though three years ago we should hardly have looked on them as such, decline apace. In the interest of fuel-economy College baths are on alternate days confined to showers, and the increasing shortage of staff has obliged the occupants of certain rooms in Whewell's Court to do their washing in lavatories downstairs in order to save labour in bedrooms. Further, from November to March Bedmakers do not return to staircases in the afternoon. Privately I suspect that the Matron is terrified of losing any more, but in fact this is not unreasonable for there is not a great deal for them to do in the afternoon and some of them have to come what, in black-out conditions, is a weary way to do it. Still, I shall not pretend that I enjoy being left without attendance from 11 a.m. until next morning, and the little my Bedmaker did in the evening — clearing away lunch, black-out, hot water bottle in bed, etc. — contributed more than its face value to my comfort. However, as my waiting room is now no longer needed for tutorial purposes, I have taken to bolting my frugal lunch there in order to leave my inner room clear; and of all these things I say, as Odysseus said before me, 'Endure, o heart; you have stood worse than this in the past' — indeed, considering the hardships some of you support, I should be ashamed to mention them if it were not the duty of the P.M. to present a detailed picture of Cambridge in wartime. It is, by the way, something of a mystery to me where the Bedmakers and Helps have gone to, for I cannot readily picture the absentees disguised as Wrens or Waafs or even Land-girls. I suppose, however, that, with husbands and daughters earning more, family budgets have swollen, and that some at least have downed mops for that reason.

We have, as perhaps you observed in the papers, elected two new Fellows — a scientist and a historian; and as the latter is a Russian prince the social tone of the High Table may be supposed enhanced. I should myself be more inclined to congratulate ourselves on acquiring a Russian who spoke excellent English, for though I was brought up to believe that all Russians were superlative linguists, local experience has sometimes suggested that they have only a considerable capacity for making themselves unintelligible in several languages. But we are getting into deep waters over our Fellowship elections for very few men are now at liberty to sit down to academic research and to produce dissertations in the normal manner; it is highly unsatisfactory to elect to a Research Fellowship anyone, whatever his abilities may be, whose capacity for research is untested; and the handicap bears very unevenly on the different subjects. For whereas most of the ablest scientists and some of the mathematicians are now engaged on research which, if not strictly germane to their natural bent, is at least research on which some kind of report may be available, the ablest humanists are either in the fighting forces or in

Government offices, and from this point of view either marking time or moving backwards.

One of the problems lately before the Council of the Senate was who should sign documents connected with the rationing of the University in footballs, tennis racquets, and other sports-gear. It was settled easily enough though we have not, like the sister University, an authority ready-made for the purpose. I learnt last year from the Oxford journals that as Colleges there had found a difficulty in arranging matches the University had appointed a gallant colonel at a salary of £500 a year to do it for them, and to advise individuals on what form of exercise to take. Naturally games for some while past have not been very easy to arrange here either, many matches have been scratched, and those who want exercise often get it by filling gaps in the sides of other Colleges. Still, when we make a similar appointment you will be able, and have my full permission, to knock me down with a feather.

FORTIETH LETTER

29.11.42

I HAVE had enquiries from three sources as to the advantages or otherwise of taking an M.A. degree, and as those who became B.A.'s in 1939 ripen for M.A.'s in January, two of these enquiries are probably due to the receipt of a circular from the College Office. The matter is obscure, and as your lessons in *The Mysterious University* have been long inter-rupted it may feature as *Lesson* 9. Learn, therefore, that so far as the College is concerned you may, as an M.A., dine (and wine) at the High Table four times per annum free of charge, and at your own charges you may dine further provided that you do not do so more than four times per quarter without special leave. (This sounds churlish, but it is not that we do not want your company. The H.T. is already numerous, and there are so many Trinity M.A.'s about that unrestricted liberty might easily create a problem.) The College M.A. fee is £1. The University charges you £3; in return you may take books out of the University Library, and will in two years time become a member of the Senate, which will entitle you to a vote on certain matters. It is true that they are not very important matters (Election of a Chancellor, Presentations to Livings, and the like), and that weightier proposals are voted on in the Regent

House; true also that the machinery for appealing from the R.H. to the Senate, though it exists, is so cumbersome that the Commissioners who made it can hardly even have intended it to work; but as under the present dispensation it is the rarest thing for a proposal to be contested even in the R.H., you need not feel yourselves unduly out in the cold on that account. You will observe that the College offers you more for your money than the University, but as the latter exists in part on degree-fees there is some piety in proceeding to the degree which will round off your University career. And I may add that you are getting it at a bargain price, for I had to pay about £20 for an article no more valuable, and moreover during the period of the present emergency you can take the degree by proxy without incurring the usual proxy fee of £3. Q. What is the Regent House? A. Under the statutes of 1926 it is composed (roughly speaking) of residents who are, or have been, actively concerned with teaching or administration in the University or Colleges. The title, however, is a revival (which will probably mislead in the future), for under the Elizabethan statutes, and down to 1856, it meant the lower of the two houses into which the Senate was divided. It then consisted of all M.A.'s under five, and all Doctors under two, years' standing, together with certain officials; and proposals did not come before it until they had first been unanimously approved by the small council of six called the Caput, and then passed in the Non-Regent House — a method of legislation which, whatever else it may have achieved, must at least have secured that nothing was done in undue haste.

The Middle East seems less interested in degrees than in the case of Mr Downing set out in no. 36, and I have been asked thence whether I think he had really cheated in the Tripos. I can, however, say no more than that there was an obvious prima facie case against him. Exactly how strong it was would take more time to estimate than I was disposed to devote to the question whether a man now dead cheated in an examination held before I was born; and in any case the details of the defence are not on record. I ought, by the way, not to have said that my father had ceased to be a Fellow when he was asked to act as a referee. I had forgotten that he held under old statutes, and therefore did not vacate until his marriage two years later.

12.12.42

Term ended on December 5 and in retrospect might be counted agreeable. Chestnuts and limes lost their leaves before the end of October, but with an absence of sharp frosts and of high winds the elms and most other trees kept many of theirs a full month longer; and as there have been some fine sunny days the Backs have at intervals been looking very lovely. Hereabouts it has been a remarkable year for quinces and medlars, and it is sad that the circumstances of the times have probably prevented most of them from reaching their proper destination in jam and jelly pots. I wouldn't say that I have found the term altogether agreeable myself, because, apart from a hot-water bottle for the hands (or rather wrists, for they are the vulnerable point), I did not until it was ended allow myself any artificial heating in my rooms. This you may put down at choice to patriotism or pig-headedness, for I have a sufficient equipment of both to account for it, but I attribute it myself mostly to the latter quality, and I have little doubt that if I had rooms which could be made comfortably warm and not merely less cold I should not have persisted. Nor perhaps should I have done so if the newspapers since the beginning of November had been less full of calories.[1] As it was, though cheerless, I have not found it intolerable except perhaps late at night, when, if I am reading and not writing, I have been apt to take my book to the Combination Room. My principal stand-by has been a motor driving-rug with a strap round the waist which prevents it from falling off when I get up to consult a book. This inestimable garment is blue in colour and has a median pocket, and thus imparts to me some resemblance on the one hand to a butcher and on the other to a female kangaroo, though art has here improved upon nature by equipping the pocket with a zip-fastener. Naturally I have had a bad cold, but I should presumably have had that in any case. Chilblains set in by mid-October. During the last two winters I have attacked these with calcium, which was not wholly without effect since it gave me a slight sore-throat. On the chilblains, however, it had none, and this year I have substituted halibut-liver oil capsules, at the mere taste of which they vanished incontinently. Fellow-sufferers take note of this, and consult your biochemical friends on the effect of Vitamin D on calcium-assimilation which is no fit theme for the P.M.

[1] The Eighth Army, advancing from el Alamein on Nov. 4, had reached el Agheila; hostilities in Madagascar ceased on Nov. 5; Allied forces landed in French N. Africa on Nov. 8; heavy naval losses inflicted on the Japanese in the Solomon Islands were announced on Nov. 16 and 19; Stalingrad was relieved on Nov. 24.

Term began with the usual scurry and fuss to recruit for College A.R.P. services and get them at once into working order. The Fire Party had, indeed, been working on a reduced scale throughout the vac., and a First Aid Party was functioning within a couple of days of the beginning of term, but there are now close on a hundred and fifty people assigned to one College A.R.P. duty or another, and it was near the end of the month before I could sit back with all the lists complete. These labours were complicated by the fact that the Regional Commissioner had ordered a big Civil Defence exercise in the Borough at the end of the first week. The incident handed out to us was formidable — the Library and D Nevile's Ct on fire and people trapped in the latter; the Hall also on fire. It was, in fact, too formidable, for an amateur party cannot be expected to cope with two major fires at once, and if this really happened we should have to call for the N.F.S. at the outset, whereas in the exercise we were not allowed to do so until the umpire gave the word. However we did our best, and, though some things went wrong, as they always must, the F.P. put up what I thought a very creditable show. By the time the N.F.S. arrived we were deemed to have extinguished the first fire and had five branches playing on the Hall. By then the Hall was no doubt burnt out, and this, though regrettable in itself, was probably some relief to the Junior Bursar since at the Bursars' inquest next morning he had not to submit a scheme for feeding those hypothetically in need of hospitality. Had you walked through the College on a Sunday afternoon ten days later you would have come upon a massed stirrup-pump practice with some 40 s.p.'s attacking imaginary incendiaries from behind the pillars of Nevile's Ct — an impressive and unusual scene. It was, indeed, unprecedented, but I have been taking my staircase-marshals' organisation more seriously than heretofore, thinking that if we had a lot of simultaneous fires in College amateur parties could at least hold some of them at bay until reinforcements arrived. With the same idea in mind I might have been found a fortnight later supervising in the greater privacy of the Lodge garden a s.p. practice for the Master, his wife, and his domestic staff.

Since I am no longer a Tutor, and since you learnt in my last that I have a good deal less supervision to do, your agile imaginations will no doubt have pictured me devoting most of my time to research; and my immortal work has indeed lain on my table and been pecked at from time to time. But the tutorship, though a tax on time, was also a good excuse for declining other corvées, one of which was examining in Entrance Scholarships; and with this I am now occupied. Moreover if you have too many engagements Providence, having no option, arranges that some of them clash; and free of tutorial hours I have been freer to keep appointments for which they have hitherto provided an unimpeachable alibi. Consequently I have been more regular in attendance at fire practices; and as there are six squads, each of which has a weekly practice, regular attendance has taken up a good many hours. I have, besides, been more assiduous in climbing St John's Chapel tower to encourage my observers posted there; and this, besides taking time, is exhausting, for it is up about two hundred steps, and the top two-thirds of the ascent are by the steepest and narrowest spiral staircase known to man. If anyone hereafter mentions the Bloody Tower to me, it will not be that in which the Little Princes were smothered of which I shall think first, and I frequently point out to the Fellows of that great foundation that any decent College owning such a tower would long ago have equipped it with a lift.

This no. carries with it, and will, as usual, deliver very late to some, all my best wishes for Christmas and the New Year. It carries also my hopes that you will go on writing to me. Your letters have been a real pleasure through the many dark months of 1942, and they will be no less welcome in 1943 when I trust such months may be fewer. I shall offer no speculations on the future, but Horace, as you may remember, observes that if your route lies either through the sweltering Syrtes or through the inhospitable Caucasus your best protection is integrity of life and innocence from crime — and neither Hitler nor that bloated exhibitionist in the Palazzo Venezia seems very well equipped for the journey.

FORTY-FIRST LETTER

25.12.42

I NEVER mention the annual Fellowship election at this College (as I did last in no. 39) without receiving enquiries as to how this mysterious rite is celebrated, and since I see no prospect of any other matter to fill this vacation issue I shall at last answer them. It is a College affair, but may be entitled *The Mysterious University: appendix* (or *epimetrum*, if you prefer) 1.

In normal times there are, under the present dispensation, usually four Fellowships on offer, and fifteen to twenty candidates, each of whom has submitted a dissertation. The case of each has been entrusted to an elector in his own subject, who handles it at electors' meetings; and each dissertation is reported on by at least one other person — an elector if one is competent, or a referee, who may be asked to attend the electors' meetings in order to answer questions. The reports on all candidates are circulated to all electors before they meet. At the first meeting the candidates are gone through, each elector speaking on the man or men for whom he is responsible and answering questions from other electors. This meeting usually last about three hours and it is pretty exhausting, but by the end it is always plain that a certain number of the candidates are not in the running, and usually plain that one or perhaps two have outstanding claims and will certainly be elected. Sometimes one can make a shrewd guess also at a third. A week-end intervenes between the two meetings, during which it may be necessary to collect further evidence on some of the dissertations. At the second meeting the election takes place. Probably the weaklings are withdrawn by their representatives almost at once and the outstanding candidates are elected quite soon; the real trouble begins over those left competing for the remaining places. Their representatives are closely cross-examined by the other electors; the cases gradually grow a bit clearer; a third is elected; and ultimately, after much searching of heart, a fourth. You may say that as between four candidates whose dissertations deal respectively with, let us imagine, the manuscripts of Palaephatus, the interior of the fixed stars, the fungoid diseases of cereals, and the administration of a mediaeval monastery, there is no basis of comparison; and of course this is the difficulty which makes electing such anxious and arduous work. On the other hand all the electors really want to get the best man and are therefore not apt to press their own candidates beyond their proper worth; and also by the time the last places are reached there is a number of electors whose men are either elected or withdrawn, and these form a nucleus who can devote their whole attention to the cases presented by those who still have cases to present. It doesn't sound very satisfactory, but I have elected a good many times in the last seventeen years and I can truthfully say that though I have often thought the last man out a little unlucky not to get a Fellowship I have only once thought him better than the last man in.

The election, as you see, is based essentially on the dissertations. In addition to these, however, the candidates have, in peace-time, done two three-hour papers, one mildly philosophical, the other on general aspects of literature, art, and history, which all the electors have read. In theory the answers should help to decide between two candidates otherwise indistinguishable, but in practice they hardly ever do, and as they are a nuisance to candidates and electors alike and there was talk even before the war of abolishing them, I expect and hope they are now dead. The electors also have before them the academic records of the men, but to these they pay no more attention than they would, if they knew them, to their personal characters or habits — indeed an elector who drew attention to the fact that somebody had failed in a Tripos would probably advance the chances of the candidate in question, and one who said that he had an odious temper or ate peas with a knife would cause such a reaction as almost to secure the man's election — though I am not suggesting that the rarity of these characteristics among the Fellows is wholly due to the discreet silence of electors.

It is an odd affair, and of course there is an unavoidable element of luck. A good man may be running in an unusually hot field and fail to come in; or he may have been unlucky in his choice of research and find after two years that a seemingly promising line led nowhere — and in some subjects, Classics in particular, it is uncommonly hard to find problems from which a young man can hope to produce valuable results in two years. Still, in spite of all this, the machinery works. If one surveys past fields after an interval of years it is possible to point to men who were unlucky for one of the above reasons, and to others who have developed later in life qualities they did not show at 24 or 25; possible also to point to others whose early promise has not been sustained — for, as Degas remarked in another connexion, 'tout le monde a du talent à vingt-cinq ans; la difficulté est d'en avoir à cinquante'. But taking the long and the large I do not think it can be denied that the record vindicates the system.

I have received a number of Christmas cards from parishioners, for which I hereby return thanks, and among them several Christmas Greetings Letter-cards from the M.E.F. As to these I hope I shall not seem ungrateful, or give the senders the impression that I was not pleased to have their good wishes, when I say that if I sat in the H. of C. I should ask the Postmaster General who conceived the idea that a galleon in full sail across a map of Asia Minor would be a suitable emblem for the occasion, and who framed the incoherent sentiment which accompanies it; also who is Edgar Longman who apparently executed the design, and whether he is responsible for the lettering of almost unexampled horror set about it. I have long suspected that we are not a truly artistic race.

15.1.43

Term began two days ago but shall rest in peace while I record the few events of the vacation. No. 40 was sent out during the intervals of a scholarship examination which reached its conclusion on Dec. 17 — candidates rather more numerous than last year and of decent quality. (I loathe examining of all kinds and see with some dismay that the new regulations for calling up will probably compel us to hold another Entrance Scholarship exam. sometime in the summer.) The following day was spent in interviewing R.A.F. Cadets in danger of being withdrawn from the course. A hectic week therefore, which was made worse by coinciding with a week of Warden's duty, for when I sleep in my clothes I sleep ill. Further, I was denied a long lie on the following Sunday by the Regional Commissioner who elected to set our Library alight at 8 a.m. as a little surprise for the N.F.S.; and by the College Fire Party who, having in any case to be there, decided to play for a while with their own fire before their big brothers came and took it from them, and so caused me to be abroad by 7.30. Here, however, we displayed some excess of zeal, for the N.F.S. did not arrive until 9.45, by which time the umpire had deemed us to have extinguished the fire and to have earned our breakfasts. The moral is: Burn early if burn you must, for the early incident catches the N.F.S. — though 8 a.m. seemed early enough to me.

Recovered from all this, I spent the interval before Christmas in setting half a Tripos paper on a subject in which there are few possible questions and most were asked by me last year. Christmas passed tranquilly enough. Quite a decent dinner, though the plum-pudding had obviously felt the pinch; and rather more guests than usual, including a dozen undergraduate firemen, one of whom did not like oysters and was mercifully sitting next me. Thereafter I fell to my books and got through a certain amount of rather drudging work until Jan. 5 when I had to go to London for two nights. I brought little news thence for I was too lame to get about much, and the weather being inclement transport was correspondingly more difficult. There is, however, an excellent show of 19th century French painting at the National Gallery. It contains some eighty pictures, and so far as the second half of the century is concerned the standard is high. There are admirable works by Degas, and by Renoir, who is rather better represented than the other Impressionists strictly so-called: and these two would in any case hold my eye even in a full-dress peace-time show of the same period. But Cézanne, if you are among the idolators, is probably better represented than either, and so is Camille Pissarro, a painter I find it easier to respect than to enjoy. In short, the most refreshing exhibition there has been since the war.

On returning from London I found the temperature of my rooms well below 40, and decided that I had done my duty by the Fuel Controller, having had a fire on the last two evenings of the year in honour of a parishioner who was staying with me but having otherwise contented myself with my hot-water bottle. I take no pride in this — indeed, as I said in my last letter, I regard it as idiotic; and I make no pretence of having been comfortable. But, when all allowances have been made for the mildness of the winter up to date, I am surprised how little real hardship it has involved. However, having now switched on my electric radiator, I shall try and keep at least my evening temperature nearer 50 than 40.

FORTY-SECOND LETTER

31.1.43

Term began, as I said in my last, on Jan. 13, but up to date it has produced lamentably little to write about. The number of freshmen matriculated was 138 — about a hundred less than at this time last year, though our own entry — 28 — was up by four. I do not know how many went down, but it may be safely assumed that the population is rather larger than it was last term both in the University and the College. It is, however, a very temporary increase so far as these freshmen are concerned for apart from a few medicals and technicians none are likely to be here for more than two terms. I received at the end of last term a document showing the number of men reading different subjects, from which I learnt that, excluding six-month Cadets, there were 786 men reading Natural Sciences and Medicine, and 463 Engineers; and that apart from these only three other faculties had more than a hundred male students — History, Modern Languages, and Mathematics, who mustered between them 412. I gave comparable figures a year ago, from which it seems that scientists have since then diminished a bit, engineers remained steady; also that mathematicians have risen to the century, but that lawyers and classics have dropped from it. No doubt the rise in mathematics and the drop in scientists are correlative and mean merely that more men are starting with mathematics on the way to physics. The fall in Arts students is general and more significant; and here the prospects for next year are pretty grim, for the Ministry of Labour seems quite firm in declining to allow any further postponement of service for any but technicians. There will be, I suppose, a certain number of women; what men will be here is quite uncertain at present but they can only be aliens, the unfit, and probably a few who come up young with no expectation of lasting out the year. One cannot complain — indeed we may congratulate ourselves on having survived four years as well as we have; but it is devoutly to be hoped that the flow will be allowed to start again as soon as it possibly can, for it will not be a very brave new world in which only the scientists and engineers have completed their education.

I do not know whether you saw in the *Times* about three weeks ago a rather mischievous letter saying that in the larger Universities, this among them, only 50-60% of the men in residence were undergoing military training. The figures supplied were true so far as they went, but they were quite misleading because they made no mention of the H.G. and of Civil Defence Services; and as the medicals and many other technicians are destined for non-combatant services they have very properly been directed to discharge their obligations of part-time national service by joining these rather than the S.T.C., which has its hands quite full enough in equipping those who will need it with Certificate B. The real number of men unaccounted for is here almost exactly 10% and I have no doubt that it is almost wholly composed of aliens and the unfit. Admittedly service in the H.G. is somewhat less onerous than that in the S.T.C., but, whatever it may mean elsewhere, it here means a regular five hours weekly with frequent but less regular addenda. Almost all the men concerned are engaged in squeezing three years work into two, and most of them are also involved in A.R.P. duties in their Colleges or the University for which they are not legally liable. I do not think, therefore, that anyone need worry about undergraduates not being adequately occupied. My own worry for a long time past has been that they can hardly call their souls their own, and are therefore missing a good deal of what in more spacious times the University has to offer them.

13.2.43

News is still in short supply, and I continue with snippets.

A faintly humorous situation has arisen over the Botanic Garden, which has long been a Cinderella among University institutions and dependent to a considerable extent on private subscriptions. One Reginald Cory, a former member of this College who lived for a while in Cambridge, took a great interest in the B.G., was a generous benefactor, and married, I think, a lady employed in them. Subject to certain large annuities, he bequeathed his estate to the University for the B.G., £30,000 to be for upkeep, the rest for general purposes other than upkeep. When he died in 1934, however, the income of the estate was insufficient to pay the annuities, and though the B.G. could look forward to a valuable endowment when the annuitants died, it has hitherto been no better off than before. Cory owned, among other property, a number of shares in a family business which had never paid a dividend. Recently the brother who managed this business died, the business was sold, and the shares, to which at R.C.'s death only a nominal value had been attached for probate, brought in £350,000. Consequently the B.G. will now receive annually for upkeep something over £1000, and about £8,000, rising when the annuities end to £12,000, for general purposes – the largest pecuniary bequest the University has ever received. It is, of course, more than the B.G. needs, but though one may regret that some of it was not left to other University purposes, we are all glad that Cinderella should have found her fairy godfather at last. The aspect which is faintly humorous is that the money available for upkeep is far too small to maintain the buildings or extensions which will result from the annual expenditure of the larger sum; and unless the lawyers succeed in extracting this substantial fly from the ointment the result of the benefaction might be to put the University to great expense. However I have the utmost confidence in the capacity of lawyers to thwart the express instructions of testators; and meanwhile the subscribers to the B.G. (of whom I was one) have received the unusual but not unwelcome invitation to discontinue their subscriptions.

A British Restaurant lunch, you will perhaps be relieved to hear, is no longer served in Hall, that organisation having foundered midway between Scylla or the Ministry of Food and Charybdis or the Borough Council. First of all S. said that though the undergraduates of King's and Clare might have a B.R. lunch in our Hall, our own undergraduates might not because they resided on the premises. Then C. said that the scheme for these three Colleges had not sufficiently relieved the pressure on the other B.R.'s in the town, and that it proposed to annex the Hall and use it as a B.R. open *urbi et orbi*. Since S. had by now withdrawn its objection this would have meant that we could indeed lunch in Hall; but as our own kitchen staff would inevitably have given notice it would also have meant that we got no other meal during the day. On this point S. was quite reasonable, and C. was firmly told that it had no power to commandeer our premises and that this was the place at which it got off. So, after a deal of palaver and waste of time, we reverted to an offer, made before all the fuss began, to provide lunch for fifty undergraduates from other Colleges — a generous offer, for it is some trouble and no advantage to us. King's to whom it was first made, have, however, responded but coyly to our advances, and as I go to press the Steward is turning his glad eye also towards Clare. So far as the congestion in town restaurants is caused by undergraduates the situation would be met if those Colleges which cannot provide lunch came to such terms as these with those that can, included lunch in their weekly charges, and sacrificed for the duration the inalienable right of the undergraduate to lunch where and how he pleases; but I suppose the truth to be that in these parts at any rate the restaurant problem is getting out of hand. The B.R.'s and all the little restaurants mentioned in no. 38 were meant for war-workers who could not conveniently get home to lunch, but others, who could, have discovered that by lunching out they can save labour and make their domestic rations go further. Consequently they lunch out. Then the Ministry of Food, partly in consequence, reduces domestic rations, increases the temptation, and swells the numbers who fall to it — and, in short, there is set up what economists are too wont to call a vicious spiral.

I have been reading *Pilote de Guerre*, by Antoine de Saint Exupéry — sketches of the fall of France and reflections thereon, for the most part as they present themselves to a pilot on a desperate and futile reconnaissance flight (*Flight to Arras* is the title of a translation which I see in the book-shops). It is a vivid and moving book — much more vivid than any of the more objective accounts I have read; and though the flight is hardly more than background it is good, for St E., as I said once before in these pages, writes well about flying. He is, indeed, the only writer known to me who does so. I suppose the difficulties of the subject are much less obvious to a professional airman than they are to those who, like me, take to the air but seldom, and usually with ample attention to spare for their surroundings; but a terribly difficult subject it is all the same. So, no doubt, is the sea; but long centuries of familiarity have thrown up a few prose-writers who could manage it, and probably the air will in time do the like. So far I have encountered nothing in English worth considering, and I have been sorry to see fighter-pilots in so much haste to write books — sorry, not surprised, for with such tales to tell the temptation is obviously strong, and if their discretion outweighed their valour they would not be fighter-pilots. Still, it is a pity that matter which in the naked sentences of a log-book or report-form would hold one breathless should be bedizened or bedrabbed into insignificance by writers who are necessarily too inexperienced to see the full difficulty of the task they have taken on themselves. However I admit that I have no more than dipped into one or two of their books and that I may have been unlucky (I do not remember their names and should not tell you if I did), and I am pulling my coat over my ears against the deluge of protest which I expect these remarks to provoke.

FORTY-THIRD LETTER

13.3.43

Term ends today, but even by turning my retrospective gaze beyond its beginning I cannot see very much material for this letter.

It has been a very mild winter. A few cold days in January caused me to cut off the water from my bathroom, which I cannot protect from frost and have in any case vacated in the cause of fuel-economy, but they had no sequel. Aconites were well out by mid-January; snowdrops and even crocuses making a display before the end of the month; the willows on our Backs, which still had a few leaves at Christmas, showing a faint mist of green a month later. Apparently, however, our particular strain of willows is exceptional in this amiable characteristic for I have noticed that aliens bought in recent years from nurserymen lost their last leaves a full month earlier and are also much less precocious. However we now have our own nursery for these short-lived trees and shall in future supply replacements from the old stock. And, talking of willows, I watched at very close quarters in December a woodpecker (greater spotted) making three holes about the size of teacups in the one at the north end of the Library—a business I do not associate with mid-winter. I take no sides in the seemingly everlasting dispute whether a woodpecker drums by hammering with its beak or vocally, but the statement that the noise is identical whatever the consistency of the wood on which it is at work (and that it must therefore be produced vocally) was given the lie by this particular bird. The only other ornithological note I can muster is that for the first time I have seen a swan in the Great Ct. It landed in the Bowling Green, and being unable to take off wandered into the Court and was meditating on one of the grass-plots. A fire-squad then practising was about to come and steer it waterwards when one of the gardeners, seizing it under each wing, deported it protesting feebly and threw it into the river. 'Wonderful lectern it would make' said a parson we passed en route. I record finally in this section a slight but general plague of mice in the Christmas vac. My own solitary specimen disregarded the traps which I set on either side of its hole, but undeterred by the failure of this pincer movement I annihilated it by a brilliantly executed attack *a posteriori* — or at least it was found dead by my bedmaker in the seat of my armchair.

My own avocations have followed their usual monotonous round of teaching, committees, and A.R.P., and I seem to have been busier than usual, or at least I have had less time for my own work and have been more tired at the end of the day, though the addenda don't amount to much — rather more teaching both in lectures and supervision, rather more regular attendance at Fire and First Aid Party practices (nine per week), Tripos papers to set. These are straws, but the dorsal concavity of this particular camel has been increasing noticeably of late. The only positively new burden has been the chairmanship of the Classical Board which I could no longer stave off on the grounds that I was Tutor; and though this has meant no increase in the number of meetings to attend (since I was regular in attendance before), a chairman must always devote a good deal of previous time to the agenda, and there happens this term to have been before Faculty Boards some rather troublesome business.

The usual business of Faculty Boards is little likely to interest the wider world to whom the P.M. is addressed, and is indeed seldom unduly exciting even to their members. 'I see the Classical Board yawn before me', said a historian preaching in our Chapel some years ago — or at least so the Dean thought. He was puzzled by this apocalyptic vision, for a historian is naturally not a member of that Board, and the C.B., however it may react to the allocutions of a colleague, might be trusted, he thought, to listen without open discourtesy to a stranger. However enquiry disclosed that it was not the Classical Board but the Chasm of War which had yawned. (What *is* the usual business of Faculty Boards? — *The Mysterious University: lesson* 10 — They appoint lecturers and examiners, fix schedules for examinations, compose lecture-lists, and in general organise University teaching in the subjects with which they are concerned. They also between them elect eight members of the General Board, whose full title is G.B. of the Faculties, and whose essential duty is to coordinate the practice of the nineteen different faculties.)

The unusual problem which has been perplexing them this term is the filling of vacant professorships and lectureships, of which I said something in no. 35. I revert to it now for it concerns the whole war-time policy of the University and has been taking up the time not only of Faculty Boards but also of the Council of the Senate and of the General Board — as well it might for it is not at all simple. It is not a problem which much concerns the existing needs of Faculties, for where a Chair has been vacant in a faculty which is working at full pressure and urgently needs the teaching-power or administration of a Professor steps have all along been taken to satisfy the need either by appointment or, where that has not been feasible, by making other arrangements. As regards the other Chairs, when appointments were suspended in 1939 the argument chiefly in our minds was financial; and since these three years have treated us more kindly than we then had right or reason to expect, this argument, though it still exists, has admittedly lost a good deal of its cogency. There is, however, another powerful argument for suspension, namely that in war-time you cannot be sure of getting the proper field of candidates. It is said that Boards of Electors have power to invite those who have not applied to stand, and so indeed they have; but, besides the objection that the electors can hardly ever be sure that they have not forgotten somebody, there is a difficulty which weighs more seriously with me. In peace-time a man comfortably established in a good post elsewhere must often find it very hard to make up his mind whether he shall or shall not apply for another which, though it may be somewhat better, will involve a move, a change of milieu, and the possibility of a less congenial and successful life than he is already leading. It seems to me that the uncertainties of the times must in such a case weight the scales heavily both against standing and against accepting if invited. On the other hand it is argued that since other Universities are filling their Chairs, some who should be here will go elsewhere; that faculties, though they can carry on without their proper Professors at present, may need them urgently and immediately at the end of the war, and will need not new-comers but men who have had time to learn the local ropes; that the task of filling twenty or more Chairs in a brief space of time will impose an intolerable burden on the Vice-Chancellor and the various electing bodies. And in these arguments there is much force. A fourth argument which, though little avowed, has weighed heavily with some, is that, since for one or two of the Chairs there is an obvious candidate who is certain to be elected, it is hard luck that he should be kept out of promotion by the suspension. This indeed answers, in the cases where it is true, the objection that you cannot be sure of getting the right field, but *per se* I think it a bad argument. There are necessarily as many potential Professors being kept out of promotion as there are professorships vacant; all are suffering, as a consequence of the war, that blighting and abbreviation of hopes and prospects which, in a greater or less degree, has come upon every one of us; and I do not think it a relevant consideration that the names of one or two such victims should be known, or that they should be, if they are, persons whom we chance to like or respect. However, the Council, after long pondering, asked those Faculty Boards which had a Chair vacant to state a case if they wanted it filled now. A good many did not want but we are about to try and fill six or seven. The ice being thus broken, the General Board, which has charge of lectureships but not of professorships, addressed a similar enquiry to the F.B.'s on that subject, but the results have not yet come to hand. The problem here is different though not easier, and you may hear more of it next term; but for the moment I judge you to have had enough of this.

I can't think of much other academic news, but you may like to know that for the time being mortar-boards are no longer an essential of academic dress because they are unobtainable. The Proctors, who had perhaps been reading what magistrates said to people who could not get batteries for their cycle-lamps, were rumoured to have had the bright idea that the situation would be met by reducing the fine for not wearing them to half-price. However the Council is capable of taking a realistic view, and on this occasion took it.

Diversions have been few. I have been to the cinema (for the first time since that mentioned in no. 28) to see *Coastal Command*, and thought well of it — better, in fact, than of the book so titled, though that too is quite interesting and contains some good photographs. I also watched quite an entertaining game of rugger, in which Oxford were defeated by a satisfactory margin (16-3), most of which, however, was compiled in the last ten minutes — as, from the spectators' point of view, it should be. The result was described by the *Oxford Magazine* as flattering to Cambridge; and in the matter of the margin perhaps it was. The same journal explained a similar result last term by the suggestion that most of the Cambridge side were probably evading military service.

News from the West (culled many months ago from *Life* and lately brought to light again): 'The average U.S. female is not only short (5 ft. 3 in. tall) but chunky (133 lbs.)'.

FORTY-FOURTH LETTER

28.3.43

THE Easter vac. no. is usually occupied in part with a list of books, which some parishioners seem to welcome but I welcome only because it tides over a dearth of other materials — for I am increasingly ashamed to confess to so desultory and unprofitable a course of reading. True, it represents only, or almost only, what I read in bed, and could be made to look less frivolous by the inclusion of the professional matter which occupies me by day (even by *Simple Hydraulics for Firemen* which catches my eye on the table at which I write); true also that the fault is partly due to reviewers. Nearly forty years ago Housman remarked at the end of a highly damaging review that a conscientious reviewer must feel some compunction at the thought that much worse books than he is slating 'are elsewhere receiving that vague and conventional laudation which is distributed at large, like the rain of heaven, by reviewers who do not know the truth and consequently cannot tell it'. (He consoled himself with the reflection that 'after all a portion of the universal shower is doubtless now descending, or will soon descend, upon Mr —— himself; and indeed, unless some unusual accident has happened, he must long ere this have received the punctual praises of the *Scotsman*'.) Still, I think things have grown much worse in recent years, and the sloppy notices which I see usually leave me in complete doubt whether a book is good, bad, or indifferent, well written or ill; often even of what it is about. Hence, it being impossible to choose from reviews the books worth reading, my literature is mostly picked at random from the Library shelves. Do not, however, suppose that I do not blush for it.

The most serious work I have read since my last list is W. W. Greg's *Editorial Problem in Shakespeare*, a very acute mind handling a problem of almost intolerable complexity — interesting, but not light reading, and coming near to the professional matter which I do not record. Of a historical character I have read a *History of Modern Greece* by E. S. Forster (short but informative), *The Legacy of Egypt* (essays, mostly good and readable, by various experts), *High Lights and Flights in New Guinea* by L. Rhys (in spite of a catchpenny title a serious account of the exploration and development of N.G.), Wavell's *Life of Allenby* (interesting, but did not persuade me that I should have liked A.), *Grey Eminence* by Aldous Huxley (about Father Joseph, Richelieu's Capuchin adviser: much belauded, but I should have preferred more of the subject and less of the author), Lord Cockburn's *Memorials* (Edinburgh society in the first thirty years of the 19th century; readable and sometimes amusing). The rest is almost entirely betwixt autobiography and reminiscence, and can be to some extent classified by subjects. About foreign parts: L. V. Cummings, *I was a Head-Hunter* (sensational but apparently true adventures in Colombia. Very readable if you like that kind of thing; but if you must use finite sentences for your titles I beseech you at least to abjure the first person); G. Klugel, *Inagua* (zoologising in the W. Indian island so named); M. Collis, *Trials in Burma* (the trials are mostly judicial); C. S. Jarvis, *Desert and Delta* (by an ex-governor of Sinai who writes an agreeable weekly page in *Country Life*); D. Lamson, *We who are about to die* (inside a Californian prison); A. M. Cleaveland, *No Life for a Lady* (an entertaining volume about ranching in New Mexico). Then four books mainly about Ireland: R. Conner, *A Plain Tale from the Bogs*; J. Eglinton, *Irish Literary Portraits*; L. Robinson, *Curtain Up* (mostly about the Abbey Theatre); E. Starkie, *A Lady's Child*. The last two are wholly devoid of Irish charm, and the last I should hardly have finished but for some interest in the author's father, an Irish civil servant and a Classical scholar of some distinction. (He was a member of this College, but I never met anyone here who knew him, and have never seen a book from his library — which is odd, for books from deceased scholars' libraries usually appear in second-hand catalogues and thence fill gaps on one's own shelves.) Two from Scotland: A. A. MacGregor, *Vanished Waters*; J. Curtis, *Mists and Monsoons* (the monsoons are Indian and less agreeable than the mists). Three from Oxford: H. Fisher, *Unfinished Autobiography* (rather disappointing); E. L. Woodward, *Short Journey*; A. L. Rowse, *Cornish Childhood* — the last two by Fellows of All Souls, both interesting, the former urbane, the latter in places disagreeably arrogant. Finally some oddments: F. Kitchen, *Life on the Land*; G. A. W. Tomlinson, *Coalminer*; M. Dickens, *One Pair of Hands* (highly coloured reminiscences of a lady cook). The only fiction to add is *The Moon is Down*, by J. Steinbeck, about the invasion of Norway — good, but hardly more than a short story; and *England is my Village*, by J. L. Rhys, short stories about flying recommended by a parishioner who took exception to my remarks on flying literature in no. 42. I did not, however, think it very good, and in any case it is mostly about pilots and machines, not about the air.

The only Penguin-like volume in this list is *Trials in Burma*, on the jacket of which you may read some pretty examples of the modern style of reviewing. Where I have said nothing of contents they may be discerned from the titles; and where nothing of merit you may assume the books to be readable; and indeed I have suppressed one or two which did not attain that modest standard. Still, after a while I grew weary as well as ashamed of this hand to mouth existence and for the last six weeks I have been engaged on the *Collections* of Thomas Hearne, which contain the journals and correspondence of that learned and industrious but embittered Oxford scholar and antiquary, extend from 1705 to 1735, and fill eleven substantial volumes of which I have now read seven. Much of them consists of extracts from books, copies of inscriptions, notes on coins, and the like — matter to be skimmed or skipped, and interesting for the most part only as contributing to the picture of his daily life; but they are enlivened by a good deal of gossip and scandal, and by H.'s venomous characterisations of people of whom he disapproved — a large body since it included almost all who were not

Jacobites and non-jurors like himself. Example of the first: the high-handed behaviour of Dr. Dobson, President of Trinity, who, being entitled by statute to expel from the College only *super crimine Haereseos, Simoniae, Perjurii manifesti, furti notabilis, Rapinae, Homicidii voluntarii, gravis percussionis socii vel (quod deterius est) ipsius Praesidentis*, nevertheless expelled Mr Henry Knollys, a Fellow-Commoner, against whom (according to his supporters) no more was alleged than that 'he laugh'd in the Chapell of the said College at the time of the Divinity Disputations and that he kick'd at the Cat of Thomas Hasker, Clerk and Bursar of the said Coll., which Cat (as it was said) ran afterwards into the Chapell'. Examples of the second: 'Oct. 6, 1709. This day, at one of the Clock, that old, hypocritical, ambitious, drunken sot, Will. Lancaster, Provost of Queen's College, was admitted Vice-Chancellour'; 'James Parkinson, A.M., Fellow of Linc. Coll., a rank, stinking Whigg, who us'd to recommend Milton and such other Republican Rascalls to his Pupills'; 'Mr. Rob. Watts, of St John's Coll., a busy, pragmatical, conceited, confident Coxcomb, and son of a Profess'd Presbyterian.' (I fear I am too apt to harbour such rancorous thoughts as these myself, but I cannot envisage myself setting them down on paper day by day, and as T. H. seems with advancing years to be growing, if not sweeter-tempered, at least more reticent, I doubt if I shall pursue him to the end.)

17.4.43

I sent out no. 43 on the last day of last term, which was also our Commemoration and celebrated by a pleasant small dinner attended by an unusual number of ex-Fellows. I cannot summarise for you the Commemoration sermon which should have preceded it for there was none, but in case you should be disappointed in this I append a memorable thought from one preached many years ago in St Catherine's by the Rev. W. T. Southward, Tutor of that College, who died in 1920: 'Had it not been for the learning, the liberality, and the piety of these men, we might still be worshipping Mercury, the ingenious pilferer, Mars, the indiscriminate butcher, and Venus, the blasée adulteress' ('What was it he called her?' said an undergraduate on the way out of Chapel: 'a blasted adulteress?'.) Vacation set in for me on the following morning like a lion, for from 10 a.m. on Sunday until 4 p.m. on Wednesday I was engaged in interviewing R.A.F. Cadets and recommending them (or not) for commissions at the end of their course. A board consisting of two

Directors of Studies and a Wing-Commander, with me as President, was charged with this duty when these courses started, and though it was largely time wasted (since the great majority of the Cadets get adequate reports and the recommendation is automatic), it was then no great matter for there were only sixty of them. Now there are three hundred and it is far past a joke — so far indeed that I have told the Air Ministry that it really can't be done in future. The same Board has also to interview during the course those Cadets who seem likely to fail or are in other ways unsatisfactory — often a troublesome and disagreeable business, for some of them are men with good officer qualities and desperately keen whom one has to send away because they will never get through the technical subjects. This term there are to be two hundred Naval Cadets and I shall have to discharge the same office for them, sitting this time with a Lieut. R.N.V.R. in place of the Wing-Commander — though I hope and think that here there will be less to do.

At this point I was chewing my pen (only it was a typewriter) in the effort to recollect what had happened since those sessions, when it occurred to me that I had already written quite enough; and so it proved. The product of my deliberations is therefore put by for a month, but I warn you to expect no delirious excitement from it for, apart from a couple of days in town, I haven't been away.

FORTY-FIFTH LETTER

18.4.43

THE end of the last issue left me at the very beginning of the vac., when I would willingly have gone away for the weather was singularly inviting and I was sick of Cambridge. However my arthritic joints fell on me with such violence towards the end of last term that I could scarcely hobble to the end of the Avenue, and though they have let up a little since, I had nowhere in particular to go, and no inclination to tether myself to a chair in a hotel lounge, so I stayed here except for two days in London largely spent in Turkish baths. In the intervals of these I saw some friends and crawled round some picture galleries but found nothing very memorable in them; though if you are interested in utility clothes a room full of them affronted my eye at the Victoria and Albert Museum when I was on my way to look at a loan collection of drawings. Since all the lesser dealers of Europe seem now to be congregated in

London, galleries and auction-rooms are over-congested with groups of little men muttering together in hoarse gutturals, and what pictures there are are hard to see and often prove to be what one saw three months ago somewhere else. However if the stationary pictures were dull the one movie I went to — *Desert Victory* — was not; I thought it a most impressive film, and it is equipped with a commentary both instructive and restrained. It made me think a lot about parishioners and other friends in the Eighth Army (though I think about them a good deal anyhow), and feel even more wormlike than usual. This is my second film in three months, my previous average being about one in three years. Do not, however, cherish the hope, or fear, that I am becoming a fan, for I was so nauseated with the quarter of an hour which, owing to my mistiming, preceded *Desert Victory* that I stayed the course with difficulty.

In Cambridge it has, in a tranquil way, not been unpleasant, for the spring has so far been of astounding beauty — lovely clear days and warm sun. The flowers have been rather below average — I suppose we have not replenished our bulbs for some years and time or mice begin to tell; in particular I have been hard put to it to find a fritillary, which is rather a favourite of mine. Still, crocuses and daffodils, if below par, have been good, and blossom naturally hasn't suffered from the war, so that I was, I dare say, as happy here as I should have been elsewhere, and incidentally got through a good deal of work, mostly on the composition of a paper for a learned journal. Nothing very much happened but the University and College have suffered a severe blow by the death of the Registrary, Ernest Harrison, whom some of you probably knew. He went out for his usual evening stroll and fell dead in the course of it — an enviable death, but it leaves the University in a difficulty, for the business of the Registry will be hard for a new man to pick up without a predecessor to initiate him, especially at a time when we welter in emergency regulations and war-time committees. E.H. was, too, a Classical scholar of the first rank and had edited the *Classical Review* with extraordinary competence for twenty years; and he will be a loss to the College, particularly to the Classical staff, who have the salutary habit of submitting their learned works to a colleague before they loose them on the world and were wont to profit much from his critical mind and punctilious accuracy. He had been a friend of mine for nearly forty years and I shall miss him a good deal.

Term began on Apr. 19 (on which day I was woken by a first and too importunate cuckoo), and, as you see, I had written down impressions of the vac. before the shades of the prison house should close about me and obliterate them, for I foresaw that I should be busy. Term brought with it after a day or two some needed rain but an unwelcome return of cold weather and a long spell of high wind which blew the top off an elm in front of St John's new building and cut short the life of the blossom. The cherries in our avenue were still wearing white for Eastertide but it was a somewhat battered and bedraggled white, and, what with early spring and late Easter, decorations in churches were mostly of lilac and tulips — which must be very unusual.

The University happens to have some rather heavy business on hand and meetings of the Council and General Board have therefore been long and weary. The death of the Registrary has made it necessary to look into the relations and duties of the three officers housed in the University Offices — the Registrary, Secretary General, and Treasurer — and make some adjustments of Ordinances before proceeding to the appointment of a new Registrary; there is a troublesome question about the future of Addenbrooke's Hospital and its relations with the University Medical School, and this is entangled with the vacancy in the Regius Professorship of Physic since it will affect the duties and prospects of a new Professor when appointed — and there are other matters of like difficulty which weary me but need not also weary you. Meanwhile the Vice-Chancellor wears a harassed look because he is, as reported in no. 43, trying to elect some new Professors and is not finding it easy. The electors are required by statute to meet at least twice and on separate days, and since, also by statute, all Boards contain at least two non-resident electors, meetings are usually held in the afternoon of one day and on the following morning (compare the practice of the ancient Persians who were wont to reconsider when sober the conclusions reached when drunk, and vice versa). But in cases of difficulty two meetings are often not enough, and what with electors being busy or out of the country, the task of collecting a quorum on any one day is proving very difficult.

The Fitzwilliam has on view some French pictures (Cézanne, Renoir, etc.) collected by Lord Rothschild, and some English (Gainsborough, Reynolds, and the like) collected, I suppose, by his grandfather. It has also some minor Italian from its own stores, and a rather amusing room of paintings, drawings, and what-nots, of animals, gathered from various sources. As I don't seem to have mentioned the Fitzw. lately I may say that I think it is still doing more than other galleries to keep the flag flying in very difficult conditions. Also that it had earlier in the year two rooms of the Tate Gallery's wartime accessions selected from a larger display which I mentioned a year ago when it was on view at the National Gallery. This last collection, and the Rothschild pictures, came here under the auspices of the Council for the Encouragement of Music and the Arts, commonly called C.E.M.A., a more or less official body (its exact nature is still mysterious to me) which is at present engaged in making a splash. I see its initials on theatre and concert bills besides on those of exhibitions, and I think it may discharge a useful function; but in these parts there are at present too many people engaged in splashing, and as the ripples they create are by no means concentric the Fitzw., though glad to have these shows, has been put to a good deal of unnecessary trouble over them.

As for me, I am, as I foresaw, busy. I have rather more teaching to do than last term (because one of my colleagues is helping in the depleted Registry), proofs of Tripos papers begin to come in, and A.R.P. pursues its usual course. A good deal of extra time has been and will be taken up by a scheme for coordinating the fire defences of all College and University buildings, under which an N.F.S. officer (who is in normal times Professor of Hebrew) controls all parties and when he judges the attack to be at an end sends out pumps and personnel from the undamaged sites to those which need help. It is quite a good scheme but it is not nearly so simple to get going as the gallant General in the Regional Commissioner's office who invented it supposes; and though we have now been stewing over it for a good many months there is still a tangle of loose strings lying about and waiting to be tied up. We, Trinity, said that in view of our large area and the importance of the Library we could not agree to send our pump off the premises on the possibly mistaken conviction of the N.F.S. that the danger was at an end, but that if they would help us to obtain another pump we would do our best to man two and hold one at the disposal of the control. Consequently the N.F.S. have lent us a second pump until we get one of our own and also an elderly Ford V 8 which is to tow it about the town in case of need. You may see a little grey home built to house the pump under the Clock Tower, and might for a while have seen the Ford on the cobbles outside the Great Gate. But if you want to put out a fire you need water as well as a pump, and the new one is mounted on a chassis meant to be towed and therefore too wide to go through the doors and passages between the Great Ct and the river. Hence the little grey home now houses the old pump (for which we had originally built a special chassis adapted to the eyes of needles), and the Ford is in the New Ct. Among the problems set by this scheme and despised by the General was that after four years of petrol-restrictions the number of undergraduates really competent to drive a car is extremely small. I may add, by the way, that a knowledge of Hebrew is not the only, or even the chief, qualification of the N.F.S. officer at the head of the scheme, for he was, inter alia, a rugger international.

P.S. I have taken to my bed with lumbago and as I can't sit up this will have to go out without the usual word of personal greetings. I am sorry for this but it can't be helped.

FORTY-SIXTH LETTER

23.5.43

No. 45 was sent out at the end of the second week of May — a week full of good news, not unexpected but not expected quite so soon by me or, I think, by most in England though those in the know seem to have had a pretty shrewd idea of the right date.[1] The First and Eighth Armies have received some handsome bouquets from the Great in various continents and my small garland will be faded by the time it is added to the pile, but I hope parishioners in those forces will accept it as none the less sincere for that. I did not look to see how the *New Statesman* bore the news, but admirers of that journal (and possibly one or two others as well) will remember that less than a year ago it was advocating the abandonment of Egypt. (July 4, 1942: 'We should not waste our limited forces too prodigally in an attempt to delay the occupation of Egypt. We shall need every tank and gun we have got to hold Palestine and Syria.')

No. 45 I couldn't send out with my own hand, having been, as I said, struck down with lumbago — a humiliating complaint, for, when any

[1] Resistance to the Allies in N. Africa ceased on May 13.

movement may be rewarded by a jab of excruciating pain, you scarcely dare to move at all, and at the same time your gingerly attempts provoke the most charitable observers to un-Christian merriment. Anyhow, I had, as I thought, defeated a mild onset when a formidable counter-attack developed in a moment, and with great difficulty (and the aid of a porter for whom I telephoned) I got myself dinnerless into bed. My bedroom, however, though a very nice room for ordinary purposes, is too dark for all-day habitation, and no College bedroom is a good place for one who might perhaps be able to manoeuvre himself out of bed but would have little assurance of getting back if he did so. Consequently, after thirty-six hours there, I had myself carried groaning downstairs by two stout Borough Ambulance men (I confess to having been glad that I was not dependent on the College First Aid Party), and was trundled away in a tempest of wind and rain to the Evelyn Nursing Home where I could be properly looked after and could ring the bell for somebody to stand by if I was contemplating any adventure. Once there I was happy enough lying abed and indulging in luxurious thoughts about the meetings, fire-practices, and other diversions from which I was absenting myself — for when red-hot needles are menacing the small of your back the prick of conscience ceases to be perceptible. As a matter of fact a short stay in a Nursing Home is a real rest, for one drops all responsibilities at the door and resigns oneself to eating lightly, sleeping heavily, and being looked after; and since in these circumstances one takes up a novel after breakfast without awakening the sense of sin, you will find a good deal more fiction in the next Literary Supplement than is usual there. It is true the day begins disagreeably early, but you can end it when you choose, and, once my complaint had subsided sufficiently to enable me to move a bit more freely, I enjoyed the relaxation, especially during the last six days, which were radiantly fine and hot and were spent by me in an armchair in the garden. I restored myself to circulation yesterday, without enthusiasm, for I am still pretty stiff and sore, but I could at a pinch have come a little earlier. However, since Triposes begin to-morrow, it was not worth while to resume my lectures, and a day or two more in the sun seemed well worth the skin off my nose which was their price.

I emerged from the Evelyn capable, given time, of dressing myself and of shuffling round to necessary rendez-vous, but not in very riotous form and expecting a leisurely week in which to form some opinion as to the answers to the questions in Part 2 of the Tripos, and no great labour thereafter in correcting them; for there were only nineteen candidates and I had but one paper from these and two from a section of three to correct. However a Professor who should have been chairman of the examiners had meanly jockeyed me into that position, and not having occupied it before I did not at the time realise that I was being had for a mug. I have now learnt that it involves a good deal of responsibility, and in particular that one has to calculate the amount to be paid to each examiner — for in this exam. at any rate the University assigns to the examination a lump sum together with a payment for each paper set and a capitation fee for each candidate, and then leaves the examiners (whose work varies a good deal in amount) to wrangle over the carcass. And I am not so fond of arithmetic that multiplying and dividing sums of money by nineteen, or indeed by other numbers, affords me any substantial pleasure. However, like other afflictions, this passed, and though the Tripos and the numerous meetings which regularly beset the end of the Easter term have kept me occupied, I haven't really been overworked.

I do not think there is much local news. After long toiling and moiling we have acquired Professors of biochemistry, engineering, and genetics, and may before we are much older amass one or two more. Meanwhile the General Board has been advancing cautiously upon the question of teaching officers who were in one or other form of probationary period at the outbreak of war. There are always more of these than we can absorb into permanent jobs, and, since all permanent appointments were suspended in 1939, they have, as their probationary periods ended, been reappointed for a year at a time on the same basis. Meanwhile they grow older with their futures still uncertain, and the large number of them who are away on war service are not providing any evidence of their suitability or otherwise for promotion. What the G.B. now proposes is to give leave to Appointments Committees to make permanent appointments next year in cases where they have sufficient evidence to do so, also to extend the probationary periods of those who return from war to academic life, and to create for the years immediately after the war some additional probationary posts so that the road may not be blocked for those who were snatched away before they had reached the foot of the academic ladder. I summarise this report remorselessly because there are parishioners whose future it may affect; others will perhaps be more interested to hear that we have knocked off claret from the High Table during the summer months, not because we are very near the dregs but in order to make our stocks last longer. I hope, however, that this will not discourage those in the neighbourhood from coming to dinner.

It has on the whole been an attractive term, for though there have been some disconcertingly sudden variations of temperature, we have had a lot of warm sun and enough rain (mostly in conveniently short spasms) to keep gardeners and others from complaining too noisily. On top of an early spring, however, this has brought on high summer sooner than I myself should wish for I am always a little sad when elms and chestnuts take to their duller liveries and the copper beech on the John's Backs which I view from my dressing-room turns as near black as may be; and it used to be one of the pleasures of Italy in September to find the greens so much fresher than those one left behind in these cooler and damper climes — though I have never understood why they should be so. However it is nice to be warm, and I do not remember the local nudists coming abroad so early before. I never see them sun-bathing, or punting, or playing tennis, in shorts (or less), without some surprise at the change which has come over us since I was an undergraduate. I do not think that in those days we should have dreamt of canoeing or punting even on the upper river without our shirts, and if any young woman had appeared there in a bathing dress even of Victorian or Edwardian amplitude she would, I am sure, have been clapped into the Spinning House in a trice so long as that remarkable edifice still stood, and similarly dealt with when the University surrendered such cares to the town. Contrariwise there were plenty of places within easy reach where one could and did bathe unencumbered with any costume, but I doubt if there are any now — certainly not Byron's Pool which used to be a favourite. My own bathing days being more or less over, I bear the latter restriction with fortitude; and since I have no prudish horror of the human form even in its less divine aspects, I rather approve than otherwise of the former licence, though there be those who wag disapproving heads. The College Library lately acquired a mid-17th cent.

notebook in which some undergraduate of the day had written various matters, among them a set of rules seemingly dictated to his pupils by James Duport, Fellow of this College, Professor of Greek, and afterwards Master of Magdalene. Among them is: 'Goe not into the water at all or very wareily once or twice in a Summer at most, but better it were I thinke if you could quite forbeare'. The Reverend Gentleman would be concerned to see the reckless behaviour of the 20th century in such matters — as, indeed, at the neglect of some of his other precepts — 'Speake Latine always in the Hall, if not elsewhere or at other times', for example, or 'Dispute alwayes Syllogystically, at least Enthemematically and as much as you can Categorically'. Even such as 'Slubber not over your exercises in a slight and careless perfunctory manner', or 'Goe to your Tutor as to your Oracle upon all occasions, for advice, and directions, as also for resolution of any scruple, or doubt, or difficulty in religion or learning', are not as universally observed as might be wished. However, if your laxity would have shocked Duport, his would have shocked Whitgift, who, as Vice-Chancellor in 1571, issued a decree that any undergraduate caught bathing should be sharply and severely whipped in the Hall of his College in the presence of all Fellows and undergraduates, and should be whipped again next day in the Public Schools by the Proctors before the lecture-class of which he was a member.

FORTY-SEVENTH LETTER

17.7.43

No. 46 was sent out, unusually, at the beginning not the end of the week, for though Full Term ended on June 10 I had a week full of fusses in front of me. And when I say fusses I mean (1) meetings of Tripos examiners, (2) ditto of electors to College scholarships, (3) ditto of ditto to University studentships, (4) ditto of the Exemptions Committee to deal with people absent from examinations, (5) ditto of the Council and General Board, each of which was bogged in a problem compelling it to meet out of term, (6) ditto of board for R.A.F. Cadets, (7) ditto of ditto for R.N. Cadets — a new board whose procedure needed careful handling, (8) Entrance Scholarship papers to set. The last is due to the necessity of having an exam. in August for those who will be called up before they can compete in December. It will not be very interesting, for in Arts subjects, if we see the successful candidates at all, it will, I suppose, not be until after the war; and it is hard on those who examined last December and have just finished with a Tripos. It is true that there will be no exam. next December, but this sugar-plum is administered too long after the medicine to afford much present consolation.

Having swallowed these draughts I went to Eton for a week-end, and spent nights on either side of it in town, without collecting much news from either place. At Eton I fell in accidentally with the Winchester match, discreditably drawn by Eton who hardly even attempted to make the 200 runs required in the four hours at their disposal. However it was a fine day and the first cricket I have watched for an age; and if it was dull, as it was, there were plenty of friends to talk to. In London I had business to transact, but I got round most of the galleries though without much profit. The National Gallery has a memorial exhibition of Wilson Steer which contains some excellent pictures though not as many as it would in peace-time. It deserves a visit from those within reach, but the ground-floor rooms now used for such shows are narrow, crowded, and awkwardly lighted, and they are therefore particularly ill-suited for land-scapes, which one wants to contemplate in tranquillity and from a certain distance.

I was back here before the end of the month, and my occupations since then have been dull enough. I have addressed myself to some proofs which needed correction, to my immortal work, and to A.R.P. arrangements for the Long Vac. — and to all with distaste, for my bout of lumbago has left me rather feeble and its relics still hang about me. Long Vac. A.R.P. is always tiresome and is likely to be particularly so this year for the joint College and University scheme mentioned in no. 45, which ought to have been in operation two months ago, came into head-on collision with a new national block and sector scheme, and both have since been in a state of suspended animation. Both are now showing signs of rising to their feet again, and whereas they could have been taken on comparatively easily by a full and experienced Fire Party at the beginning of the summer term, they will be very tiresome to get going with a vacation crew which comes and goes. However of this more (I fear) hereafter.

We have suffered another severe blow by the death of Stephen Gaselee, Librarian of the Foreign Office, for his help and advice were often very useful both to the University (e.g., when there was a question of giving an honorary degree to some non-academic foreigner) and to individuals here (*e.g.*, when they wanted to convey books or MSS to or from the continent). He was probably known to some parishioners, for he was a Fellow of Magdalene, came up in peace-time for most week-ends, and often lunched at the Pitt; others probably knew him by sight for he was a conspicuous figure in scarlet socks, tweed tail-coat, and scarlet or Old Etonian bow-tie, wearing, if in academic dress, a top-hat with a gown, according to the ancient custom of non-resident M.A.'s. He was learned in a strange assortment of very recondite subjects, and I shall feel his loss severely for he had been a great friend of mine since my early under-graduate days and always dropped in on Sunday mornings when he was in Cambridge.

I have been reading (in a recent History of St Catherine's Coll., followed by pamphlet literature and an unpublished account by Winstanley) about the election of C. K. Robinson to the Mastership of that College in 1861 — the most sensational historical example of the troubles, touched on long ago in these pages, which may arise when the Fellows of a College elect their own Master. There were at the time only five Fellows, of whom two, Robinson and Jameson, were candidates. Two Fellows voted for J., J. and one other voted for R., R. voted for himself and was elected. You will observe, however, that if R. had voted for J. or if J. had voted for himself, J. would have been Master. It appears certain that J. emerged from the election with his arm round R.'s neck, accepted from him the post of President, and walked about with him for the next few days on the friendliest of terms; also that it was quite customary to vote for one-self in such circumstances, and that J. voted for R. against R.'s express advice. R. had to leave Cambridge shortly after the election and found on his return that J. had turned completely against him, that he was accused of electing himself, and that the scandal was all over the Univer-sity, the common report being that R. and J. had agreed to exchange votes and that R., who voted after J., had secured the Mastership by voting for himself instead. In view of the talk in the town R. and J. published a joint statement showing that there had been misunderstanding on both sides. J. had voted for R. thinking that R. had said he would not vote for himself; R. had voted for himself thinking that J. knew he was going to do so. It was not explained how these misunderstandings had arisen, and feeling continued to run so high that when, six years later, R. applied for a D.D. degree *jure dignitatis* (as Heads of Houses were then entitled to do) the Grace was opposed. Thereupon the Fellows of St C.'s, who were all new since the election, published a fly-sheet in defence of their Master, J. published a long reply, the Fellows issued a rejoinder, Mr. Browne, a Fellow, printed (in a pamphlet of seventeen mortal pages) the correspondence in which he declined further acquaintance with Mr. Shilleto of Peterhouse who in King's Combination Room had connected the name of Robinson with robbery; to which Mr. S. retaliated by printing a letter from Mr. B. to Mrs. S. repudiating on behalf of Mrs. B. and himself the further acquaintance of Mrs. S. and daughters. No doubt if the fires needed stoking all this paper stoked them, but it is the fact that R. was completely boycotted by the University for the rest of his life — a most unfair and unfortunate result, for R. remained Master until his death in 1909, and for nearly half a century the whole College lay under a cloud acquiring an inferiority complex.

Why J., after welcoming R.'s election, turned against him remains a mystery (for the explanation proffered in the History explains nothing)[1] but, quite apart from that, it is an extraordinary story. R. apparently offered to resign, and J. declined the offer; but supposing J. to have had a real grievance, of which there is no evidence, it was nevertheless a purely domestic affair, and it is astonishing to one familiar with the place nowadays that it should have been aired outside the College, and that, if aired, anybody should have paid attention to it. I can remember in more modern times one or two cases of people who failed to support with dignity a disappointment about an election to a University (not a College) post, and they were universally condemned or ridiculed. I would not say that the reactions to the Robinson case were discreditable to the University, but they were highly so to those who then composed academic society. I am also astonished at the readiness of our grandfathers to betake themselves to print. The volume of tracts which contains some of the documents in this case contains three pamphlets, of 29 pages in all, about an undergraduate (described as 'upright, temperate and diligent, frank, open-hearted and magnanimous, who would be an acquisition and an ornament to any society') who had been rusticated for brawling in Hall. A casual turning of the pages suggested that he was the victim of an injustice, but I still cannot conceive a matter of the kind nowadays coming before the public in print unless somebody on one side or the other was demented.

[1] See p. 195.

And (to return to the election of Heads of Houses) there were times when it involved physical as well as mental discomfort. In January 1743 the Fellows of King's seem to have spent 48 hours in their Chapel before any of the three candidates secured an absolute majority. One of them described the scene at 2 a.m.: 'Some wrapped in blankets, erect in their stalls like mummies; others asleep on cushions like so many Gothic tombs. Here a red cap over a wig; there a face lost in the cape of a rug. One blowing a chafing dish with a surplice sleeve; another warming a little negus, or sipping Coke upon Littleton, i.e., tent and brandy. Thus did they combat the cold of that frosty night, which has not killed any one of them, to my infinite surprize'. Tent, by the way, is a red Spanish wine, and very comforting, I can well believe, in such circumstances. It is sometimes used now for Communion wine, but I suppose it hardly follows that they had been breaking into the vestry cupboard.

FORTY-EIGHTH LETTER

12.8.43

THE Parish year has been wont to end with a retrospect and shall again, though there is not a great deal to record. A few parishioners have fallen away, though none, I am thankful to say, from enemy action; and all those reported missing last year in the far east are now known to be safe, though out of reach of the P.M. Errant sheep have mostly been replaced by others who have returned to the fold, and numbers have not fluctuated much above or below ninety. I had expected them to fall more, for in present conditions, as I said last year, it is unlikely that more than a stray new-comer will be added (I think there were only two in the twelvemonth), and indeed the contents are now so bare of news that though old subscribers may continue their subscriptions from force of habit I can't suppose that new ones would be attracted. As for the Parish boundaries, they grow increasingly hard to beat as the tides of war wash over them. In the west the U.S.A. have joined South America in outer darkness but have been replaced by Canada. In Africa, Tripolitania, Tunisia, and Algeria are, or have been, within the boundaries. As to the south of that continent I hesitate to guess, for when I included the Transvaal last year a parishioner disclosed that he had received copies there long before but had not been allowed to say where he was. I have had for some months, but have no more, a correspondent in Cape Town; and since I have not been conscious of one in Natal for a long time I mention that one parishioner has retired with a smashed leg from el Alamein to a military hospital at Pietermaritzburg. I have become conscious during the year that one parishioner is in Persia, and another in Madagascar — both new countries. And Sicily?[1] Well, I should like to report that the circulation had extended so far since it would be a sign and a portent, but though I have no doubt that it has, no direct evidence has so far reached me.

For two years past I have said that I no longer consider it an ineluctable obligation to write letters of such portentous length, and this has, in fact, been my creed for two years. It has not been put into practice because, somehow or other and somewhence or other, sufficient material has so far been found. However it requires but little imagination on your parts, and none on mine, to realise that this can't go on for ever, so I bid you remember that in the words of another Don (Lewis Carroll) 'what I tell you three times is true'.

If no portent has reached me from Sicily here are two small events nearer home which I should like to regard as such. First I have lately received a large book on some niceties of Latin syntax sent me by a learned and charming Swedish professor named Löfstedt who has a remarkable gift for making this somewhat austere subject interesting and even exciting. Two years ago a French Professor in occupied France wrote and asked me to look at a manuscript for him, but with that trifling exception I have been completely cut off from continental scholarship since the fall of France. One swallow doesn't make a summer but it is at least a welcome harbinger. Secondly, a friend of mine has lately acquired a bronze Victory which once stood on an orb in the hand of the statue of Napoleon at the top of the column in the Place Vendôme. There have been at least three different statues there, but this no doubt comes from the figure smashed in 1870 when the column was pulled down in the Commune, and the painter Courbet, who, having lately and imprudently taken to politics, signed the order, was presently told he could pay for putting it up again — a bill of 300,000 odd francs which caused him to retire hastily to Switzerland. The Victory is not in itself a very attractive object but I hope it is a portent, and that before long some Frenchman will have earned it as a present — and that it will be clear which one.

[1] The Allies landed in Sicily on July 10.

News from the Cam is parochial indeed compared with that from the tideless dolorous midland sea, but it is my business to be parochial and what little there is I chronicle. The Long, though enlivened by welcome visits from several parishioners, has not otherwise been very agreeable, partly because it was overshadowed by the threat of the scholarship examination in which I am at present engaged, partly because the first three weeks of July were overcast, tempestuous, and, for the time of year, much too cold, and August has not so far been much better. We have two more Professors, for the Dean of College (Hollond) has become Rouse Ball Professor of English Law, and a new geologist has also been elected. We have also a new Registrary — Dr. Grave, of Emmanuel, who is not known personally to me but may be to some of you since he was a Proctor shortly before the war. Otherwise the only thing I can think of is that the University is entangled in discussions about war-bonuses for University teaching officers. This doesn't affect me personally, and it is the kind of business which I am quite incapable of understanding, so though I sit through long discussions I do not bend my mind to them with unremitting attention. The matter arises because the Civil Service and two other Universities have instituted such bonuses owing to the rise in the cost of living. My private impression is that any rise in the cost of living in England is offset by the absence of things on which one can spend money, and though I do not dispute that such a bonus may be desirable I fancy that it is high taxation rather than increased cost of living which causes shoes to pinch. Apart from these diversions I have been occupied fitfully with my own work, and with A.R.P. for next year. I think I should have resigned my A.R.P. duties but for one fact, for I am now so lame that I cannot really attend practices, climb towers, or crawl about roofs, as sedulously as seems to me desirable, and the *Times*, which lately published an announcement about me under the heading Ancient Monuments in War Areas, came pretty near the truth. However, by a great stroke of luck, the College is very well off for A.R.P. personnel since six eminent firemen are also eminent scientists and will be doing war-research in Cambridge, and the leader of the First Aid Party will also be up next year. Thus we shall start the year far better off than we have ever been before, and once the services have got going in October they can be largely left to these efficient n.c.o.'s.

As soon as the scholarship election is over I am going down to Wales (if I can get there) for ten days or a fortnight. I have hesitated about this a good deal, for travelling is very disagreeable and the afflictions which gave me pause about A.R.P. duties give me still more at the possibility of having to stand for hours in a train-corridor. However I am very jaded both in body and mind and shall make the attempt for the sake of a little rest and change, and to get out of the din of aeroplanes — a sound to which familiarity does not reconcile me. It is true that I much prefer the sound of British engines at night to that of German and that it is now by far the commoner, but Air Chief Marshal Harris's[1] war, though I have no doubts whatever about its utility or even necessity nor any of the efficiency with which he conducts it, nevertheless horrifies me. Humanitarians will be shocked to hear that it is not so much the slaughter involved which shocks me, nor even the fact that the slaughter is necessarily indiscriminate. The chance that your bomb or theirs will kill a potential Michelangelo or Shakespeare is negligible, and not much higher that it will kill anybody whose death will affect the course of history or even of the present war; and if it kills a harmless civilian, myself or another, the event is much too insignificant to matter in such times. I am not even sure that when an aggressive nation learns, not as a theoretical possibility but as a bitter fact, that by going to war it exposes not only its soldiers but their parents, wives, and children to death or mutilation the lesson may not be salutary. Still, wholesale destruction, whether of lives or property, must needs be sickening, and destruction of property on this unexampled scale sickens me the more by the danger it necessarily involves to the cultural heritage of mankind. The bomb that wrecks a Wren church in the City, a Baroque palace in Genoa, or a Greek temple in Sicily, destroys something utterly irreplaceable and of more value than almost any individual life can possibly be; and since in objects of this kind, exposed in any case to the accidents and attrition of time, accretion gains but slowly on normal wastage, abnormal destruction horrifies me. I would blot Rome or Cologne or any other town from the map rather than lose this particular war, and, if we must, should count it the lesser loss to Europe. But even now the losses are already heavy, and the drone of British bombers overhead by night and of American by day holds a menace which disturbs more than my sleep or my work. I do not mean that it gets on my nerves, for it does not; but all the same I would willingly not hear it for a while.

[1] A.O.C.-in-C. Bomber Command.

FORTY-NINTH LETTER

THE scholarship exam. on which I was engaged when last heard of produced only a moderate crop of candidates — as was to be expected, for many of them were very young and in any case it was not the harvest of a full year. As soon as it was over I hurried away to Wales for a fortnight's holiday. I wasn't lucky in the weather, for though it was not remorselessly wet there was much more rain than sun, and the boisterous winds which have blown almost continuously throughout the summer in England pursued me across the border. Hence my project of basking long, idle, days in the garden was frustrated. However I took a great deal of fresh air, butter, cream, and other country commodities, slept much sounder than I am apt to do in Cambridge, and lifted my eyes to green remembered hills, which is a refreshment even when one can no longer walk on them. On the way back I spent two agreeable nights with cousins at Stone in Staffordshire, and by catching a different train to London from Stafford evaded the nightmarish experiences of last year at that station. In fact my journeys, after a good deal of anxiety about a seat at the start, were in the end not uncomfortable, and here I count myself lucky for travelling has become a terror. I suspect that this is largely needless, and, if needless, I have no doubt that it is both wrong and foolish, for the ordinary citizen (not to mention his wife), often harder worked than usual, and often without many of the amenities to which he is accustomed, if he is to do his work efficiently, needs an occasional holiday as much as a Civil Servant or a soldier; and he ought, if possible, to be enabled to take one without being subjected to acute and deterrent discomfort. For my own part I do not find, after four years of this, that a fortnight is enough.

On the way to Wales, and again on the way back, I slept a night in London, but did little there except see a friend or two, and look at a few moderate pictures which do not deserve record. No more do the paltry and tiresome jobs which have occupied me since my return, and I proceed, as usual in September, to give some account of my recent reading.

Contrary to the expectations raised in no. 44 I finished reading Hearne's *Collections* when I was laid up. It is a feat which I dare say but few have achieved and H. is not everybody's meat, but I laid down vol. 11 genuinely wishing that there were more to come. The last two or three vols. are rather different from the earlier for they are less encumbered with extracts from the books he had been reading, and since his personal grievances are somewhat fading with the lapse of time (he had been under-librarian of the Bodleian but was deprived as a nonjuror), his venom is mostly expended upon departures from proper practice in the University and the universe, and upon those responsible for them — for instance the use of the Sheldonian Theatre for concerts given by Handel and his orchestra, variously referred to by H. as 'a parcel of Pickpockets' and 'a lowsy crew of foreign Fiddlers'. I found in these vols. a great deal of mildly entertaining matter but shall only retail here the spirited behaviour of Mr Humphrey Wanley (afterwards librarian of the Harleian Library) who was entered as a freshman at St Edmund Hall. However, after attending his tutor's first lecture (which was on logic), he exclaimed 'By God, Mr Milles, I do not nor cannot understand it', and going away entered himself at Univ. instead. Hearne led me on to Anthony à Wood, an earlier Oxford antiquary whose papers cover the years 1632-1695 and fill three fat volumes. W. was as cross-grained as H. but more reticent, and though his diaries contain weightier matter (for King and Parliament were sometimes at Oxford) they are less amusing. From Wood I passed to John Aubrey's *Brief Lives*, but these are too frequently mere raw material and I was disappointed with them. Aubrey was a friend of Wood and supplied him with biographical material — a service which Wood repaid by tearing pages out of A.'s notebooks and describing him as 'a shiftless person, roving and magotie-headed, and sometimes little better than crazed'. I have also read in 17th cent. biography Roger North's life of his brother John who was Master of this College from 1677 to 1683 — a learned and worthy man though I dare say not a very good Master; at any rate he desired to be buried in the Ante-Chapel 'that the Fellows might trample upon him dead as they had done living.'

My more miscellaneous reading includes in biography Lord Ponsonby's life of Henry P., private secretary to Queen Victoria (which contains a devastating portrait of Her Majesty in the form of her own letters and notes), C. E. Jarvis's life of Peake Pasha (called *Arab Command*), and an autobiographical volume called *Half a Life* (both moderately interesting); S. Sassoon's *The Weald of Youth* (rather disappointing); and *Portraits of a Lifetime*, by Emile Blanche, a French painter and writer who has known a lot of interesting people but has little of interest to say about them. Among travel books I have read M. Collis, *The Land of the Great Image* (adventures of an early 17th cent. Portuguese friar in Arakan; good); M. Cable and F. French, *The Gobi Desert* (a very attractive book by two missionary ladies); Sven Hedin, *The Wandering Lake* (Lop Nor, also in the Gobi; less interesting to me); E. S. Drower, *Peacock Angel* (about the Yezidis in Kurdistan; pleasant); K. Bradley, *Diary of a District Officer* (N. Rhodesia); R. G. Massock, *Italy from Within* (by an American journalist). Miscellaneous books include W. Trotter, *Instincts of the Herd in Peace and War* (an interesting book written during the last war and mostly about Germany and England); W. T. Whitley, *Art in England* 1800-1837 (two vols. taking year by year and containing material from newspapers and similar sources; quite entertaining); F. H. Colson, *The Week* (about the origin of the week as a unit; interesting but not light reading). I have also skimmed rather than read the Place-Name Society's new volume on Cambridgeshire, from which I learnt, among other things, that Petty Cury was not, as I had been brought up to believe, the Little Stable (*écurie*) but the Little Cookery, for in 1330 it was described as Parva Cokeria.

Fiction is better represented than usual owing to my sojourn in a nursing home. *Le Silence de la Mer*, by a writer who calls himself 'Vercors', was clandestinely published in France and is about a Francophil German officer in occupied France (a short story well worth reading). S. Townsend Warner, *The Salutation* (short stories); J. Collier, *Tom's a cold* (both written with some distinction); R. Macaulay, *Orphan Island*; E. Waugh, *Black Mischief*, and *Scoop*; A. Thirkill, *August Folly* (all four quite amusing, especially the first); X., *The Greatest People in the World* (short stories); J. L. Rhys, *Flying Shadow* (these two about flying); C. S. Forester, *The Ship* (Mediterranean convoy; good — I am not sure how far it is fiction though); G. Green, *England Made Me*. I also re-read in the Nursing Home *Wuthering Heights* (which, despite its obvious faults, is a better book than I have been wont to think), and a good deal of Jane Austen.

I have, as usual, marked cheap editions with an asterisk and omitted some books which I am not prepared to describe as readable, among them Duff Cooper's *David* (the Psalmist) which I have seen praised but could not stomach even in a Nursing Home.

Two parishioners have asked for the explanation given in the History of St Catherine's for Jameson's change of attitude to Robinson after the election described in no. 47. It is that J. learnt that R. was about to be married. R. had made no secret of this but J., who had not heard of it, is alleged, on doing so, to have said 'Married! he's deceived me'. I cannot, however, understand this. It is true that if R. had married before the election he would have forfeited his Fellowship and therefore have had no vote, but he might have been a candidate all the same, and to postpone his marriage (if he did postpone it) until he knew whether he was to live in the Lodge or retire to a country living was mere common sense and I do not see that it provided J. with any sort of grievance. This story comes from Edward Perowne, afterwards Master of Corpus, who knew them both and informed J. of the marriage, but it is not recorded what relevance he saw in it. (Perowne is associated in my mind with a pleasing incident in an examination where he was invigilating, perhaps as Proctor. Perambulating the room he noticed about half-time that all one candidate had so far written was a verse:

> Teddy Perowne
> Has gone to his own,
> Has gone to his own in a chariot.

Flattered by this reference and curious to see if the composition had proceeded further, he collected the paper from the man's place at the end of the examination and was rewarded with the next verse which ran:

> He is sitting in state
> On a fizzing hot plate
> With Pilate and Judas Iscariot.)[1]

Others have enquired from the Middle East about the Spinning House, to which I said (in no. 46) that young women would have been committed not long since if they had appeared on the river as scantily clad as is now fashionable. This is a longer story and must wait, but I was amused to learn, à propos of this subject, that the Eighth Army on arriving in Tunisia were shocked to find that the First Army had not brought their bathing dresses with them.

[1] See p. 221.

FIFTIETH LETTER

1.10.43

OBSERVE with reverence and awe the number at the head of this letter. Also reflect that it indicates two hundred pages and, if my estimate is correct, about seventy-five thousand words. (Parishioners with a conscience and a taste for airgraphs and arithmetic should now be in a position to calculate their debit balances.) The Jubilee number of the P.M. has evoked demonstrations both inside and outside the Parish. From within Parishioners in Africa and Sicily have, I understand, very kindly despatched tributes of lemons in my direction; from without Marshal Badoglio has acknowledged as he should this display of bulldog tenacity, though candour compels me to add that he slightly mistimed his gesture which was made public just as I was sending out no. 49.[1] Still, better early than late, and I sincerely hope that other marshals and suchlike folk will not stand on a punctilio and wait for my centenary issue before following suit. As to the coloured supplement issued on these occasions by properly conducted journals, I fear I must leave it to your imaginations — a portrait, perhaps, of the editor tearing his grey hairs for want of copy.

I shall have, now and henceforward, to add whatever I do add to these letters in pencil, for the mountainous stocks of paper which I bespoke some years ago are exhausted, and the best now obtainable, as you probably noticed in no. 49, though it takes the stencil-ink well enough, blots and blurs under the pen. However my greetings will not be less sincere for that and may, I hope, be more legible.

The reference to the Spinning House in no. 46, as I said last month, provoked some enquiries. It was a building in St Andrew's St opposite the New Theatre, originally founded by Thomas Hobson, the celebrated carrier, whose name is attached (erroneously) to the Conduit, and it was part workhouse, part prison, shared by the town and the University. For under the Elizabethan statutes of 1561 the University was empowered 'to make scrutiny search and inquisition for all public women, procuresses, vagabonds, and other persons suspected of evil', and to punish by imprisonment and otherwise all who were 'found guilty or suspected of evil'; and this, with other similarly autocratic powers, it exercised down

---
[1] The surrender of Italy was announced on Sept. 8.

to the Cambridge University and Corporation Act of 1894. I fancy that the town had long given up its share in the Spinning House which was used as the University prison. I do not know what befell the vagabonds incarcerated in it; the ladies of dubious virtue there were, in the eighteenth century, whipped by the town-crier at the expense of the Vice-Chancellor, but in the nineteenth they seem to have been treated with less drastic remedies for they got sevenpence a day together with a pint of beer, and were prescribed a diet which, if plain, was not unsubstantial.

I read some months ago an account by Winstanley of the disputes which led up to the act of 1894. Most of them are dreary but the part involving the Spinning House has a certain sordid picturesqueness and provoked a reverberating scandal at the time. Since, therefore, I am likely to have little else to fill this letter with, and some parishioners seem to enjoy academic scandal (no doubt for its rarity), I shall briefly record it here. I remark by way of preface that the rights of the University under the old statutes, though tenaciously upheld by the University, had long been a source of friction with the town and had been the subject of protracted and futile negotiations since 1853. Even before that the Spinning House had led to scandal; for instance, when in 1846 one Elizabeth Hare died of rheumatic fever, the report was spread abroad that she had caught it from a damp bed in the Spinning House where she had lately spent the night. This particular charge was easily disproved (for the lady who had shared the bed testified to its excellence) but most or all of the University privileges were obviously anomalous, and the town might well complain that the Vice-Chancellor should possess the power unknown to civil magistrates of imprisoning on suspicion.

The final racket over the Spinning House began in February 1891, when Jane Elsden, who was known to the Proctors and had indeed been released from the S.H. the day before, met the Proctor (R. St J. Parry, afterwards Vice-Master of this College) in Petty Cury. She took to her heels but was caught by the Bull-dogs after a spirited pursuit and on the following day sentenced by the Vice-Chancellor (H. M. Butler, Master of Trinity) to three weeks in the S.H. In the afternoon, however, owing to the negligence of the matron, she escaped and modestly withdrew to her parents' house in a neighbouring village. The Vice-Chancellor thereupon had her re-arrested and charged with prison-breaking. This he was fully entitled to do, but it was nevertheless imprudent, for this charge had to be made not in his own court but at the Assizes, where her counsel, though he could not challenge the original sentence, could, and did, denounce the proceedings in the V.-C.'s court — they were held in camera, the evidence was not on oath, the prisoner was not allowed counsel, the offence was unknown to the law. Naturally Jane was convicted, and naturally too she became a martyr. Questions were asked in Parliament, discussions between town and University were reopened, and some reforms were introduced into the procedure of the V.-C.'s court. Meanwhile, feeling running very high, the Proctors were told to avoid arrests if they decently could. Unfortunately in December one of them encountered Daisy Hopkins, whose virtue was well below suspicion, not only in the town but in the company of an undergraduate. She was arrested, appeared before the V.-C. next day 'fashionably attired in a navy-blue costume trimmed with gold edging and a fawn-coloured felt hat', and, the evidence as to her character being plain, got fourteen days. D.H. then applied for a writ of Habeas Corpus in the High Court, which quashed the original sentence not on its merits but on a flaw in the indictment — which was one up to the town. Next she sued the University for damages for false imprisonment and lost, which was one up to them. At this point the name of D.H. fades from the chaste page of academic history. I suppose, however, that by now the scandal had become too flagrant, and though the negotiations dragged on for a while, an agreement leading to the act of 1894 was presently reached. Under this the University handed over its police jurisdiction to the town and therefore had no more use for a prison. Soon afterwards the Spinning House was demolished, I think in 1901. At any rate it had vanished without a trace when I came up in 1905 though the circumstances leading to its abolition were still the subject of ribald merriment among certain junior Dons of my acquaintance.

15.10.43

Full Term began on Oct. 8 but its products still await digestion and I complete this issue with what little has befallen me in the six weeks since I returned from Wales. I meant to do some work of my own and have in fact done a little (including the composition of a note for a learned journal on the best recipe for producing swarms of bees from the carcass of a cow, though this is not a method I should recommend to commencing apiarists) — but only a little, for distractions have intervened.

My solicitors having at long last completed some legal business on which they have been engaged for eighteen months, I have had to do a good deal of tidying up of my affairs, and, as usual, A.R.P. has occupied time. I meant to produce a new edition of the weightiest College manual on the subject, but have not because the new national Fire Guard Plan and the University and Colleges Joint Scheme are still locked in internecine conflict, and when I ask the Borough authorities for enlightenment on the former they point accusing fingers at me and say I am suffering from an N.F.S. complex — a fault of which conscience at any rate acquits me. I have also spent a good deal of time having short-wave treatment applied to my damaged joints whose deportment during the last twelve months has far passed the limits of decorum. For some years it has been impossible to get this treatment here, but a local practitioner has now set up a cage within which the rays may be loosed upon my hip without disrupting communications with aircraft, sabotaging radiolocation, and otherwise misconducting themselves; and they have perhaps reduced my immobility a little. Two days were occupied with interviewing R.A.F. Cadets at the end of their six months' course. This was much less laborious than in April (when it took four days) because the Board interviewed only those whose qualifications were in doubt and signed up the rest on their record. Still, it was a hard two days, and embittered by one Cadet who had transcribed his neighbour's papers with a sustained and punctilious accuracy worthy of a nobler cause. Finally, I have been to London for two nights, where, besides seeing some friends, having some Turkish baths, and tottering with little profit round some picture-galleries, I took the opportunity of getting my hair cut and buying some chocolate. And this I mention because the first of these exploits now involves in Cambridge a test of endurance to which I submit more and more reluctantly, and the second a test of opportunism in which I am invariably unsuccessful. Not a very profitable six weeks I fear, but it hasn't been unpleasant, for the weather has on the whole been fine. But the arrears of summer for which I had hoped have not been forthcoming and there has been an autumnal nip in the wind which was unwelcome. I confess that though I do not intend to practice all the austerities of last year I am not looking forward to the winter.

FIFTY-FIRST LETTER

13.11.43

Statistics in these pages regularly set in with November frosts, and strike with a similar chill upon some of my correspondents. They are, however, no less inevitable, so learn that the number of men in residence is 2651, and of women 483. The corresponding figures for last October were 2700 and 475. The 2651 men comprise 185 B.A.'s, Research Students and 4th year men; 212 3rd year: 724 2nd year: 1530 freshmen: and all these totals are within ten of those corresponding for last year except that the 2nd year men have gone down by 56, no doubt owing to the fact that there can be practically no 2nd year men reading Arts subjects except the medically unfit. Freshmen have actually gone up by 4. In view of the bar on all but the very young Arts students this is surprising, but it is also a little misleading for two reasons. In the first place the total includes 660 Short Course Cadets of whom 200 are R.N. Cadets; and as the R.N. courses only began last April there were no sailors to include in last October's figures. Secondly, I should judge that there are quite a number of very young Arts students here; certainly I see a lot of unusually youthful faces about the place and the Steward tells me that a good many members of this College, if not exactly sucklings, are at least entitled to an extra milk-ration by reason of their tender years. Some of these would presumably have come up anyhow, but others may be ascribed to our having held our scholarship exam. in August instead of December, so that the intake of this October includes some scholars and exhibitioners and there will this year be none to come up in January. Still, make what deductions you will, the way in which very much more than a mere semblance of University life has been maintained into a fifth year of war is as surprising as it is pleasing. I add, to keep step with previous statistics, that in this College there are 270 men up, of whom 151 are freshmen, as against 289 and 149 respectively last year. Also that students from evacuated institutions now number 1761, as against 1902 last year — a drop mostly accounted for by the departure of the London Hospital medicals and some Chichester theologians for their wonted habitats.

Since this is the first year in which no reservations at all have been allowed to able-bodied Arts students, I shall here record that I am lecturing to a class composed of thirteen ordinary undergraduates (young or unfit in I know not what proportion), eight R.N. Cadets, seven R.A.F. Cadets, and ten women. There are no doubt in residence a few women and unfit men who attended the same course last year, and there are also some stray survivors reading for Part 2 of the Tripos, but apart from these my class probably represents the whole population reading Classics in the University for there are precious few lecturers left and there is therefore practically no choice of lectures. The Cadets are there because a very sensible scheme was introduced last year by which Cadets of approximately Higher Certificate standard were allowed to attend certain specified courses in their own subjects instead of taking the more general Arts course constructed for them, and probably my class in Classics is a fair cross sample of the conditions prevailing in all Arts faculties. The shortage of lecturers is due to the fact that in view of the impending reduction of the number of students the University released some more lecturers in June. Of my two colleagues here Sandbach is away on Government service, and Rattenbury, though here, is wholly employed in the Registry where he is helping the new Registrary to get hold of the strings. Consequently there reposes on my long-suffering neck all the Classical supervision for five Colleges, who have piled upon it two unfit 3rd year men, one man in his third term waiting to be called up by the R.A.F., three young freshmen, and six Cadets—not an overwhelming burden, I admit, but heavier than I expected or wanted, and made unwieldy by the Cadets, whose professional programme makes it necessary to concentrate all lectures and most of the supervision into three days of the week. However enough (or more) of this.

I have been hideously busy since term began, for the organising of College A.R.P. has always been laborious at the start of the academic year, and this year it has been worse than ever before. This is not unnatural, for it involves, one way or another, about 170 people, and when you have deducted from the total number of residents those who live in distant lodgings, the Cadets (who can be used for some purposes but are uneconomical since they must be replaced in April), and those who, by dint of being idle, tiresome, and unreliable, have succeeded in establishing that they are more trouble than they are worth, and so get off (not a large body, I am glad to say), there is now no great margin of man-power to play with, and it has taken me a full month to get my lists complete. And, by the way, the letters A.R.P., which figure too largely in the

P.M., stand in that journal, as I now tell you once and for all, exclusively for Air Raid Precautions. This belated explanation is due to the fact that after I had lately looked at a new edition of the Parish Address Book, and had boggled at the uncouth strings of initials which serve some of you for addresses, I betook myself to a *Dictionary of Abbreviations*, and there I found not indeed much help with the problems which sent me to it, but the information that A.R.P. was perhaps more familiar to some of you as Ammunition Refilling Point, and to others (though these I conceive to be a minority) as Associated Reformed Presbyterian. It seems to me that this war is even worse than the last in this respect, and that the pullulation and proliferation of initials which has been going on for the last four years will make half the documents of the period quite soon unintelligible. I am far from blameless myself, I know, for I was turning the back pages of the P.M. the other day, and, stumbling upon L.D.V., wondered how many people now remembered that the Home Guard was once called the Local Defence Volunteers.

I was turning back numbers to see what subjects had served to fill the Autumn issues of earlier years, and I found two which hadn't had their usual turn. They shall have it now, not because they offer much material but because all material is scarce and if the term has so far produced any besides statistics and A.R.P. I have been too busy or too jaded to take adequate notice of it.

I discovered that the October issue has usually recorded visible changes in the appearance of the town, but these naturally grow annually fewer as the war-years roll by, and beyond onions for carrots in the John's parterres, some unsightly stacks of coke under our Library, and some extensive repairs to the Great Gate steps, I think A.R.P. is responsible for all the novelties I have noticed in the past twelve months. Surface water-mains have been laid along a good many streets and there are a lot of new reservoirs dotted about the town and inside some courts — some unsightly, others, where there is grass to bank the sides, not displeasing, at any rate as long as the water is clean. A year ago I referred to the one at the end of King's Chapel as static water, but further study of N.F.S. literature leads me to suppose that this, at any rate in the local dialect, is a solecism and that it should be called a dam, the name static water being reserved for water in motion — in Cambridge the Cam, at Buffalo no doubt Niagara. Similarly an N.F.S. static umpire I have found by experience to be one who buzzes about like a bluebottle on a window-pane and must be followed, if at all, at a run. Another school of thought maintains that water is static when not enclosed in a pipe, but this view, though not unplausible as to water, breaks down badly on the umpires. For the rest, I have already mentioned the grey shed in the Great Ct for the second pump, and the only addendum I can muster is that the powers whom it pleased long ago (see no. 15) to erect a series of hideous surface Air Raid Shelters in the New Court have now been pleased to pull them down again — a valuable contribution to the war effort which will no doubt receive suitable recognition in due course.

My researches disclosed further that Nature Notes have long been absent from these pages. That, however, is because Nature has not of late obtruded herself much upon my notice, though perhaps I may say that the College grass, what with summer drought and neglect, is looking shabbier than I remember to have seen it; that there is a lamentable absence of walnuts on the trees in the Roundabout after a bumper crop last year; and that there have been a lot of goldfinches about. I do not recall them in the Bowling Green until this autumn, but that may well be merely because increasing immobility has caused me to sit there a good deal on fine afternoons instead of going for a walk, and I will not take my oath to their having been more numerous than usual. And here are some items which may perhaps be included under the head of Nature Notes though I accept no personal responsibility for them. First I lately came across a leaflet issued periodically by The Society for United Prayer for the Prevention of Cruelty to Animals. I confess that I had never heard of this Society, nor have I now joined it though some of you may like to do so. The leaflet, or the copy which I saw, consists of lists of Thanksgivings (*e.g.*, 'For the merciful preservation of the cows in a much-raided south coast district'), and of Intercessions (*e.g.*, 'That twenty gorillas trapped and now captive at Brazzaville, Belgian Congo, may be spared suffering'). Secondly a lady writing in *Country Life* says 'We also had an opossum which used to run down the veranda spouting every morning exactly at eight o'clock'. This seems very odd behaviour in a marsupial, though I admit that the oddity may be in part explained by the supposition that the good lady uses 'veranda' as an adjective and 'spouting' as a noun. And finally a sentence from the *Economist*: 'Millions of Americans are now coming to see that if Pan-America and the British Commonwealth are the wasp of the New Democracy, then the peoples of Russia and Asia may well become its wolf'. This I take not from the *Economist* but from *Punch*, which quoted it without comment, thereby causing me to wonder whether the great British Public was more adept at textual criticism than I supposed. However some light will be thrown on this question if you will all take stop-watches in hand and tell me how many seconds you have required to make the necessary emendations.

FIFTY-SECOND LETTER

28.11.43

TERM ends in a week's time and my impressions of it are sufficiently mature to be issued to the Parish though they are not very exciting. So far as weather is concerned it has on the whole been pleasant, and until mid-November there was a fine display of autumn gold and brown and a good many sunny days to set it off, though I here record with displeasure that St John's have been cutting down some elms on their Backs (to the prejudice of the view from my bedroom window) on the paltry pretext that they might fall on Johnian heads. There have been some cold days and some very cold nights and of late it has been rather persistently foggy, but I have endured no great hardships, partly because I have renounced the austerities of yesteryear and allowed myself a little electric heating in the evening, partly because a pair of corduroy trousers to which I have lately taken are considerably warmer than their predecessors — and this is not surprising since I took to them not so much to be in the fashion as because the pair which they replace exhibited to the public gaze larger areas of skin than seemed becoming. Be prepared, therefore, when next you see me to find my lower limbs cased in material of a shade which in battleships is known as elephant-grey and in trousseaux as oyster-grey. (Strange, for those that go down to the sea in ships might be expected to think of oysters before elephants. Memo: to look into this for next instalment of Nature Notes.) Be prepared also to see me wearing a soft collar, and very much against my will for I detest them. However my laundress says she can get no starch, and meanwhile my whole supply of stiff collars has long since accumulated in her hands. It is among the minor inconveniences, which cannot be expected to grow less and in fact do not. Another is the cluttering up of the University Library by young women; and this has been forced upon my attention by the fact that my lawful occasions have taken me there more than usual of late and it is sometimes almost impossible to find a seat. I shouldn't mind this so much if I thought they were advancing learning or even materially improving their own minds, but observation leads me to fear that a good many of them spend their time powdering their noses and corresponding with their boy-friends, and it is not for the furtherance of such innocent ends as these that University Libraries exist. I fear too that they foster a spirit of malevolence among senior members of the University, whom I sometimes catch eyeing their serried ranks with positive venom.

A more serious but not less natural inconvenience is the growing shortage of staff in every department. At the beginning of the term the Steward asked for undergraduate volunteers to help peel potatoes and the like (at 1/3 per hour, aprons provided) and was vexed at the small response. I wasn't surprised at it myself, for undergraduates, heaven knows, have plenty else to do at present and they were wanted only against a possible shortage which hasn't as yet arisen. If it does I have no doubt that help will be forthcoming, as it has been (whether voluntary or forced I do not know) in other Colleges for some time past. Meanwhile the College food seems to me to have improved rather than the reverse; rabbits are mercifully in short supply, and the High Table dinner is usually better than that obtainable at my own club and not worse than that served at two other clubs at which I chance to have dined in recent months. It is long since I dined in a London restaurant but reports do not encourage me to think I should fare better if I did.

University business, unlike the rabbits, is in plentiful supply but would make poor copy, for the questions before us are largely technical and the answers still obscure. The Medical School, the Regius Professorship of Physic, and their future relations with an enlarged Addenbrooke's; the establishment of a school of Veterinary Science; the post-war needs of the University; the numbers of the Women's Colleges (they have a ration of 500, but having indulged in excesses of freshwomen to fill up the vacancies caused by 3rd year deficiences will find themselves in a mess as soon as the 2nd year are free to stay on) — these are a fair sample of the themes that occupy my Monday mornings and Wednesday afternoons — not agreeably, but it is something to be thinking not of war emergencies but of post-war construction.

For the rest, I have done nothing of the faintest interest — not even seen Cambridge beat Oxford at Rugger yesterday, for the Senior Tutor, who has a soul above such matters, called for that time a meeting of the

College Education Committee (which hasn't met for five years) to consider needs of the College staff. One of its needs is that I should sit back and recuperate for a bit, but of this no mention was made.

13.12.43

I have had lately some instruction in the art of letter-writing, a subject, as you will readily imagine, of constant and painful interest to me. First I read in Max Beerbohm's lecture on Lytton Strachey that Dr Joad had told a questioner who wanted to write good letters (I suppose a Brains Trust question) that all you had to do was to think out clearly what you wanted to say and then set it down in the simplest terms; and no doubt one might sometimes write a good letter so. There comes to my mind one written long ago to a Bishop's wife of my acquaintance by a protégée on her way to Australia: 'Dear Madam, I hope this finds you as well as it leaves me. The ship is in the middle of the Red Sea, and it is fearfully hot. I am in a terrible state of melting all day long. But, honoured Madam, I know you will be pleased to hear that I am still a member of the Church of England.' Max B. characterises Dr J. as an 'agile and mellifluous quodlibetarian'; the terms which occurred to me were less choice and, I confess, less urbane. Still, since it seemed there were those who claimed to have a specific sovereign for those in my condition, I expended some pence on a work which I saw in a shop entitled *The Secret of Good Letter Writing*, and this contains much useful information. It told me, for instance, when I might suitably begin my letter 'Hullo Darling', and said that in the improbable event of my wishing to address a Peer the librarian would be able to advise me as to the proper style. It also bade me be careful not to confuse 'shall' and 'will', and gave much other valuable instruction of a like nature; but the Celt in my blood is, I believe, sufficiently subjugated not to interfere in my handling of those difficult auxiliaries, and, truth to tell, it is not in these departments that I most feel the need of aid. Miss Mitford once wrote in a letter to her father, 'Mamma says the great art of letter-writing is to construct an epistle without one possible subject', and what Mamma said in 1811 is no less profoundly true in 1943. My handbook, unlike Dr Joad, did indeed address itself to this aspect of the matter. It said that if I examined the events of a seemingly uneventful day I should find many items suitable for inclusion — for instance, quaint things the children said, and details about that lecture at the Women's

Institute. Even my hour's gossip with Ethel before going to bed would probably contain enough material for a lengthy letter. But, alas, I never gossip with Ethel before going to bed, and as the only lectures I attend are my own, whose contents are wholly unsuitable to the Parish Magazine, it will, I fear, profit little or nothing from this course of instruction.

My last lesson in the epistolary art comes more unexpectedly from Hitler or one of his gang, who, I read in the papers, has lately issued to the troops an order on the subject. It said that those who thought letters were for the purpose of expressing the writer's opinions were under a delusion, and that thenceforward all letters would end on a cheerful note. If I were a German and saw my armies heavily defeated on one front and disastrously on another, my chief cities laid in ruins, my submarines paying no dividends, my principal ally in arms against me, the rest wavering, neutrals no longer concealing their opinion that I was beaten, and the peoples I had oppressed straining to get at my throat, I should, apart from any personal discomforts I might be enduring, have some difficulty in writing a cheerful New Year letter. And though I do not think the P.M. has ever disseminated gloom and despondency, I confess that in past years it has not always been easy to sound cheerful. However, if we have had long to wait for good news, we have had it in full measure in 1943, and though the prospect of 1944 is, for obvious reasons, not calculated to inspire cheerfulness, it is at least possible for the first time in the history of the P.M. to look forward to a New Year with some confidence that the last siren will sound before the Last Trump. And in that spirit of tempered optimism I send you all my warmest wishes for it, and for Christmas.

FIFTY-THIRD LETTER

26.12.43

IF this number gets filled it will at best be a patchwork affair, and since on Christmas and Boxing Days extra turns of Warden's duty confine me to my rooms while the Head and Second Porters take their ease beneath their family Christmas trees, I may as well stitch some of the rags and tatters together now though the vacation has so far produced few of them. It has indeed hardly deserved its name, for the business mentioned in no. 52 has kept committees sitting far past the end of term, and I have also had to spend two days interviewing R.A.F. and

R.N. Cadets. One incident, however, it has produced, for I have suffered a heavy misfortune. One night when I was in Hall some loathsome brute invaded my rooms and stole my typewriter. There has been a good deal of stealing from College rooms (and from London flats) recently and no doubt I ought to have sported my oak; but it is a nuisance to do so, I am on the whole of a confiding disposition, and since a thief was lately caught red-handed stealing the Junior Bursar's collars and consigned to jug, I thought the danger was past. However the detective told me that six or eight typewriters have lately been stolen here, and this was no doubt a specialist, for, though he went through my drawers, he left some gold studs and other valuable objects, taking only some chocolate. The loss of the typewriter is much more than a bore, for though I do not use it continually, I need it sometimes very badly indeed and the Directorate of Office Machinery has peremptorily refused me a permit to buy another. Moreover its loss seriously affects the production of the P.M., for often when a long day's work has left me too tired to do anything else I still have sufficient energy to type, but not to write, a paragraph for it; and, besides, my only method of calculating the length of the letters is to count the lines of typescript.

Misfortunes are proverbially gregarious and a lot of lesser contrarieties have since befallen me which I should scorn to chronicle in detail except to say that, as my laundress now has influenza, visitors in the near future are likely to find me wearing not only soft but dirty collars. It may be true, as the hymn cheerfully observes, that

> These slight disappointments are sent to prepare
> For what may hereafter befall,
> For seasons of real disappointment and care,
> Which commonly happen to all,

but I will not deny that since I sent out no. 52 my frame of mind has been prevailingly peevish.

Besides being peevish I am qualifying not slowly for the madhouse under the deluge of paper which descends on me in reference to the Fire Guard Plan. One of them lately said that when I detected a small unexploded anti-personnel bomb, among my numerous and immediate duties would be to inform the headmaster of any school in session and supply him with a picture or poster of the bomb. Another said I was to equip my Sector Point with 'table, chairs for Message Clerk and messengers, black-out, mobilising slate, chalk, log-sheets, spare N.F.S. message forms, Sector Point sign, Sector Diagram, and some form of emergency lighting' (in the next paragraph it said the Sector Diagram must be kept in my personal possession). It also said 'Sector Point Messengers must be earmarked', and if anybody has a humane branding-iron or similar appliance which he can lend me I am prepared to do my best. More seriously, however, this scheme, which in fundamental outline is quite sensible, seems to me in danger of foundering under the weight of detail loaded on it. *Ex hypothesi* it has got to be operated in their spare time by men and women of average intelligence, and I hope I shall not seem unduly conceited if I say that documents which Broad and I study with growing bewilderment are not likely to convey their meaning with instant clarity to other people. It may be, for instance, that the majority of Fire Guards more readily remember the distinctions between blocks, sectors, areas, wards, zones, and regions than we can, but I doubt it. Meanwhile my tin hat has been taken away and painted with so chic a design in black and white that if it were less hideously uncomfortable, and if my duties did not as a rule tether me to the telephones in the Wardens' Post, I might sometimes even be tempted to wear it.

And talking (as usual) of A.R.P., I ought to have recorded somewhere during the summer that the College Fire Party was photographed by *Life* for the edification of America, and filmed by the British Council for the edification of all neutral nations. I doubt if America will profit, for the photographs were dull and did not appear in a number which contained a good many pictures of Cambridge; I haven't seen the film, but if the Portuguese, Swedes, Swiss, and Turks (not to mention the Irish) suddenly take up arms you will now know the reason.

I might have mentioned among the impressions left upon me by last term that the shortage of stuff for gowns was beginning to make itself visible, for an undergraduate who regularly appeared academically naked at my lectures said he could not get a gown (I doubt if he had tried very hard), and a freshman of this College who wears a Caius gown was assured by the tailor from whom he procured it that it was 'just as good'. Whatever view one may take of this sentiment it has some historical justification, for the distinguishing patterns of College gowns are said to be only about a hundred years old, and until 1769 only scholars and graduates wore mortar-boards. (If any parishioner was ever fined for not wearing one he will derive comfort from the thought that they became general because undergraduates themselves petitioned the Duke of Grafton for them in order to attend his installation as Chancellor more becomingly dressed.) The subject of academic dress for undergraduates is, however, shrouded in mystery, for though history is vocal on University costume, its remarks are mostly directed to graduates and based either on religious grounds, as when the Puritans denounced mortar-boards as borrowed from the priests of Baal, or else on its extravagance in non-academic garments. Thus in 1600 Henry Pepper B.A. of Corpus went to a play at the Black Bear Inn 'having deformed long locks of unseemly sight, and great breaches undecent for a graduate or scholar of orderly carriage', and was not only ordered to 'procure his hair to be cut or powled' but was suspended from his degree. About thirty years earlier I blush to record that the Proctors themselves were so utterly lost to all sense of decency as to go about wearing 'verye unseemly ruffes at their hands, and greate Galligaskens and Barreld hooese stuffed with horse Tayles, with skabilonions[1] and knitt nether-stockes too fine for schollers', whereby godly men were much offended. Lord Burghley, who was Chancellor at the time, assigned the too elaborate dress among Fellows of Colleges to 'the great stipendes of Tutors', who have since been relieved of all temptation to the like extravagances, but I shall here recall a favourite sentence of mine which I used to think of suspending over my tutorial desk. It comes from a letter addressed to the Seniors of this College in 1648 by the Master, Thomas Hill: 'I am confident many pupils (and it may bee their abused poor damned Fathers) lie roaring in Hell, cursing eternally their negligent yet covetous Tutors'.

Among the impressions of last term I might also have mentioned that the Fitzwilliam has lately filled two rooms with a very remarkable display of French engraved portraits, books, medals, and autographs, from (roughly) Louis XI on. It is not my line of country, but it would do credit to any museum even in peace-time and has elicited an ecstatic sonnet from a French visitor. The same post delivered to the Director a letter from a parcel of women who call themselves 'the artists living in Cambridge' complaining of the total neglect here of all arts except music. Their names are mostly unknown to me, but I suppose what they really want is to see their own works in the Fitzwilliam. If they

[1] See p. 215.

were less ignorant they would know, as I have said before, that the Fitzw. has done more than any museum except the National Gallery to keep things going during the last four years — and the N.G. naturally has far more staff, funds, and other facilities than we have. It is exasperating that the Director, who has worked like a black and deserves everybody's thanks, should be treated to impertinences of this kind.

15.1.44

Having borrowed an ancient and unfamiliar typewriter and tapped out my Boxing Day maunderings, I find with surprise that they extend even beyond my needs and will supply a small nest-egg for no. 54. I shall therefore only add here my thanks for numerous Christmas cards (a high variety from the Middle East and much superior to the design on which I commented last year), and tell you, in case you don't know already, that the Master has lately published a brief and very readable history of the College in just over a hundred pages. It supplies a real want, for the only comparable book (by Rouse Ball) has long been out of print, and my copy was removed from my waiting room by an ungrateful pupil so many years ago that I hardly remember what it was like. I should have mentioned this in an earlier issue but did not because the book, like most others one wants, immediately became unobtainable. However there are now new supplies in the shops.

FIFTY-FOURTH LETTER

30.1.44

I REVERT to the Christmas vac. — stale news, if news it can be called, but all my so-called news is some months out of date before it reaches the outlying parts of the Parish so perhaps it is as well that it is so seldom of any moment.

We had quite a pleasant little Christmas dinner which I ate seated between a Belgian, whom I knew because he was one of my firemen, and an unknown negro. Both liked oysters so I got no more than my fair share but they had no other defects as neighbours, and a little diversion was welcome for I was working very hard all through the vac. You may suppose me to have been engaged upon my immortal work, but, if so, you suppose wrong for I have not been able to touch it since October having undertaken to write a memoir of Stephen Gaselee (whose death was mentioned in no. 47) for the British Academy, which is wont to publish a substantial brochure on its deceased Fellows. It is not an easy task in any case and some of it depends on memory; and memories, or at any rate mine, don't always stand the test of research. For instance Gaselee was interested in exotic foods and before the last war he was Steward of Magdalene. Until a few weeks ago I should have been prepared to swear that at that time I had seen in a poulterer's shop an unfamiliar corpse labelled 'WALLABY. Reserved for the Master and Fellows of Magdalene.' Not feeling quite sure, however, whether it was a wallaby or an opossum, I instituted enquiries among the few surviving Fellows of the period, and as none remembers having been invited to partake of either animal I now begin to wonder if I really saw it or whether it is merely a plausible invention of my own or another's. Some light might be thrown on this dark passage of history if any parishioner chances to know whether wallaby (or opossum) is edible.

This same task twice took me to London for two nights to make some enquiries — not very agreeably, for blacked out London in December or January fog is no place for me, and the trains, besides being crowded, were very late. I did nothing very exciting there and had not time to get round all the galleries, but those I did visit seemed to me rather more entertaining than they have been on recent visits. I surprised myself by acquiring a drawing by Matisse, an artist who has seldom seemed to mean much to me. However it may be that I have other such surprises in store for myself, for I fancy that in my declining years my taste grows a trifle less reprehensibly eclectic. I do not think I brought back any news unless it should be that it doesn't now seem much easier to get one's hair cut in London than in Cambridge (see no. 50), but I did bring back a typewriter very kindly lent me by a cousin, so that unless this too is stolen the mechanical future of the P.M. is rosier. Meanwhile I daren't stir from my rooms without locking the door, and I have continued to assail the Directorate of Office Machinery, exasperated to find that they have lately given an undergraduate the permit to buy a typewriter which they refuse to me. However the Master, who kindly intervened on my behalf, was told that, though a suitable machine could not be released for me, the College might acquire a second-hand one on my behalf. Since there are no second-hand ones in the market, and since, if there were, I or the College could buy one of the type required without a permit, this soft answer has failed to turn away my wrath.

I occupied my train-journeys with the *Mémoires* of André Maurois who has had an odd career. His real name is Herzog and he is by origin an Alsatian Jew who was for a time a successful business man in the family textile concern at Elbeuf in Normandy. In the last war he was liaison officer with the British army, opened his literary career with *Les Silences du Colonel Bramble*, and for some time specialised on England, writing books on Disraeli, Edward VII, Shelley, and Byron, of which the last is, I think, good, the others quite pleasant but much slighter. He has lived a good deal in England, gave a course of lectures in this College in 1928, and has received much hospitality from various distinguished people. In 1939 he was again attached to the British army, this time as Official Eye-Witness, came to England for a few months in 1940, and then retired to America, where he now lectures on French literature at a College in California. I should have thought that a Frenchman who owes so much to England, which he professes to understand, and has professed to admire, might, however patriotic (and, by the way, not all French patriots have retired to California), be disposed to admit that in the last four years this country has in some respects done rather better than his own. All M.'s bouquets are for America, but I did not grudge them for I had read the book up to that point with a growing distaste for the author's outlook on most subjects. However, I also read it, especially the parts about his childhood, with some interest, and you might find it more congenial than I.

For the rest, by the end of the vac. I had finished the memoir of Gaselee except for some trifling details to be verified, had put together some emendations of his for a learned journal, and at very long last (for I have been trying since July) had produced a new edition (the 7th) of the College Wardens' manual, revised in light of the Fire Guard Plan — or rather in its darkness, for there are many points which remain obscure, partly for the reasons given last month, partly because the plan doesn't really fit our particular circumstances very well, and partly because, as I have said before, its details sometimes clash with the University and Colleges Joint Fire Protection Scheme. I was just sending out no. 53 when I received a supply of forms which I was to complete as soon as I had extinguished any fires caused by enemy action. One section asked for a census of nine different types of bomb which might have fallen (leaving, however, space for other types not specifically mentioned). I asked how, if the bomb had exploded, I was to know how much it had weighed and what had been written on it and was told that I should soon learn to distinguish them in practice. But I sincerely hope that I shan't.

12.2.44

Term had already just begun when I sent out no. 53, but it hasn't so far been either very memorable or very agreeable. I see that there are about sixty freshmen, of whom nine are at Trinity — a considerable decrease on last January's entry, but then there was no scholarship exam. last December. That pleasure has been reserved for March and is at the moment calling on me to set some papers. It may, I suppose, bring in a few men next term but not enough to counterbalance a considerable drop in our numbers in prospect owing to the fact that there will be substantially fewer Cadets taking the new courses which begin in April. I see that at this time last year I supplied some details of the men then reading different subjects, so to keep step I shall here record that scientists, engineers, and mathematicians, who number respectively 790, 451, and 104, are almost precisely as plentiful as they were a year ago, but that these three faculties now embrace considerably more than two thirds of the resident male population. This state of affairs was inevitable as soon as all postponement of service for Arts students came to an end, and one may be glad that it did not arise earlier; but nobody can think it desirable and I sincerely trust that it will not last very long.

Other scraps of news must keep for I am a bit under the weather besides being very busy. The fashionable influenza has, as usual, passed me by, but I have had a heavy cold and am menaced besides with lumbago (also fashionable), which, without laying me up, has from time to time administered a sufficiently vicious jab to the small of my back to remind me of what it did last May. Having no mind to encourage a repetition of those tasteless pranks, I have had to move warily for some time past, for until this week I have had three separate courses of lectures to give (one of which, *laus Deo*, is now ended), and also a great deal of supervision which, owing to the exigences of the men's timetables, arranges itself very inconveniently for me, and is indeed difficult to arrange at all. I am also occupied with the happy and congenial duty of rounding up all the civilian gas-masks in College and having them tested for defects. In short this is one of the not rare periods at which I am not at my brightest and best.

FIFTY-FIFTH LETTER

Answers to Correspondents (no. 53): Galligaskens are wide breeches; skabilonions (a mysterious word) apparently the hose or drawers you wear under them. Hooese I take to be merely an uneconomical way of spelling hose. I think of introducing it to the College Fire Party.

FIFTY-FIFTH LETTER

11.3.44

Term, which ends to-day, has been chiefly remarkable for the weather, for January was in the main so mild that the snowdrops grew into quite tall flowers and before the end of the month there was an appreciable display of yellow crocuses which always appear before the others. Deluded by these events the birds struck up a vigorous spring-chorus, but they have since shut up, for February has been a good deal colder with occasional brief flurries of snow and it was not until the end of it that the yellow crocuses, which had flowered gaily all through, began to be joined by small parties of blue and white. They are still going quite strong and though the carpet in our Avenue has usually been thicker it can have seldom lasted so long. Meanwhile there has been almost no rain and not enough snow to matter, and we may well be faced with a water-shortage. For many months now the Fountain has been reduced to a mere dribble, and occupants of the Great Court have listened in vain for the plash of water which I used, when I lived there, to count one of its amenities; and though this may be partly due to choking of the spring near Madingley which feeds it, the Clerk of the Works has lately produced a report on soundings in the College well which, if not wholly intelligible to me, is vaguely menacing. I haven't enjoyed these months very much myself though there have been some lovely sunny days for I have been too busy and not very well, but with the aid of rugs and hot-water bottles and a little electric warmth in the evenings I have got through them without much to complain of, and I have derived much comfort from my corduroy trousers—so much indeed that when it was announced that I could have a reasonable number of pockets I entertained the idea of ordering a suit of it against next winter. I have, however, been obliged to put it from me on the discovery that corduroy is now mostly reserved for agricultural labourers and that the only tailor in the town who has any has no workman left who can make a coat of it. True, the populace seeing me in such a suit might suppose me more Bloomsbury-minded than in fact I am, but disappointment has been little solaced by this reflexion for I shouldn't greatly care if it did.

We have collected one or two new Professors and are engaged in collecting some more, whereby I am unpleasantly reminded that of the too numerous Chairs to which I am an elector three are vacant. That of Classical Archaeology is to be filled in the summer (long notice having been given because prospective candidates are probably strewn about the Mediterranean), and the others (Latin and Fine Arts) will no doubt need occupants before long; and electing Professors tends to be both disagreeable and laborious—disagreeable because for any Chair to which one is likely to be an elector some of one's friends are likely to be candidates and one would rather not sit in judgment on them; laborious because if one knows little of a candidate one may feel it incumbent on one to read his works. Among Professors already garnered is a new Regius of Modern History, G. N. Clark, until now Chichele Professor at Oxford, whom we have made a Fellow. We have also elected Lord Russell whose previous connexion with the College (when he was Bertrand Russell) was narrated in no. 36. Since it was so, his subsequent academic adventures should perhaps be added, for they are sensational enough and have occupied a lot of space in the American papers. I don't know them in detail or very accurately, but he was lecturing in America and was appointed to a Chair of philosophy in New York. This appointment raised a hullabaloo from those who considered his views on matrimony unsound, and after much fuss and a lawsuit the appointment was either cancelled or not ratified. After a brief interlude of lecturing in the far west he was appointed for a period of years to a lectureship financed by a wealthy American named Barnes who presently quarrelled with him and dismissed him. R. then brought an action against Barnes and after several lawsuits found himself with substantial damages and without a job. It is very right and proper that so distinguished a scholar should again be a Fellow of his own College, but in view of R.'s previous relations with it there is some humour in the report that among the circumstances leading to the breach with Barnes and hence to R.'s return to Trinity was that he had defended the position of the British in India, of which B. disapproved — for a less likely stepping-stone on the homeward journey I imagine nobody could have conceived.

Otherwise the time of University bodies has been largely taken up with attempts to foresee the future, make their own plans, and answer questions addressed to them by others — and they are not finding it at all easy. There is, for instance, a general idea abroad (though I do not really know on what it is based) that there will be a largely increased demand for University education after the war, and we have been bidden to declare what is to be the size of this University and what additional numbers it could accommodate in a demobilisation rush. The answer to the first question is not too difficult, for unless the character of the University is to be fundamentally changed, as nobody, I think, desires, our numbers are conditioned by the accommodation in Colleges. This College, for instance, could only feed six to seven hundred, and, as older parishioners will remember, can barely house so many. Add your College totals together, throw in a moderate addition of non-Collegiate students, and you have an answer, which needs only to be qualified by riders saying that the University Laboratories will only house x physicists, y anatomists, and so on. The total for the whole University works out at about 5300 and is almost precisely the number which it held in 1938-9, so that if anyone has been banking on a large capacity for expansion here (or, I suppose, at Oxford) he will have to think again. The answer to the second question is also not difficult; we, for instance, could at an extreme pinch accommodate 750 provided that it was only for an emergency period, and the University as a whole could digest about an extra thousand. But these answers must be governed by the proviso that we can recover our staff both teaching and domestic, fill the vacancies which have accrued during the war, and have our premises back; and the question of buildings, both College and University, is fraught with difficulty. Many were requisitioned by the Office of Works in 1939, the occupants placed there by them cannot be dislodged by us, and in some cases they have made so free with the buildings that even if labour is available, which seems improbable, it would take six months or more to restore them to their pristine and proper uses. Other premises are occupied by evacuated institutions whom we could no doubt turn into the street; but if we did some would have no homes until bomb-damage was repaired, others until they in their turn had evicted squatters over whom they have no authority. Moreover lodgings as well as College and University buildings will be needed, and a wholesale evacuation of the town will be necessary before we can house our estimated quotas.

Then there are questions as to the future needs of faculties based on the assumption that there will be a lot of Government money available for expansion. These tend to be complicated by consideration of the implications of the Tom Report or the Dick Report, on which the Government has still to take action, or of the probable findings of the Harry Committee who have not yet reported. (Life would be at any rate a little simpler if committees were named after their subject and not after their eminent chairmen.) Take the Medical School, for instance, where reforms and expansion have long been envisaged though their nature has been the subject of strong and legitimate difference of opinion. Are we to aim at a school of clinical study? or of post-graduate research? or of both? How decide when we do not know whether Addenbrooke's Hospital is to be vastly enlarged and made into a Regional Hospital or not? The Regius Professorship of Physic is at present vacant, and again considerable and legitimate difference of opinion has existed as to whether this Chair should normally be held by a distinguished physician, who is likely to come to it at a mature age and therefore only hold it for a short time, or by a younger man actively engaged not in practice but in clinical research. Moreover, though the wishes of the University would probably be taken into account, the R.P.P. is a Crown appointment not ours. Here, then, are three problems inextricably linked. The future of Addenbrooke's (at any rate) will be decided when the report of a committee (here called the Goodenough C.) has been issued and implemented by Government action[1] But if Addenbrooke's is to be doubled or trebled in size it will take years to build the necessary accommodation, and it will take much time and thought to organise whatever extensions and reforms are ultimately decided on in the Medical School. Meanwhile we might well like the assistance and advice of a Regius Professor of one sort or the other, but how do we get him until we can tell him what his duties will ultimately be?

I take the medical problem as an illustration because the difficulties are widely, though not always completely, known in medical circles, from whom from time to time we receive memoranda on them. It is perhaps the most complicated, but there are others which, though less visible to the outside world, are hardly less so, and it shows the sort of problem which tends to accumulate in a University during a long period of abnormal conditions imposed by war. They are not insoluble of course but they will call for many years of hard thinking and organising, and though the post-war period will have the outstanding and undeniable

[1] See p. 238.

advantage of being post-war, I confess that I don't see much else to look forward to in its initial period.

The constant presence of Cassino in the headlines has reminded me of what St Benedict says about it in the *Paradiso* — 'The mountain whose summit was crowded with the people gulled and ill-disposed'. It has also reminded me that the last time I passed that way I was pleased to observe in the station a large L.M.S. poster saying 'Visit Peebles'. I have sometimes wondered whether many of the Cassinesi obeyed this exhortation and, if so, whether they really enjoyed themselves.

FIFTY-SIXTH LETTER

15.4.44

My Easter Vacation number has usually been occupied with literary tittle-tattle, which once had a point since it indicated to some parishioners, or so it was hoped, books which they might like to read. I doubt if it serves that purpose now, for all readable new books go out of print and disappear from the shops in the twinkling of an eye. The book trade is in fact in a sorry plight for lack of paper, and the University is beginning to worry about the shortage of text-books. Had you read the *Cambridge University Reporter* diligently during the past two or three years (an improbable contingency) you would often have noticed changes in the schedules of books set for examination (especially in English and Modern Languages) owing to those originally prescribed being unobtainable, and a sudden return to anything like normal numbers would probably cause great difficulties in most faculties for the same reason. However the unlikelihood of your being able to find the books shall not deter me from following my usual custom for there is little else to write about.

As usual when I review the books I have read I am dismayed by the desultory character of the list, and though this time a good many of them deal with the Far East I will not pretend that this is more than an accident, for it was not until I came to write them down that I became aware of the fact myself. I may as well begin with these. M. Collis, *Lords of the Sunset* (about the Shan States), and *She was a Queen* (a picturesque book about the Tartar invasion of Burma in the 11th cent.); H. R. Robinson, *A Modern de Quincey* (rather a sordid record of opium-smoking in Burma); and two books about the war in those parts — G. Rodger, *Red*

Moon Rising (with excellent photographs), and J. Morrison, *Malayan Postscript.* (Some interesting matter about the war in Malaya by A. H. Hill has lately been appearing in *Blackwood.*) Thence into China: *Through Jade Gate and Central Asia*, by M. Cable and F. French, is an earlier and less good travel-book than one by the same authors commended in no. 49: *Autobiography of a Chinese Girl*, by Hsieh Ping-Ying is rather an attractive book by a young woman who is advanced enough to have joined the army but not enough to have shed the queer and rather engaging naïveté which clings to Chinese life. H. Mears, *Year of the Wild Boar*, is a curious account of life in Japan by an American woman; C. Crockett, *The House in the Rain-Forest*, is a pleasant book about New Guinea by an anthropologist. Next I may mention two good Penguins about Africa: *Guerrilla War in Abyssinia*, by W. E. D. Allen, and *Into Madagascar*, by K. C. Gandar Dower, a former pupil of mine, lately, I am sorry to say, reported missing. Other books between travel and autobiography are *Africa Drums*, by R. St B. Baker (Kenya and Nigeria); P. W. Ranier, *Green Fire* (emerald-mining in Colombia); *Young Man of Caracas*, by T. R. Ybarra (Venezuela; amusing); *The Track*, by A. Barea (a grim book about Spanish campaigns in Morocco; sequel to *The Forge* mentioned in no. 32). I have also read in autobiography a much older one by W. P. Frith, painter of *Derby Day* (rather entertaining); the second volume of Henson's *Retrospect* (with further remarkably candid opinions on Church and Churchmen); *Myself*, by X. M. Boulestin, probably better known as a cook than as a writer though he was both and had known some interesting people; *Good Neighbours*, by W. Rose, a picture of village life; *Malachi Horan Remembers*, conversations with an Irish nonagenarian recorded by G. A. Little (I recommend both of these); *Four Score Years*, by G. G. Coulton whose lectures some of you may have attended — a very pleasant book though little concerned with Cambridge. I have also read two biographies of archaeologists — *Time and Chance*, about the Evans family by the younger sister of Sir Arthur Evans, and *The Traveller's Journey is done*, a life of Humfry Payne, a very distinguished young archaeologist whom I knew, by his wife, who uses her maiden name of Powell. With these may go the *Letters of G. S. Gordon*, President of Magd., Oxford (whom I also knew slightly) which I thought rather disappointing, and an apparently autobiographical novel called *Highland River* by N. M. Gunn.

That about exhausts my list (and probably my readers) but I will throw in some strays—a book by G. M. Richter about Andrea del Castagno, a painter who interested me a good deal when I was a more serious student of Italian art than I have time to be nowadays; *Target: Germany*, a record of the American 8th Bomber Command which I recommend; and two novels, *Portrait in a Mirror* by C. Morgan which I found readable, and an immense novel in two parts about India in the time of Akbar, called *The Near and the Far* and by L. H. Myers. This from time to time vexed me by its leisurely progress and by the unconscionable number of loose strings which festoon it but it seemed to me to deserve the perseverance which it certainly demands. I have also skimmed (heaven knows why) a work on poisonous fishes by H. M. Evans called *Sting-Fish and Seafarer*, where I read that when the Psalmist promised me that I might with impunity tread the young lion under my feet he really meant that I might step on the poisonous spine of the Lesser Weever: and this privilege, if I were more addicted than I am to paddling, would at least be more advantageous than I have ever reckoned the other.

Coulton's book, by the way, contains a slightly different, and I think somewhat inferior, version of the poem about Teddy Perowne going to his own which I recorded in no. 49, but says nothing about its having been discovered in an examination; and I suspect that this story, like many another, had been polished up before it reached me. Also that the poet may have plagiarised. One parishioner knew a similar rhyme about Lloyd George (which is too late to matter), another one about Gladstone (priority here uncertain)—though no doubt if you wish to stigmatise your enemy as Iscariot in verse, unless he is complaisant enough to be called Marriott, you fall back upon chariot as the obvious rhyme. Another University anecdote in which the limelight has revealed flaws concerns the feat of jumping our Hall steps from bottom to top. The other day General Montgomery being here told the Master that his father had performed it, and bade him publish the fact—as he duly did in the *Times*. General M. being News, other papers copied it, with the incidental result that for some days we were beset by aspirants to the same distinction, and by press photographers recording their mostly unsuccessful attempts. No doubts are here cast on the prowess of the General's father, but the tradition, recorded in the Master's book, that Whewell, when Master, seeing some young gentlemen at this exercise, clapped his mortar-board firmly on his head and accomplished it, has thus been brought under a scrutiny which it doesn't seem to stand very well. For one thing, whatever Whewell's faults may have been, an inadequate sense of his own dignity was not among them. For another, W. was forty-five when he became Master, and over sixty when Sir George Young, who claimed to have witnessed the exploit, came into residence. Therefore, though no doubt within reach of an athletic undergraduate, I decline on present evidence to believe that W. (who, incidentally, was built like a prize-fighter) achieved it, at any rate as Master. As a result of all this we have had in the *Times* a sort of silly-season correspondence about feats of endurance and agility performed by undergraduates, which caused me to think how nice it would be if the papers should ever again be empty of news. 'There's nothing I like better on a Sunday or a holiday', says someone in *Faust*, 'than a gossip about war and rumours of war'; but few now can share this taste, and I look back myself to an Arcadian day before the last war when all one evening paper could find for its placard was 'Sad Death of a Gentleman'.

For the last six months, however, we have been plagued with other feats of undergraduate prowess of the kind which result in inappropriate objects being affixed to inaccessible pinnacles from which our decrepit and overworked staff must risk their necks to retrieve them, stealing of notice-boards difficult or impossible to replace, and removal of man-hole and coal-hole covers from the pavement so that those who walk the darkened streets by night may break their legs. I do not count it among my many faults as a Tutor that I took an unduly censorious view of youthful levities, but I confess that even in peace-time I used to think this kind of joke singularly unfunny. In present conditions it is a good deal less than that, and if it fell to me to interview these heroes I would undertake to mend their sense of humour. However as they are practically never caught, and would in any case be no affair of mine, they will no doubt escape that experience. If they are never caught, how do I know that they are undergraduates? Well, I admit that I do not — but I have my suspicions. It is perhaps not wholly *à propos de bottes* to record that an R.A.F. Cadet whom I was interviewing for a commission the other day, when asked whether he felt he had sufficient self-confidence to impress his personality on a tough crew of colonial air-gunners, replied (rather pertly, I thought) 'Oh yes, I think so; I've been six months at . . .' (well no: perhaps it would be indiscreet to say which College he mentioned).

23.4.44

No. 56 was sent out just at the end of a vacation which was an insult to the name. It began with two days spent on interviewing R.A.F. cadets, I had some laborious Tripos papers to set, there were committees to attend, and there was an Entrance Scholarship exam. which occupied the last ten days of March. This last was an intolerable imposition. It is bad enough (at least for those who loathe examining as much as I do) to have three of them in fifteen months, and I suppose that the poor standard of candidates, which made it worse, was partly due to this increased frequency; add that those responsible planted it in the very middle of the so-called vacation and you will understand why it made me peevish. As it was drawing drearily to its end we were, for four nights, more or less driven from house and home by a military invasion. In prospect this was unwelcome, and to me a source of some anxiety, for A.R.P. is one thing and P(assive) A(ir) D(efence) for aught I know another. In the event, however, it proved very pleasant. No doubt the ghosts of ancient Dons gibbered shrilly together on the Combination Room stairs as they passed notices directing them to Ante-room and N.A.A.F.I., but the inconvenience to us was inconsiderable, the Army of Occupation seemed appreciative of its quarters, and it included a parishioner and other pupils and acquaintances whom I had not seen for many years. It also entertained a few of us to a Mess Guest-night in Hall which, if weak on drink, attained an almost pre-war standard in food. Do not, however, believe the papers, from the *Times* downwards, which said that Eisenhower and Montgomery were there, for they were not.[1]

Apart from this interlude a brief visit from another parishioner almost completes the record of my diversions since I last wrote, unless you should count among them that, as the end of last term found me about as energetic as a piece of chewed string, I took, not without some effect, a course of ultra-violet rays as a tonic, and had a rheumatic shoulder massaged. I had intended to crown these joys with some more short-wave treatment for my arthritic joints, which have been troublesome, but this cup was dashed from my lip by the discovery that the apparatus was out of order. I have not been away, could scarcely have done so if I had wished, and in fact hardly wished. I had hoped to do a little work of my

[1] See p. 232.

own but what with one interruption and another I did not really get started until the last fortnight before term, and by then libraries were closing for Easter. My immortal work has been almost at a standstill since October, partly owing to other demands on my time, partly because I am bogged in a sticky patch of it, but more, I think, because, as these weary years roll on, the odd hour or half-hour at the end of the day which I might devote to research finds me too jaded to do so to any good purpose. However I do not delude myself with the belief that the sum total of human knowledge or happiness is thereby much diminished, and no doubt many another scholar finds himself in the like case.

For light vacation reading I was supplied with a volume of two hundred odd pages in which are printed the answers of the Faculties and Departments when asked what their post-war development plans might be. When totted up they involve capital expenditure of about a million, and increased annual expenditure of about a quarter of a million. These figures are not necessarily preposterous, for an unofficial Parliamentary and Scientific Committee not long ago recommended that the Treasury should raise its annual grant to Universities from two and a quarter to six or seven millions, and should assign them ten millions for capital expenditure; and, if it did, our share might come to something like the sums which the various development-plans are now seen to involve. There are, however, three dragons lurking on the first stage of this path. One is that the calculations are based on pre-war costs of building, equipment, and maintenance, and must therefore be much below the true figure: the second that maintenance-costs for what we already possess are likely to be much heavier after the war than they were in 1938: the third that we have already incurred an increased annual expenditure of £30,000 in war-bonuses and allowances for assistants for which new money must be found, and unless we do something comparable for teaching officers (to the tune of, say, £100,000) we shall be unlikely to get the men we want. It is all very complicated. However in the meantime we cannot do more than forward our plans to the University Grants Committee who originally asked for them. When it is known what money is available no doubt the General Board will wrap towels round its heads and sit down to compose an order of precedence and settle whether (let us say) a Demonstratorship in Anthropophagy is more, or less, urgently needed than a Lectureship in Ooscopy and Coscinomancy.

And if by then I have ceased to be a member of the Board I shall support my exclusion from these deliberations with fortitude.

Somebody, by the way, on reading no. 55, said that all this post-war planning was too optimistic. If so, the optimism proceeds from the Grants Committee (on whom see no. 11) not from us; but unless it is too sanguine to assume that the future of British Universities is likely to be planned by the British and not by the Germans (and I hope it is not), I do not consider that much optimism is involved. The enquiry assumes that the war will end some day, and may, like the last, end suddenly; I do not think it implies any view as to when the day will be.

13.5.44

Term began as long ago as April 18 but it has produced no startling incidents and its brief and unexciting chronicle had best be reserved until it is complete, for one term now is much like another. I say 'now', but I sometimes wonder whether a *revenant* from 1938 dropped unexpectedly in the Great Court would immediately notice anything amiss. The average age of undergraduates is of course much less, but he would not immediately miss the older section; many have uniforms, but they don't wear them all or every day; and I am not sure that among the outward and visible signs of war the earliest to catch his attention might not be the number of undergraduates who carry loaves of bread about under their arms. Quite right they should too, for, as I have said before, they are of an age for which the ration is really insufficient, and (in Dr. Johnson's words) 'I look upon it that he who does not mind his belly will hardly mind anything else'. No doubt they would carry cakes if they could, but cakes, I am told by those who know, require much diplomacy, and the young woman in *Canticles* who clamours in the Authorised Version to be stayed with flagons, and in the Revised to be stayed with raisin-cake, would find in this town at any rate her revised demand deemed at least as unreasonable as the first. And even in London I notice that the fat man in my club who used always to have for tea two muffins, two crumpets, and a piece of Boodle's Cake (an order which, with long practice, he would give almost in one syllable) is now woefully shrunk within the embrace of the chair he once largely overflowed. Meanwhile the College, having extracted no satisfaction from the Ministry of Food on the ration question, has given undergraduates the option of contracting out of lunch in Hall, thinking that if enough did so breakfast and dinner might be made more substantial. It also seemed possible that they would create such a congestion in the British Restaurants that the Borough might join in beating on the doors of the Ministry of Food. As in the event less than a dozen have availed themselves of the option neither result will ensue; and I think the majority have chosen wisely, for all the restaurants are crowded out and the bother of getting things to eat in your rooms is excessive. And the Kitchens, if they no longer, like the Johnian Kitchens of whom Wordsworth so beautifully sang, 'make a humming sound, less tuneable than bees, But hardly less industrious', produce on the whole edible if not very appetising meals and quite large enough for me. Indeed I suppose that a sudden return to the flesh-pots of pre-war peace would result in a heavy mortality among us from surfeits and apoplexies. I turned up the other day with amusement the menus of dinners I had given to the Family (my dining club), where seven courses and dessert were almost *de rigueur*, and wondered whether I could cope with such a dinner after four years' rationing. I used to think them over-long even at the time, and mine were airy trifles compared to some I recall designed by the older members of the club, who were apt to produce about course five a saddle of mutton or a beefsteak pudding. However I ought perhaps to say that my present contentment is partly due to generous support from the Parish, from whom I have lately received tributes of Italian lemons, Canadian olives, and Australian cheese — all excellent, and the more welcome because cheese and fruit are what I most miss.

It is likely, I suppose, that the storm whose approach has held us tensed for a long while now will have broken before I send out another letter — may even have done so before this one has been duplicated and dispatched for I go to press on May 8. I shall not write about it except to say that those of you who will be in it are much in my thoughts.[1]

FIFTY-EIGHTH LETTER

14.6.44

Y ou will, I am sure, neither expect me to write about France nor suppose that I think of anything else. This letter was fortunately finished by June 6.

Full term, of which a retrospect was reserved for this number, ends

[1] Allied forces landed in France on June 6.

on June 9, having provided some delicious sunny days in April, and a really hot week towards the end of May which brought in high summer sooner and faster than I could have wished. For the rest, though we are still dreadfully short of rain, it has been mostly cold and overcast, and there was a frost early in May which is said to have done much damage. Consequently, though I heard swifts outside my bedroom window on May 8, it was close on three weeks before they took up their usual evening gambols in Nevile's Ct. I heard no cuckoo until May 6, and have heard none since, but that is partly because they do not much frequent the Backs and I as seldom get beyond them, partly because the din of aeroplanes has for many weeks been so continuous and insistent that for much of the day and night a cuckoo might almost discharge its eponymous function on my window-sill without making itself heard. My phenological notes might indeed record when, let us say, a Marauder first swam into my ken, but I suppose the censor would disapprove of such a record and I am not very well equipped to make it. I understand that natives of the Solomon Islands, to whom any aeroplane was lately 'schooner-belong-Jesus', now distinguish a Zero from a Mitshubishi with unerring precision, but my own progress in these studies has been less spectacular, and though a round score of species frequent the Cambridge skies I confess that I am decidedly shaky on the rarer specimens.

The population of the town has decreased a bit because a Government Dept. received a letter to the effect that we should like University buildings evacuated in the near future. We meant laboratories and lecture-rooms, but the G.D., pardonably unable to distinguish between University and Colleges, withdrew the occupants of certain Colleges at a moment's notice — to the considerable annoyance of the said Colleges, who were left with rooms they could not staff and for which they receive no rent. This College, which could have spared its lodgers without flinching, has only recovered one staircase, and that for a different reason. The population of the University has also declined, for there are some two hundred fewer Cadets in the present six-months course than in the last though the Services concerned contemplate a return to the old numbers in September. Owing to this decrease I have had less supervision to do, for the five Colleges who cast all their Classical cares on me muster only two Classical Cadets as against six last term. I haven't minded a slight let-up, as you may imagine, but of late Cadets have been more amusing to teach than the few ordinary undergraduates, who would not be here unless they were very young and in consequence immature and ill-read. There are still, however, a good many Classics in the University and I have been lecturing to a class of forty about equally divided between the sexes — on Martial, a subject in my repertory which always reminds me that in my young days, when lectures were College lectures and you couldn't attend those in another College without leave, a Newnhamite who asked the then Master of Caius whether she might come to his on Martial was said to have received the answer 'No decent woman would wish to attend my lectures'. But I must warn you that if you must draw inferences from this incident they should relate to Classical lecturers not to Newnhamites, for my discourses on this poet would draw no blood to the most modest cheek.

And, talking of the Classics, the University has just received a legacy for their advancement which will bring in about £1,500 a year — a tribute to the subject the more handsome in view of the fact that the testator was bracketed bottom in the Classical Tripos four years before I was born. But, like the legacy to the Botanic Garden mentioned in no. 42, it bids fair to prove somewhat embarrassing for it is strictly tied up for scholarships, of which the faculty already possesses about as many as it can profitably award in an average year. And if you wish to draw inferences here also, they are that if any of you contemplate leaving large bequests to the University you should either give that body a good deal of discretion in disposing of them or should consult somebody on the spot as to the way in which they can be most profitably employed.

University business has been very dull. I have been sitting on a committee which is trying to draft a general rule which shall allow those who return into residence after war-service reasonable latitude as to the date at which they shall take examinations — a nightmarish task, for the standing of candidates for examinations is a complicated matter and scarcely two faculties have framed their regulation alike. For the rest we have been busy with the published reports of such committees as were mentioned in no. 55 — the Norwood Report (on *The Curriculum and Examinations in Secondary Schools*: 150 pp.), the McNair Report (on *The Supply, Recruitment, and Training of Teachers and Youth Leaders*: 176 pp.), and the Loveday Report (on *Veterinary Education*: only 35 pp. but it is a second report). Have I read them all? Well, no. I read the last, but have only dipped into the others, for, truth to tell, though I have spent my life in the practice of education, the theory of it repels me. I believe in my own subject and wish a sufficient number of suitable persons to study it both for its sake and for theirs; but when I am bidden to consider at what age boys shall take the examination which, in a new and better world, will replace the School Certificate, how many subjects they shall offer, whether they shall devote two periods a week to geography or three, and the like, my spirit, though I know it should not, shrivels within me. I did, however, read the bit about Youth Leaders, and was filled with compassion for those who would henceforward be cast on the world with this hideous label attached to them and that without even a hyphen to their names. I do not know whether it is due to the influence of Hitlerjugend, Giovanezza, and such, but the word youth', like the equally respectable word 'people', begins to stink.

The Fitzwilliam has been unusually active for it received last year several large gifts. Consequently it has rehung four rooms with quite an entertaining display of newly acquired drawings and prints, and it has also, for the first time since the war began, had some of the Courtauld rooms open, to house a Greek exhibition on the lines of those which have been held recently in London and Edinburgh. Naturally few of the larger objects were of the first water, but they looked very well in that setting and it was a real pleasure to have some more of the Museum open if only for a month.

Other diversions have been few. The Prime Ministers of Australia and New Zealand received honorary degrees last month, but I was not there to see, partly because I have little taste for such ceremonies, partly because I was at the time queued up among the out-patients at Addenbrooke's whither I have been resorting twice a week for the treatment which, as I said last month, I failed to obtain in the vac. — a bore, but one sees life, and that not so proletarian as you might suppose for I usually encounter the Vice-Chancellor in the same queue and on the same errand as myself. One Sunday afternoon I attended a private showing of the British Council film of Cambridge mentioned in no. 53, wherein you may see (for it will soon be released) some excellent views of the town, diverse aspects of undergraduate life, and a number of eminent and less eminent persons negotiating their hoops with the customary address. You may also see the College Fire Party running a line of hose up to the Chapel roof and feeding it from the Fountain — very efficiently too, though I will not take my oath that the projector does not speed them up a bit. Of its kind a good film I thought.

The Fire Party leads naturally to A.R.P., but from that front there is little to report except that I have had to spend a good deal of time to very little purpose at a refresher course for Wardens, and that the Regional authorities, having discovered what I told you and could have told them many months ago, namely that the Fire Guard Plan and the University and Colleges Joint Fire Protection Scheme are incompatible, have substantially modified the former and more or less scrapped the latter, with the result that the seventh edition of my manual for College Wardens which, as recorded in no. 54, was, after long labour, brought to birth in January, is out of date and has needed much amendment. Another consequence of the alterations in the F.G.P. is that we are now in the same sector as St John's, and that, as the Sector Point is now there, I am degraded from Sector Captain to a paltry Block Leader and am faced with the appalling humiliation (if anybody remembers) of having my tin hat removed in order that someone may paint out one of its noble black stripes. Amid all this I preserve my sanity (in so far as I do preserve it) partly owing to the fact that the second in command of the local F.G. office has a sense of humour, and when I told him, as I did a month or so since, that our Sector Point Sign had been stolen he was merely convulsed with laughter. Still, I hope that certain precautions which I have taken may preserve for us the Block Point Sign which now adorns or disfigures the Great Gate in its place.

FIFTY-NINTH LETTER

25.6.44

No. 58 was sent out just after the Second Front had been established, and I suppose that to me as to most people, participants and spectators alike, the event was in a sense a relief, for, as Brutus says, Between the acting of a dreadful thing And the first motion, all the interim is Like a phantasma — and the interim had been long. But too much is at stake, and too many friends of mine are involved, for it to have brought more than a change of anxieties, and parishioners will not, I know, mistake the trivialities with which this letter must be filled for the real subject of my thoughts.

The war, too, has moved into districts better known to me than any hitherto and has roused a jumble of memories. I remember, as I was setting out for Caen, meeting Stephen Gaselee, who said 'You will have there some very good tripe', adding as an afterthought, 'You may also see the tomb of William the Conqueror'. But I was going there primarily to look at a very small number of Italian pictures in the gallery, there are better ways of cooking tripe than *à la mode de Caen*, and though I hope its two gaunt Norman abbeys still stand I have pleasanter recollections of Bayeux and its cathedral. Cherbourg stands in my mind for a dreary and tempestuous evening spent waiting for a boat, and for seeing a Frenchman catch a fish — an event which, from long observation of the serried ranks of anglers which line the rivers, canals, lakes, ponds, and piers of that country, I had supposed never to occur. In Italy also the names have associations. Orvieto, where I have stayed several times, competes with Urbino for the first place in my affections among the smaller hill-towns; it is a fascinating place, and its black and white zebra-striped cathedral is perhaps my favourite in Italy. I think also of a good day spent motoring from it to Viterbo, past Bolsena and Montefiascone in the country which produces the most attractive white wines of Italy; and of another from Viterbo, by way of Toscania and its vast empty churches, to Tarquinia, where you walk on an airy upland looking across the town and the Maremma to the sea, and dive from time to time into an Etruscan painted tomb-chamber which your guide unlocks for you. Less pleasantly I remember there a Good Friday procession in which a grubby urchin imperfectly disguised as a gilt-winged angel fainted, and was brought, expectorating freely, into the *trattoria* where I was dining to be refreshed with spirits; also the hotel whose discomforts drove me after one night to Civitavecchia. All these were in the news soon after the fall of Rome;[1] north of them, except on the Adriatic coast which I do not know south of Loreto, most places of any size, and some of none, are in varying degrees familiar, and their names in the paper stir anxiety as well as memory for many of them are delightful places and most hold treasures too easily destroyed.

The prospect of the Second Front, in addition to the anxieties common to us all, was responsible also for some local worries. It was thought possible that when it started the Home Guard might be called out, and if this had happened in the middle of Triposes there would have been a pretty academic mess to clear up. In fact the H.G. was not called out and Triposes had ended before the hour struck. It was thought that if it started before the Final M.B. exams. were over many of the candidates and some of the examiners would be called off to emergency hospitals;

[1] June 4.

and in fact it started before they began, and a few candidates, though not, I think, any examiners, were unable to appear. There was also a difficulty about patients for the clinical examinations as some of the wards at Addenbrooke's had been cleared for casualties. However the immediate effect upon the University was small, though I have felt glad that I had not to prepare for an examination during the long period of tension we have been going through and was thankful that there were only ten candidates in Part 2 of the Tripos in which I was examining at the time.

I suppose I can now reveal that the military occupation of the College mentioned in no. 57 was occasioned by an enormous conference during which the Great Court positively blushed with Generals. Naturally I didn't ask what they were conferring about, but it was not hard to guess, and the College now has in its archives a letter from the presiding General reporting the successful execution of the Combined Operation 'Conqueror' on June 6 and following days, and conveying the thanks of the three Services for our hospitality during its planning. It was kept very secret and the *canard* that Eisenhower and Montgomery were here probably arose from the discovery in the town that the College was closed to the public and had military pickets on its gates; also you will now understand why the A.R.P. arrangements caused me some anxiety.

14.7.44

The end of term was accompanied by the usual flurry of committees but I shall not chronicle their proceedings though I have nothing else to chronicle unless it should be that on June 20 I made my first, and presumably also my last, public appearance in a cope — not the ecclesiastical vestment but the sleeveless scarlet cloak with ermine hood and tippet worn by all Doctors in medieval Universities, and here by the Vice-Chancellor, by Doctors of Divinity at the Ash Wednesday Litany, and by those presenting people for higher degrees. This last duty may fall to chairmen of Faculty Boards and I was presenting a Classic for a Litt.D., a degree which, for one reason or another, very few Classics have taken in recent years. I had to go straight from the Senate House to a Board convened either to dismiss, or else to chasten, idle and refractory R.N. Cadets, and I rather regretted that I could not take the cope with me, for it would be a refractory Cadet indeed who should remain unshaken by an allocution from a President so formidably attired.

The Congregation at which I was performing happened to be that for

General Admissions which I used to attend regularly, for it is the custom of the Trinity Tutors to post themselves at the Doctors' Door of the Senate House and shake hands with their pupils and acquaintances as they pass out of it fully fledged — rather a sticky occupation on a hot day but enlivened by speculation among the Tutors as to which of the men, if any, has acquired a sufficiently wide social range to exchange handshakes with all four Tutors. Indeed, if they were of that habit of mind, some brisk betting might go on between them. I hadn't been to General Admissions for some years and was rather surprised to find so large an assembly of spectators, for in these days, as you may suppose, most undergraduates are far away by the end of their third year, and proceedings which used to take two days are now easily compressed into a morning. General Admissions, however, had begun even before the war to lose something of its old character, for idle Praelectors had encouraged people to take degrees by proxy, whereas in my young days they were not allowed to do so without solid excuses and the day rounded off the academic year, and marked the end of an academic generation, with a fine mustering of parents, sisters, and aunts. I rather regret the change, for if people drift away one by one at the end of term the year peters out rather feebly, and the proceedings in the Senate House were mildly picturesque, though I suppose that academic ceremonial is bound to go on declining in this particular. How much more picturesque (for instance) when a glomerel, who had been led by the Master of Glomery[1] before three Masters of Arts and had satisfied them that he deserved the minor degree of Master in Grammar, appeared before the Vice-Chancellor to receive it. Then, said the regulations, 'the Bedyll in Arte shall bring the Master of Gramer to the Vicechauncelar, delyvering hym a Palmer wyth a Rodde, whych the Vycechauncelar shall gyve to the seyde Master in Gramer and so create hym Master. Than shall the Bedell purvay for every Master in Gramer a shrewde Boy, whom the master in Gramer shall bete openlye in the Scolys, and the master in Gramer shall give the Boye a Grote for hys labour, and another Grote to hym that provydeth the Rod and the Palmer'. (A palmer is no doubt an implement for chastising on the palm, and 'shrewde' means 'naughty'.) And when we move with the times and institute a Diploma in Youth Leadership it seems to me that we might do worse than revive this procedure for its recipients.

[1] See p. 237.

My only direct news of D Day to date comes (in chronological order) from four parishioners, of whom one landed his glider on top of another and was quickly returned to an English hospital with slight concussion; one is surgeon in a destroyer; a third is in the R.A.S.C. and has written direct from France; the fourth is a too-reticent Wing-Commander who was towing gliders. Consequently, though I can think of many who may be there, I do not know who is. Those who are may well have little time for writing letters — but they might remember that even a line would be very welcome. I should also be glad to know why it is called D Day.[1]

SIXTIETH LETTER

12.8.44

THE August no. of the P.M. usually begins with some account of its progress and regress during the year, but there is not this August a great deal to record. Twelve months ago I still did not know for certain that it was circulating in Sicily (though in fact it was), and the inclusion of Italy and France are the high spots in this year's retrospect. Other new districts are Burma, Assam (I believe), and Ceylon. Against these Persia and Madagascar have disappeared; so has Sicily so far as I know, and so certainly have some parts of Africa, but it is impossible to keep track of parishioners in that continent and I shall not attempt to guess which. Numbers have remained pretty steady; if few issues have gone to more than ninety none have gone to less than eighty-five. I have not, for a long time past, aimed at increasing the circulation and have enrolled only two new subscribers in the year. As usual a few old ones have fallen off, but, also as usual, a few who had defaulted have renewed their subscriptions. One, I am very sorry to say, has lately been killed in Normandy; two have been discharged from the army as the result of wounds received in Africa and Italy.

And so ends a fifth weary year. Hitler told Henderson that he would prefer war when he was fifty (*i.e.* in 1939) to war when he was fifty-five. I hope and believe that he did indeed find it more agreeable five years ago than he does now, and I suppose that if he had foreseen its duration he would have planned it differently or not planned it at all. And when the idea of the P.M. first floated into my mind, as it did one late-August

[1] See p. 241.

day in 1939 as I drove homeward from Wales across the Cotswolds attending to the road with half my mind and with the other half vaguely pondering this and that, I also, if I had known what I was doing, should have planned differently or not at all. However it seems now not un-reasonable to hope that before another twelvemonth is complete we shall both be relieved of our burdens. I remember during that same drive thinking of the occasion on which the word National-Socialisten had first impinged on my consciousness. It was on a Sunday evening in September 1930. I was on my way home from Vienna, had reached Dresden from Prag in the afternoon, and after dinner was sitting on the terrace overlooking the great bend of the Elbe and was smoking my pipe contentedly enough but for a loud-speaker in a neighbouring café which was blaring out election results. Most of the successful candidates seemed to be National-Socialists, a word which then conveyed no meaning to me. It was the election in which the Nazi poll jumped from under one to over six million votes and placed Hitler firmly in the limelight; but of this I had as little inkling as of what his being there was going to mean to us all. And I sometimes wonder what posterity will think of an age which has allowed such a person to mean so much.

Since the end of last term I have been on the whole less busy than for a long time past. The Long Vac. meetings of the usual bodies have had unusually long agenda to deal with, and they have been more or less coincident with meetings of electors to two professorships with which I am concerned so that I have had to spend some time reading the works of possible candidates. Otherwise, having thrust the supervision of some Cadets on a deputy, I have not had very much to do and would willingly have gone away for a few days to get out of the noise, which, after a long stretch, I find rather wearing. For the only place where one can be reasonably sure of not hearing an aeroplane is in Hall where the din is usually such that one can hear nothing. (This, as I think I once said before, is partly due to the *élan* of war-time waiters, who, having break-fast to lay as well as dinner to serve, throw the crockery and cutlery about with a feverish abandon; partly, I must own, it proceeds from the High Table itself which, ever since I have known it, has contained one or two members whose vocal organs are under very imperfect control.) However I could think of no asylum within easy reach and therefore stayed here intending to spend instead some idle days in the sun and not foreseeing that whenever there was any sun there would be a high, cold, wind which would discourage me from sitting in it. It has, in fact, been until quite recently a very disagreeable summer. It did not rain seriously until the very end of June, and would probably not have done so then if I had not, on the previous evening, put myself and the Fire Party to some inconvenience in order to water the Master's raspberries (which is not so easy with a fire-hose as you might think); but it has been dull and cold — so cold that the cockchafers prudently prolonged their four-year sojourn under the turf of Nevile's Ct into July, which is very late for them. Their emergence is an annual event much looked forward to by the College cats both for sporting and for gastronomic reasons (and if you have ever observed them quartering the grass-plots in a midsummer twilight and from time to time leaping into the air in a seemingly demented manner that is the explanation), but it is disliked by me, for a cockchafer is too apt to bumble into my window and strike me sharply in the face before I have bent my mind to the question whether it is indeed a cockchafer or merely a distant Lancaster. However I have survived these various discomforts, have held Fire Guard exercises 'Phoenixette' and 'Granta', and having some time to spare have done a good deal of my own work though I have been too jaded to do it with much zest.

My thoughts still running much on France, I have been reading two fat volumes grimly entitled *Les Fossoyeurs*, by the French journalist who writes over the name of 'Pertinax', of which the first is devoted to Gamelin, Daladier, and Reynaud, the second to Pétain. I did not read very carefully for it is hard going especially for one not well-informed about French politics, but it is a devastating indictment and in its main outlines I should guess unanswerable. But whereas Pétain, with Laval and some others, seems damned beyond mercy or compassion, I felt some sympathy with the villains of the first volume who, for all their gross faults and blunders, appeared essentially to fail because they were utterly unequal to the appalling situations they were called upon to confront. It is a hideous story, enacted against an equally hideous background of faction, intrigue, and treason, and the first of these is, I fear, deeply ingrained in French character. I do not understand what goes on in Algiers, but I see little ground for hoping that even calamity has cured the nation of a taste which tore it in two over Dreyfus, Glozel, and I know not what lessers issues; and though English and American hesitations seem to me very unfortunate, they also seem to me inevitable. I am afraid also that there are now a good many Frenchmen for whom there can be no future place in any healthy France, and I remember with foreboding that it was a Frenchman (I do not know which) who said 'la vengeance est un plat qui se mange froid'. More cheerful reading (and vastly shorter) is a booklet produced by the French underground press entitled *Angleterre* and by an author who calls himself 'Argonne'. Its theme is that France and England are essentially one, and that their numerous disagreements have been family squabbles — dynastic, religious, political, but never national. I have heard on what I believe to be good authority that even before the invasion our stock stood much higher in France than it did four years ago, but it is surprising as well as heartening that such a thesis, whether tenable or not, should be upheld by a Frenchman, and the essay begins with a moving picture of the anxiety with which some Frenchmen at least watched the fate of this country in 1940.

Answer to correspondents (no. 59): Glomery is grammar, and glomerels were those who studied it — for it has possibly escaped your notice that the words 'grammar' and 'glamour', which have somewhat parted company in modern times, are really one and the same, the common element being, I suppose, mystery. The last Master of Glomery was Sir John Cheke in the first half of the sixteenth century, and the office, which perhaps goes back to pre-University times, is appropriately somewhat mysterious. The Master was appointed by the Archdeacon of Ely, seems to have been responsible for elementary teaching in the town, and to have later acquired some obscure but not important University duties. There was a Glomery Hall somewhere in the neighbourhood of Clare, and Glomery Lane ran from it parallel to Senate House Passage. I am sorry that this has vanished, for Cambridge has lost too many of its picturesque street-names. Petty Cury is of the right vintage, but Regent St, for instance, was better named as Preachers' Streetway (from the Dominican Priory on the site of Emmanuel), and Trinity Lane as Findsilver Lane; and where is now The Duddery in which clothes and woollens were sold? I like an ancient town to have ancient and thought-provoking street-names, and shall probably (unless some parishioner chances to be able to enlighten me) go to my grave wondering how a certain dirty little street in Amiens came by the name of Rue des Corps Nus Sans Têtes.[1]

[1] See p. 241.

SIXTY-FIRST LETTER

15.9.44

No. 60 was sent out at a week-end embittered by emergency meetings of three committees (an outrage in the second week of August), a weary inquest on a Fire Guard Exercise, and a session with the dentist. This one is written in Radnorshire whither I betook myself on weathering these storms, and it will contain neither academic news nor comment on the many momentous events which have contributed no little to the enjoyment of a holiday.[1] Travelling being what it is, I had hesitated long over taking one this year, but I had been in Cambridge since last September and concluded that a change of scenery, society, and diet was overdue; and in the event, having with some kind assistance at Euston secured a seat for the longest part of the journey, I got down to Wales with but little inconvenience and was very glad I had come. On my way I spent a night in London — an unusually quiet one I was told, but anyhow, despite the traffic in the street, it was quieter than any night in Cambridge for many a month and I slept sound enough. I had not many hours there, but I took the opportunity of inspecting the pile of rubble to which an early p-plane (f-bomb, doodle-bug, V 1, or what-not) had reduced a house belonging to me — a tasteless and impertinent action which I nevertheless supported with calm, for I had intended in any case to get rid of the house on the first favourable occasion, and though I was sorry for the tenants (who were killed) I had had no personal contact with them. I have neither right nor inclination to belittle the nuisance-value of these contraptions, but in case anyone overseas thinks they have changed the face of London I add that I noticed no other damage caused by them.

This no. will also lack what the September issue has usually contained, viz, a report on the books I have read since April, for I have left the list behind and cannot reconstruct authors and titles accurately enough from memory though you may perhaps get it later. I have, however, had served out to me for vacation reading the report of the Goodenough Committee (on *Medical Schools*; 313 pp.) of which I read enough to see that the regional planning of hospitals was not (as asserted in no. 55) within its terms of reference; and the Fleming Report (on *The Public*

---

[1] Allied forces landed in southern France on Aug. 15; entered Paris on Aug. 25 and Brussels on Sept. 3; and crossed the German frontier on Sept. 11. Rumania declared war on Germany on Aug. 25, Bulgaria on Sept. 5; Finland ceased hostilities on Sept. 4.

Schools and the General Educational System; 132 pp.) which contains some interesting if not very relevant historical matter on the origin of Public Schools, and proposals for the reservation in them of a percentage of places for boys from grant-aided secondary schools which sound reasonable enough in theory. The difficulties are more likely to arise in practice, and when it comes to implementing the various educational proposals now before the public (a process I expect to see described as pin-pointing the blue-print) I think there will be trouble.

I have also been reading *Cambridge Retrospect*, a slim booklet by T. R. Glover, once Public Orator, who died two years ago. It is not a good book, but it contains some reminiscences of Cambridge (mostly Johnian) worthies which amused me because I can remember most of the people mentioned; but I doubted as I read whether it would amuse you much, and it caused me to think, as I have often thought before, that the more remarkable figures who survived from the '60's and '70's of the last century into the first decade of this, and so into my undergraduate days, really ceased to be credible as soon as they ceased to exist. When this thought occurs to me it is naturally accompanied by the thought that since my generation of Dons stands to your generation of undergraduates as they did to mine, you may be thinking of us as we did of them. This is a sobering, but also rather a comforting, reflexion, for, in the days when the one-horse tram which conveyed us in a leisurely manner from the Senate House to the station could be halted in the King's Parade in order that the passengers might savour to the full an altercation there in noisy progress between the then Registrary and an Irish professor (a good friend of mine), Cambridge life had a certain colour and amplitude which I fear it may since have lost. Still, I do venture to think that Dons have grown less eccentric in the course of time and that none of my generation would, for instance, perform such exploits as those recorded long ago in the answers to a Quiz (no. 26), or, like Peter Mason, President of St John's, publish a Hebrew Grammar in the form of letters to a Duchess ('Your Grace having, I doubt not, committed to memory the Personal Pronouns given in one of my former letters, I now beg permission to go through their respective Declensions' — and so on). And if you counter this by arguing that our eccentricities, though of a different character, are no less absurd than theirs, I shall reply from my last ditch that in one particular at any rate I know we have improved. We cannot lecture as badly as some of them did or our lecture-rooms would be empty.

I do not mean, I hasten to add, that all the instructors of my youth were bad lecturers. On the contrary most of the younger and some of the older were competent, and a few more than competent; but there were also some whose lectures were a disgrace. I do not think Classics were worse off than other subjects for I have heard a similar tale from other faculties, but I take example from the Professors of Greek and Latin for I had the misfortune or imprudence to attend them both. Jebb was not an eccentric; he was a Knight, an M.P., a friend of Tennyson, and, as a scholar, not so distinguished as his contemporaries thought but still distinguished. His idea of lecturing was to read out in a monotonous inaudible voice from a notebook or proofsheets strings of references which nobody would look up and which would not have profited them if they had. Mayor, Professor of Latin, was very learned, perhaps fifteen years older than Jebb, and much odder. His method was to ramble from theme to theme as they came into his head — the names of the Greek letters, the Old Catholics, vegetarianism, and what not — none of them remotely connected with the subject on which he was supposed to be discoursing; then when the members of his scanty audience all chanced to absent themselves on the same day the course stopped. (This, incidentally, was an improvement on Jebb from our point of view, for Jebb took offence if we were absent and wrote angry letters to our Tutors.) The only course of Mayor's I attended was, I think, on Plautus — not that Plautus had been mentioned except accidentally by the time, some weeks later, when the lectures came to their predestined end. The only other attendant was an elderly clergyman with a game leg whom I conjecturally identified with a scholar of notoriously homicidal tendencies then resident in a neighbouring College. As he sat between me and the door and was reputedly apt to knife anyone who coughed or sneezed in his presence this added a spice of adventitious interest to the lectures since it was not until long after the course had ceased that I discovered him to be not after all the homicide but a harmless retired schoolmaster. Mayor's lectures were less boring than Jebb's, and as an occasional experience they might even have been called entertaining, but both alike were practically useless and it is extraordinary that Jebb, at any rate, should not have seen this, or if he did see it, should not have done better. Nobody by exercising thought can lecture brilliantly, but to lecture with reasonable competence I maintain to be within the powers of anyone who has no natural impediment and is willing to take pains. And when you moderns complain of your lectures in my hearing, or if you complain of mine out of my hearing, I should like to plant you for an hour or two in some of the lecture-rooms where I sat in my youth and hear what you would say of them.

I shall not, as anticipated in no. 60, go to my grave wondering about the Rue des Corps Nus Sans Têtes in Amiens, not because a parishioner has since visited it (though some may have done so),[1] but because, by one of those odd coincidences which nevertheless happen, I chanced, on the very day my last letter went out, to sit in the Combination Room next to a Free French physiologist who has been a member of our High Table for two or three years, and he chanced to reveal that he had once lived in Amiens. He said that the street was the site of the gibbet on which, according to the salutary custom of Picardy, the naked and decapitated corpses of robbers were hung up by the heels. I wish the brute who stole my typewriter could have seen them. On the other hand I cannot tell an enquirer why Trinity Lane was once called Findsilver Lane. I know of it only that it had a bad reputation, that it was popularly known by a name with which the late Dr. Venn refused to sully his pages (and with which I am therefore unable to sully these), and that the Masters of Gonville Hall and Michael House once received a Royal raspberry to say that if they did not abate the *horror abominabilis* created there by the state of the drains they would shortly get it in the neck. As to D Day, the Parish has supplied some diversified explanations but the prevailing, and no doubt correct, view is that it is the Day with a capital D, or Zero Day, on the analogy of Jour J and Heure H. I gather also that the term was used for the invasion of Sicily, though whether on French or on American initiative remains obscure.

SIXTY-SECOND LETTER

14.10.44

I GOT back from Wales, without serious discomfort on the journey, on September 7, to find the lawns much greener than I had left them, a fine crop of mushrooms growing in the Great Court, and more hornets about than I have seen before here or elsewhere. I had had a very enjoyable three weeks — my longest respite from the grindstone for I know

[1] Amiens was liberated on Aug. 31.

not how many years. The weather was not too good, for there was much wind and little sun; but until the last few days there was also little rain, and as my creaking joints, though no less strident, were somewhat less painful than last year, I was able to get further up my favourite green hills. I also enjoyed a diet of plentiful butter, cream, and really fresh vegetables, nót to mention some Camembert cheeses sent to a fellow-visitor. These arrived a little tired by a long postal journey, and I have since received one in better condition which came from Normandy under the personal escort of a parishioner; but tired or not they make a very welcome change from the inferior mousetrap variety which has long been our portion. I have, I confess, been somewhat surprised to find that Camembert is native to Normandy, for its little round boxes used to be adorned with a highly coloured view of seemingly Alpine pastures and, if I remember, of snow mountains. However I have now discovered (not without difficulty, for my atlas failed me) that the village of Camembert is (or perhaps was) in the Department of Orne some fifteen miles east of Falaise. I hope parishioners who passed that way made the acquaintance of the less famous but even better cheeses of Pont l'Evêque which resemble, and are almost as good as, Brie.

I should gladly have vegetated longer than three weeks but I had things to do here — two days of interviewing R.A.F. cadets, and a week of Warden's duty, during which I found further reason to appreciate the nuisance-value of p-planes. For, awakened by an alert presumably due to one, and stumbling into a pitchy night without a torch (mine having run down), I applied my face with such violence to the stone wall at the end of the Cloisters that I appeared before the astonished Porter on duty looking more like the blood-boltered Banquo than a peevish pedant roused from his beauty-sleep. Besides these things the relaxations in the Civil Defence Services, though welcome as a symptom, have created for me far more trouble than they have removed. True, I need no longer man the Johnian tower, but the elaborate Fire Guard rules are withdrawn (since the F.G. Plan has been relegated to cold storage); what little bòttom was left in the University and Colleges Joint Fire Protection Scheme has been knocked out of it; and the task of remembering what rules were in force before these dispensations, ànd how far they are still applicable, has not been easy. We have also had to consider what College services should be kept alive — practically all, we concluded, for they were instituted long before the authorities got busy, and in so far as they safeguard our buildings it is better to be safe than sorry. I do not anticipate serious complaint from their members who, with a few inevitable exceptions, are a very willing lot; and burdens have been lightened by the removal of compulsory part-time national service for undergraduates — an obligation which could hardly have been maintained when the Home Guard, in which about half have discharged it, have only voluntary parades.

I had meant to go to Eton for a week-end before Term began, but a hitch at that end, and at this my preoccupation with the above-mentioned matters, intervened, and apart from half a very wet day in London and half a very fine one visiting a friend at Hemingford Grey I have had no diversions. I brought no news from London unless it should be that a room full of American war-artists at the National Gallery disclosed to a hasty glance no marked differences from their English counterparts, but I noticed from the train-window a good deal more evidence of p-planes than I had seen in central London.

At this time of year I usually record visible changes in the appearance of the town, but apart from a leprous incrustation of Fire Guard signs the buildings are unchanged and the only novelty of the last twelve months, if indeed that too is not older, is, I think, the numerous parties, mostly of American airmen, being taken on tours conducted by various eminent persons. In this College the Master or Vice-Master may be seen on most afternoons showing a party round, and to judge from the number of Americans whom I catch photographing their buddies or cuties (if I have the terms correctly) in front of the Fountain or the Sun-dial those objects must by now be pretty familiar in the States. I asked the Master whether he had taken much in tips but, somewhat to my surprise, he said that though plentifully rewarded with American cigarettes no cash had come his way. I imagine, therefore, that the identity of the cicerone must be explained to the parties in advance, for I well remember the Master of another College, whom a chance visitor had interrupted in conversation with me in his College Library, exhibiting the sights and accepting with a suitable expression of gratitude the sixpence proffered by the tourist on his departure — plainly the tactful thing to do, but my heart bled for the tourist, who had visibly hesitated, and I wondered how often when in similar doubt myself I had chosen wrong. I do not know how far it is these tours, which penetrate regions usually closed to visitors, and how far the general decline of manners, which accounts for the shameless readiness of strangers (mostly British, I must admit, and female) to make their way into what are quite plainly private premises and often marked as such, but at any rate it is no uncommon thing for a party to enter my rooms without knocking and, when asked somewhat coldly what they want, to reply that they are 'just looking round the College'. However, if visible changes are few, there is one audible change which may be mentioned, for 'Trinity's loquacious clock' is now reduced to complete taciturnity. The duty of striking the quarters it abandoned some months ago because the mechanism had been wrecked by one of the humorists whose *facetiae* were mentioned in no. 56. It no longer strikes the hours because the belfry was lately found to be unsafe. Consequently two of the three bells have been dismounted and must remain so until we can rebuild the belfry in what may well be a somewhat distant future.

Term began on October 10 but you must curb your impatience for statistics until next month. Meanwhile I chronicle a few trifles of academic news which properly belong to the vacation or even to last term. Both the University and the College have been filling up vacancies with a view to returning to a more normal existence. The University has acquired some more Professors, among them one of Latin to whom I was privileged to teach some rudiments of that language when he was a small boy at Eton. This makes me feel even more decrepit than I am. The College has been still busier in this direction and has appointed lecturers in French, Russian, Law, Physics, Botany, and, in Engineering, no less than three — some to fill vacancies caused by retirement and resignations, some — the Russian, the Botanist, and one of the Engineers — as additions to the pre-war staff, and the Physicist to act for Feather whom the Government have requisitioned for some time to come. We have also acquired a new Matron, for Miss Lusk has retired and gone back to her Irish home. I hope her successor will soon feel herself, as Miss Lusk of late has not done, in a position to treat with Bedmakers on more even terms, for the amount of service they provide has steadily decreased for years past. I suppose, however, that while we have with us an American Red Cross eager to pay charladies 2/6 an hour the latter will continue to turn up their noses at us. We have also suffered losses by death. Innes you perhaps hardly knew even by sight, for though he was Bursar for 30 years he ceased to be so in 1929 and he was over eighty when he died. Fowler, Professor of Applied Mathematics, was probably known to a good many scientific parishioners, and he should be accounted a war-casualty. Though he was younger than I am, and seemingly far more robust, he nevertheless had a stroke shortly before the war; but, bidden to take things easy, he had preferred to spend himself on the Admiralty work which earned him a Knighthood a year ago. Finally the University has had some financial ups and downs. Sir Herbert Thompson has bequeathed it about £60,000 for the study of Egyptology — a subject hardly dealt with here though the Fitzwilliam's small but choice assortment of Egyptian things was increased last year by the presentation of another large collection. Egyptologists are scarce in England and appointments to any teaching posts we may create will probably present difficulties, so if any of you are ambitious in that direction here may be your chance. Imperial Chemicals, as you may have read in the papers, are to provide us with £7,200 per annum for seven years for Research Fellowships, and there have been feelers in similar directions from other large concerns, for the war has made Big Business more conscious of the value of academic research (as well it might); and no doubt excess profits invested in this generous way will presently pay dividends. Per contra the Drapers' Company, which since 1919 has contributed £800 a year towards the stipend of the French Professor, has announced that owing to war-damage to its properties and other similar causes it will be unable to do so after this year.

Hints for pipe-smokers (from the Orders of a Free French unit): Par dérogation de l'Article 25 du Réglement de Service dans l'Armée et de l'Article 17 dans l'Armée de Mer, les militaires des Armées de Terre, de Mer, et de l'Air sont autorisés à fumer la pipe en ville à la condition qu'elle soit fumée avec élégance, et qu'elle ne soit pas en permanence dans la bouche des interessés.

SIXTY-THIRD LETTER

11.11.44

STATISTICS, derived, as usual, from the *Cambridge Review*. There are 2875 men in residence — B.A.'s, Research Students, and 4th year men, 215; 259, 3rd year; 793, 2nd year; 1608, 1st year. This represents an increase of 224 over last October, distributed in fair proportion over all four groups. It surprises me, and I think most other people, nor have I heard an authentic explanation. The thin trickle of ex-service men is not sufficient to account for it and it perhaps depends rather on various slight changes in the rules for reservation, with which, being no longer a Tutor, I am no longer in touch. There are 324 men in this College, of whom 169 are Freshmen, as against 270 and 151 last year; Newnham and Girton house 489, as against 483; and the evacuated institutions 1378 as against 1761. This last figure, however, really indicates an increase similar to our own, for Bedford College, which in 1943 contributed nearly 600, has gone home and it is again possible to find a seat in the University Library (see no. 52). From other sources I add that Sciences, Engineering, and Mathematics now employ more than three fifths of the total undergraduates; that History and English are the only Humane faculties to number over a hundred; that I am lecturing to a class composed of 19 Cadets, 16 women, and 8 ordinary undergraduates; and that the five Colleges for whose Classical supervision I am responsible contain 5 o.u.'s and 7 Cadets reading the subject. There will be a drop in numbers in April for there are to be substantially fewer Cadets in the second course of the year; and very possibly another drop next October when the Cadets will again be reduced and there will be no State Bursars, of whom about 270 arrived last month. It seems possible, however, that by then some favour may be shown to those whose education is still incomplete, for though no hint of anything of the sort has been dropped in demobilisation schemes or elsewhere, there has been a good deal of correspondence in the papers about it, and it is patent that unless something is done quickly to produce some people capable of teaching it will be impossible for many years to come even to make a start on the numerous and ambitious educational projects now before the public. I add, finally, that expressed as percentages of the last pre-war year the numbers of undergraduates male and female (excluding Cadets) who have been up during these six years are 79, 57, 53, 48, 42, 46. I hope we may now prove to have turned the corner; also that this paragraph will keep you quiet for a while.

When the last no. went out I was engaged in the annual reorganisation of A.R.P. parties and was struggling even more ineffectually than usual against the protective mechanism possessed by a large percentage of undergraduates which secures that an unwelcome message, however forcibly presented to eye or ear, is either repulsed by those organs or, if an initial penetration is effected, is sealed off by the mind. This peculiarity of the species is well known to Tutors, and I remember a good many years ago a suggestion that the bland ignorance of the College rules professed by our pupils might perhaps decrease if the book containing them were in verse instead of prose. Its projected revision did not proceed very far and I can now recall only two stanzas, which came from the section on discipline and ran as follows:

> If our landladies lay a complaint
> That their lodgers are drunken or riotous
> Our Tutors apply the constraint
> Best suited to sober or quiet us:

> But if we are guilty in College
> Of conduct profane or obscene
> The matter is brought to the knowledge
> And left in the hands of the Dean.

However I doubt whether mechanical remedies of this kind would have produced an organic change, and the fact remains that if you put out a notice summoning people to an A.R.P. or other meeting and only 20 out of the 30 whom it concerns turn up there is nothing for it but to send individually for the missing 10 and then to repeat to each the substance of whatever it was you said to the 20 — and this is a weariness of the flesh.

Besides, I read in *Country Life* last August a letter from a gentleman who said that he had been awakened one night in his country cottage by a man in the garden shouting at a barking dog which he repeatedly addressed as 'Thunderbolt'. Enquiry having shown that no dog in the village answered to the name of Thunderbolt, it became plain to him that the incident, as he elegantly expressed it, 'savoured of the supernatural' — a conclusion presently confirmed by the discovery on the rockery of a peculiarly shaped flint. Since the flint, of which a view was provided, bore no resemblance either to a dog or to a thunderbolt I did not quite follow this bit. However the gentleman went on to say that though he had seen a ghost or two in his time he claimed no psychic powers, but in January 1918 he had predicted that the then war would end on Nov. 11 and he now had a premonition that this one would end on Oct. 9. This seemed a very suitable date to me as Term began on the following day, and though I wouldn't go so far as to say that I regarded the matter as settled, I could well have spared the drudgery which in the event occupied all my spare time for the ten days thereafter.

My reading-list got squeezed out of the Sept. no. and I will not resurrect it now, but as one or two people have enquired after it here are half a dozen of the books which have seemed to me most worth while in recent months. First two volumes of letters by artists, both poor, both passionately devoted to painting, and both engaging characters — Camille Pissarro and J. B. Yeats (father of the poet). C.P., as I think I once said before, is not my favourite painter, though a watercolour of his which hangs in my bedroom has so far stood the hard test of familiarity; but his letters, unlike those of his contemporaries which I have read (Degas, Renoir, Cézanne), are instructive on French painting and painters, and his indomitable courage and confidence in face of grinding poverty, a large family, and a querulous wife, are very impressive. His letters, however, are published not in French but in very expensive and rather clumsy American and most of you would probably prefer Yeats, who writes well, had a less one-track mind, and being less poor could exercise it more freely on subjects other than paint. A life of William the Silent (of Orange), by C. V. Wedgwood, is about the liberation of the Netherlands in the 16th century and interested me even before the subject became topical, but as the authoress is my cousin I forbear to puff it further. *No Outspan*, by D. Reitz, is a third volume of very lively reminiscences by a distinguished South African politician who died lately in London where he was High Commissioner. The *Longhorns*, by J. F. Dobie, is a very readable and entertaining account of the cattle-ranching industry in Texas by an American Professor who was lecturing here last year; and *Shearwaters*, by R. M. Lockley, is, as perhaps you have already guessed, about shearwaters, birds in which I take a mild interest, partly because their nocturnal pranks have been held to explain some ancient Mediterranean bird-mysteries, partly for the pretty example of scientific nomenclature which they present. For you might suppose that a bird known to ornithologists as *Puffinus puffinus puffinus* would probably prove to be a puffin. Not at all; it is a Manx Shearwater, and a puffin is known to them as *Fratercula arctica arctica* — of which I will only say that if you must call something a small female brother may be a puffin is as suitable as any other victim.

I have also been looking again at the Master's little history of the College which I had read only rather hastily when I recommended it in no. 53. It well bears re-reading, but I am sorry that it does (as I think) a good deal less than justice to Essex as an architect. Essex was the son of a Cambridge builder, and was responsible for much work in Cambridge — notably the front of Emmanuel, the interior of the front court of Christ's, and the 18th century building at Queens'. Privately he was an admirer of Gothic architecture which nobody wanted at the time, but that did not prevent him from building not indeed with genius but with taste and talent in another style. For us he altered the north and south ranges of Nevile's Court in 1755, built the bridge in 1764, and the Kitchen Building in 1774. No doubt it is lucky that a scheme for rebuilding the whole of the Great Court in that style fell through, and no doubt it is a pity that Essex was let loose in it at all, for much of its beauty is due to the proportions and the irregularity of the older buildings, of which the east and south ranges at any rate are in themselves of no great distinction. Still, that ought not to blind us to the fact that the Kitchen Building, though it now harmonises ill with the rest of the court, is a very dignified piece of work, and the same, or more, might be said of the bridge (which the Master does not mention). As to Nevile's Court, where Essex renewed the stonework, substituted the level balustrade for a row of dormers, and pared off some gimcrack Jacobean ornament, the alterations seem to me masterly. I should have thought them an improvement anyway, and certainly it is entirely due to Essex that the sides of the court make a harmonious unity with the Library — and since I contemplate it daily from my window I have the best of reasons for not underestimating the debt which the College owes him. His journal of an architectural tour in the Low Countries, which I have read, suggests that he was a nice, as well as an intelligent, man, and there exists an entrancing silhouette of the Essex family showing Miss Milicent E. embroidering at her tambour opposite to Mr E. who is plying his compasses at his designing-table; under the table a spaniel, on it a tame squirrel which Mrs E. is feeding.

SIXTY-FOURTH LETTER

10.12.44

ERM ended on December 8 and has not been agreeable; for if
since mid-November it has mostly been unseasonably mild, it was until
then unseasonably chilly, and I do not remember a wetter Cambridge
autumn. No harm in that after so long a drought, and by the beginning
of November the Fountain, dry for many months, had begun to drip
again; but cold and wind and wet had pretty well stripped the trees by
the same date, and a slow autumn in the Backs can be the most lovely
of the seasons. As part compensation I have again, to my great delight,
heard the pipe of curlews overhead at night; and since their return
coincides with some relaxation in the black-out I suppose their absence
was rightly ascribed to that cause, in no. 34. To the relaxation I ascribe
also the fact that some undergraduates now veil their academic nudity in
gowns visibly made of black-out material.

Other academic news is scanty. Eddington's death, at the comparatively early age of 61, you have no doubt seen in the papers, but he
was probably known to few parishioners except advanced Applied
Mathematicians, nor did I know him well myself though when he was
a B.A. and I a Freshman our attics in the Great Ct adjoined — a shy
man, though not unfriendly, and silent; it was a surprise to me to discover
how eloquent he could be on paper. You may also have read in the
papers that on Nov. 5 there was a riot; but this, though highly discreditable to all concerned (the majority, I understand, not members of
the University), owed its excessive publicity to some injudicious observations by the Mayor. The Council of the Senate has been bogged in some
troublesome problems (finance, training colleges, and the like) which
would not interest you and do not much interest me for I have nothing
to contribute to their solution. Partly for this reason I am glad that my
membership of that august body ends with the year, but, apart from it,
the business of the Council is too miscellaneous to be continuously
interesting and the five years I have served are enough. For the rest, I
record that rabbits and parsnips have again invaded the High Table in
revolting force. I sometimes think that in lieu of these familiar and
unwelcome expedients we ought in time of scarcity to revive some of
the olde worlde cates which pleased our ancestors and might please as
well as sustain us. Take Porpoise Pudding for instance: now there is a
dish evidently nutritious and to the haggis-minded I should suppose

even appetising, yet when have I been invited to partake of it? (Recipe, for the use of R.N.V.R. parishioners: Take the Blode of hym, and the grece of hymself, & Otemele, & Salt, & Pepir & Gyngere, & mingle these togederys wel, & than putte this in the Gutte of the purpays, & than lat it seethe esyli, & not hard, a good whylys; and than take hym uppe, & broyle hym a lytil, & than serve forth.) However what, as Shakespeare enquires, is a sorry parsnip to a good heart? I console myself in these tribulations by the reflexion that there are other austerities to which even the sixth year of war has not yet reduced us. For example I read in a book by the late American ambassador in Tokyo that in Japan even before Pearl Harbour the exigences of the China Incident had made it necessary to deprive all concubines of telephones.

And now I have to announce that this is the last issue of the P.M. in its present form. This news ought to surprise nobody; I am myself surprised, as you should be, that these letters have been maintained on the same scale for more than five years, for the daily life of a Don is no inexhaustible quarry, and, as I said in no. 24, the shortage of subject matter had begun to trouble me before the second year was out. From the beginning I have had two objects in view. The first was to keep in touch with friends whom I could seldom hope to see, and whose whereabouts and occupation might shift from month to month. That object I do not renounce, for I shall continue to write to you (or at least to those of you who maintain your subscriptions in the form of letters to me), though not as heretofore at regular intervals nor at such inordinate length; and I very much hope that you will go on writing. My second object was to provide what entertainment I could for those whose temporary profession I remembered from the last war to involve long periods of boredom; but my increasing difficulty in finding things to write about must have been long apparent, and I cannot but suppose that I become in consequence decreasingly entertaining. Besides, I grow older, and tireder, and duller; and since I have no desire to emulate Mary Lunn (who, you will remember, died suddenly at ninety-one Of psittacosis, not before Becoming an appalling bore), it is better to call a halt, if there is still time, before I begin to contribute to the boredom I have been trying to relieve. The P.M. nearly came to an untimely end this summer for lack of envelopes, and I had fully determined that it should turn over a new leaf on its fifth birthday last September, but the war was then in a decisive stage and I felt that I must go on as before for a few more months. Now, it is true, the war even in Europe is not yet over, and if the German people are sufficiently devoted to the loathsome masters they have chosen to serve it may even last for some time; but that it is substantially won I cannot doubt. The University, too, has weathered the storm, and though there are many repairs and alterations to be made before it is fully fit for sea again, their slow and laborious progress will provide little material for such a chronicle as this. Since, therefore, the end of hostilities in Europe will not in any case close this correspondence I choose the end of the year as a suitably clear-cut date for converting my monthly into a periodical of less regular appearance and length.

When I consider the past history of the P.M. I sometimes wonder what you may so far have learnt from it. You know, no doubt, more of me, my habits, tastes, and occupations, than you did — much more indeed than is worth the knowing; but that was a fault inherent in the undertaking, and since it could not be avoided I do not think it needs apology. In less personal themes the circumstances of the times have imposed some reticences on me; I have not been free to tell you exactly where bombs have fallen, nor what unwonted occupants have been quartered in this College or in that. These details, however, I trust I shall soon be allowed to supply. Again, some local activities (for instance concerts, plays, sports) have lain outside my own ambit and have therefore received little or no notice. But with these reservations I hope I have succeeded in giving you a truthful picture of Cambridge in wartime. The remaining contents of the P.M. are motley indeed for I have had to write on anything which came into my head, and in only one particular have I been consciously didactic. For I will here confess that when short of material I have rather welcomed opportunities of telling you a little about the working of the College and the University and of recounting episodes in their history. It has always seemed to me a pity that undergraduates should go down knowing so little of the microcosm of which they have formed a part and to which most, I hope, owe a good deal. It is inevitable that it should be so, and though in my undergraduate days I probably knew more of these things than the average undergraduate of today (for academic politics made more noise then than they do now) it was only a little more. Still, it is a pity; and if the P.M. has caused you to think rather more about the place and its organisation, and to think of it, if not with more affection, at least with more understanding, I shall consider myself to have done some good.

Some of you will hear, this time with a legitimate surprise which a few months ago I should have shared myself, that the Parish Magazine is presently to appear in print — an event for which certain parishioners are more responsible than I. For about a year they have been expressing the hope, or even the belief, that it would presently be available in book-form, and I have thereby been thrown into a considerable twitter, being on the one hand unwilling, as always, to disappoint parishioners and on the other very doubtful whether anybody but a parishioner would want such a book. The record it would contain of the impact of war on a University might, I thought, give it some day a minute historical interest, but neither that nor its other contents would make it readable now; and I remembered that the letters had often been written at times of overwork and anxiety and that they could not be the better reading for that. However, since it was impossible for me, and very difficult for anybody in Cambridge, to form a valuable opinion on the question, I made up a couple of files and asked one or two friends who were neither parishioners nor connected with Cambridge to read them. All these were in favour of publication, but I should still have been left hesitating if one of the files had not fallen more or less accidentally into the hands of Mr G. Wren Howard, who, though he was unknown to me at the time, is a member of this College and a partner of Jonathan Cape the publisher. And when he wrote to me out of the blue to ask if his firm might publish the letters it seemed to me that I might without undue presumption meet the wishes of those parishioners who had asked for them. It will never be said of them as was said of Pascal's *Lettres Provinciales* (though on much more esoteric themes) that 'elles ne sont pas seulment estimées par les Theologiens: elles sont encore agreables aux gens du monde et intelligibles aux femmes mesmes', but it is a publisher's business to know what sort of books the public wants, and since Messrs Cape think that some of them will want this sort I have permitted myself to hope that they may be right.

I have left myself little space to send you all my warmest wishes for a happy Christmas and New Year. 1944 has brought, from all quarters except China, good news almost unbroken. I hope that 1945 will follow suit, and since too many of you have been too long beyond the unplumbed, salt, estranging sea, in particular I hope that its early months will see these at any rate home again — and visiting Cambridge.

POSTSCRIPT

(Extracted from a later letter)

June 1945

MANY momentous and welcome events have happened since I wrote to you last, but I need only record here that Cambridge celebrated VE day[1] with a good deal of noise but with no serious disorder; that the Mayor lit a large bonfire on Midsummer Common, but without my assistance; that our undergraduates had a glass of champagne in Hall; and that selected firemen had a glass or two more after Hall in my rooms. I had, as a matter of fact, celebrated a VC day more furtively just a week earlier, for reading in the evening paper that the Ministry of Home Security had instructed local authorities to liquidate their Civil Defence Services on the following day, I removed from my key-ring the Golden Plover call which has served me these five years and more for a Warden's whistle, and sneaked out at midnight to post a notice disbanding the College A.R.P. services. I confess that I do not regret having no longer to sleep in my clothes or to attend five or six practices a week, but my relief on these heads is nothing to my relief that the College buildings have come through the war with no worse than a few pock-marks on Whewell's Ct.

I imagine that I am now free to fill in two of the gaps which, as I said in no. 64, prevented the P.M. from being a full picture of Cambridge in war-time — bombs and billets — and I will deal with them in that order.

Bombs were dropped in the town on, I think, fifteen occasions, and about thirty people in all were killed — the largest number (10) in the first raid in June 1940, when some small houses down in the Barnwell direction were demolished. The last fell in August 1942, but Alerts went on until March of this year. A number of V1's buzzed past within earshot, and one or two within eyeshot, but none dropped very near, and such few V2's as were reported in the district also behaved with discretion. Damage to the town was very slight; that to the University negligible. Apart from the windows and stonework of Whewell's Ct, which suffered when the Union was set alight in July 1942, I think Sidney had then some incendiaries in their garden; and Emmanuel and Downing had the like from a shower recorded in no. 19 when one extinguished itself in a sink

[1] May 8.

254

in the Cavendish Laboratory. No other Colleges or University buildings were hit so far as I know.

The war-time visitors, though not to my knowledge responsible for any loss of life, have done far more damage to College property than the bombs, both by turning it inside out for their own convenience and by setting it on fire. From the start we had R.A.F. Initial Training Wings (at first two; later one with other R.A.F. units). These had their headquarters in Jesus and occupied the requisitioned parts of eight other Colleges; these it was to whom Pembroke ascribed the fire mentioned in no. 20; and these who stood not on the order of their going, as recorded in no. 58. Queens' housed the Bart.'s medical school; Christ's the London School of Oriental Studies; Peterhouse, King's, and St. Catherine's portions of London University. King's had also an R.A.F. transport unit which parked its lorries, omnibuses, and what-nots under the trees in the Backs and has left scarce a blade of grass behind it. Caius, Corpus, Trinity, and Sidney had Civil Servants, some I think from the start. Ours in Trinity were regional offices of various ministries, who appeared only when bombing began in earnest. Until then the New Ct and Hostel were empty except for birds of passage — some short courses for officers, and after Dunkirk a company and a half of troops, whom we were more than glad to welcome.

That is not a complete list, for I omit some smaller units squeezed in here and there, and I make no attempt to record what went in laboratories — partly because I hardly know myself, I add, however, that various Colleges have put up Dominion, Colonial, and U.S.A. troops sent here for a weekly educational course organised by a regional committee; also that some of us set aside rooms and provided entertainment for troops on leave, who have been in charge of the English-speaking Union. Ours have mostly been Canadian and American officers and N.C.O.'s, who have been, I think, genuinely appreciative of their surroundings. I should judge from my contacts with them at the High Table and elsewhere that this and the educational courses had been happy experiments, and that a good many people will carry pleasant memories of Cambridge across the Atlantic.

INDEX